Making Sense of Social Research

Making Sense of Social Research

Malcolm Williams

SAGE Publications
London • Thousand Oaks • New Delhi

First published 2003

SAGE Publications Ltd
6 Bonhill Street
London EC2A 4PU

SAGE Publications Inc.
2455 Teller Road
Thousand Oaks, California 91320

SAGE Publications India Pvt Ltd
B-42, Panchsheel Enclave
Post Box 4109
New Delhi 110 017

British Library Cataloguing in Publication data

A catalogue record for this book is available from
the British Library

ISBN 0 7619 6421 5
     0 7619 6422 3

Library of Congress Control Number: Available

Typeset by C&M Digitals (P) Ltd., Chennai, India
Printed and bound in Great Britain by Athenaeum Press, Gateshead

Contents

Preface

There are plenty of good research methods books around and when Chris Rojek suggested I write one, my first thought was, do we need another? Yet like most teachers of research methods I have never found quite the right book and in my mind the present book had an embryonic form even before Chris's suggestion. Because I believe strongly in the inter-relationship of theory and method I wanted to write a book that placed emphasis on this. I also wanted to write a book that spoke to the reader in a forthright and uncomplicated way, even if that meant some over-simplification in places. My own experience has led me to believe it's best to start with simple first principles, even if these have to be revised later. Finally, I wanted to write a book that was about social research as social *science*, because I believe that, despite its faults, science and its method have the potential to lead us to more reliable knowledge and the latter is an important requisite in all of our strivings to make a more just and equitable world.

To what extent I have managed to do these things the reader must decide. If I have not done so, it would not be for the want of support from friends and colleagues. Many have helped unwittingly in helping me write this book, most particularly the students I have taught over the years at the University of Plymouth and prior to this, City University and the University of North London. Some people have given me particular help in the writing and production process. Iain Wilkinson and Steve Miles kindly provided research examples. Liz Hodgkinson, Carol Williams, Sam Regan de Bere and Roger Sapsford read and commented on chapters, as did two anonymous reviewers. The latter two provided enormously helpful feedback. One of them hated the book, but nevertheless found time to do much of the proof reading (try to get out more is my advice!). Particular thanks to Tim May for friendship, inspiration and support; to Dave Byrne, Bob Carter and Ray Pawson for useful discussions and ideas; to Chris Rojek and Kay Bridger from Sage Publications for being supportive and efficient throughout the project. Finally, my love and thanks to Liz, Laura and John for being there and putting up with my occasional Irritable Male Syndrome!

Introduction

With the enormous growth in recent years of a research culture in public life, or perhaps more specifically an evidence-based and evaluation culture, more and more people are called upon to undertake social research. Social research can appear bewildering for first-time researchers, whether they are students or those who must undertake research as part of their jobs. When is a survey appropriate, or when are depth interviews better? How big should a sample be? When is a finding 'significant', etc., etc.? The aim of this book is to help those who must undertake social research (willingly or perhaps reluctantly) to make sense of these things.

What is social research?

Social research is the means by which social scientists understand, explain and predict the social world. Social researchers may have a background in one (or more) substantive areas of social science, such as economics, social policy, human geography, sociology or political science. Increasingly, though, many who become social researchers do not have any specialist social science background, but may have received their social research training after graduating in quite a different area, or they may have learnt 'on the job'. Researchers are not just academics and many work for local or national government, health services, charities or campaigning organizations and in market research.

What we call social research covers a wide range of activities from theoretically driven 'pure' research, to the pragmatic and varying tasks carried out by researchers in the community. The former may be doing very sophisticated research, perhaps developing neural networks to model the social world (Byrne, 2002: Chapter 8), while the latter might be conducting focus groups on attitudes to local healthcare plans. In this respect the scope of social research from the esoteric to the everyday mirrors that of the science–technology continuum. Yet in the same way that theoretical physics and mechanical engineering each depend on the principles of natural science, so it is that all social research from the most complex to the most mundane depends on certain principles and techniques. These have their origins in substantive disciplines such as statistics, sociology and anthropology and while researchers may not study these disciplines directly, to learn about social research is to learn some of the fundamentals of social science.

To do basic social research is not difficult, though even in its simplest form it does take us beyond common sense and obvious everyday explanations. One way in which it is different to natural science and technology is that taxi drivers rarely give you the benefit of their views on the second law of thermodynamics, or on the Planck Constant, but they will tell you that a return of the death penalty will reduce crime, or that single mothers are a financial burden on the state. In these and many other things common sense is either wrong, or in need of modification. Society needs social researchers as much as it needs engineers. The latter can tell us how to build structurally sound bridges, roads, power stations and apartment blocks, but it is social researchers who can tell us about the need for such things and their likely social impact. Common sense, whether that of taxi drivers, politicians or even the media, is not enough and to rely on it for policy-making, or even local community planning, may prove costly. In the 1950s and 1960s British urban housing policy was dominated by the move to build large quantities of high rise high density housing. The policy was mostly the result of well-intentioned political rhetoric, but even by the late 1960s it was becoming clear that it was a mistaken policy and was leading to social problems, many of which remain with us today (Jephcott, 1971; Murie, 1983; Coleman, 1990). As is so often the case, it was social researchers who were called in to describe and explain these problems.

Not all research is about solving 'social' problems. Some research is about aspects of the puzzles that have occupied humans since the time of the ancient Greeks: what are we like, and how can we know the social world? Sometimes knowing a bit more about the social world helps us to resolve the practical problems of living in it and sometimes knowing more about the practical problems of, say, poverty or poor housing throws light on what individuals and groups are like. The resolution of these problems requires curiosity, indeed curiosity is a precondition of all science. Knowledge, in any subject, is not derived from a neutral aggregation of 'facts', but as a result of active seeking, or error and the elimination of error. The resolution of one problem, or set of problems, creates a new batch of problems. As the philosopher Karl Popper put it:

> Every solution of a problem raises new unsolved problems; this more so the deeper the original problem and the bolder its solution. The more we learn about the world, and the deeper our learning, the more conscious, specific; and articulate will be our knowledge of what we do not know, our knowledge of our ignorance. (Popper, 1989: 29)

Popper's message was that while there is a limit to our knowledge, there is no limit to our ignorance, yet despite this to thrive, or indeed survive, we continue to push out the boundaries of our knowledge, to get nearer and nearer 'the truth'. For me this is the spirit of research; it is critical, yet optimistic activity that provides me with a never ending source of puzzles.

Researching *social* life

Of course much of the foregoing would apply equally to research in the natural sciences and although there is a powerful argument which says the natural and social sciences do not sharply divide, either in terms of method or concerns, there is something special about social life that makes the job of a social researcher different to that of, say, an experimental physicist. Social life consists of complex feedback mechanisms between individuals and groups and vice versa. This leads to enormous complexity, but of course such complexity is present in the natural world, as are feedback mechanisms. It is the nature of the feedback mechanisms that is different (Eve et al., 1997; Byrne, 1998). Humans have the ability to reflect upon information and act creatively upon it. This produces the dynamic of social life, the subtle and complex arrangements of action and structure that Anthony Giddens (1984) has termed 'structuration'. Now if the actions of one individual or group can lead another individual or group to change what it is they are doing, then this has implications for researching individuals or groups. In social research, as in any area of science, the act of our investigation will have an impact upon the environment investigated, but for us it is the scale of that potential effect that is at issue. In other words, social researchers are themselves agents of change in the world. These changes may be effected by the research act itself, or as a result of the findings becoming known. Opinion polls showing that a presidential candidate's ratings are improving can lend a credibility to a campaign that might have been lacking hitherto.

Although social research transcends common sense and everyday views of the world, it nevertheless contains political and ethical issues that cannot be avoided. These will range from the choice of topic A rather than B in the first place, to how the research is conducted and how it is reported. Research is never neutral and there is always a context. This does not mean, however, that it cannot be objective and indeed moral or political commitment is often an important precursor to good research. A concern for equal opportunities often underlies rigorous research on how those opportunities are not realized. People who research homelessness often begin from a position of seeing homelessness as an evil, as do those who research poverty or substance abuse. We are then curious citizens who are interested in and care about the social world in which we live.

That this world is social, rather than a world of disconnected autonomous individuals, is likewise important. Psychologists, while not ignoring the nature of the external world, are nevertheless concerned with individual consciousness. Social researchers (and more generally social scientists) are concerned about the nature of relationships between people. Social researchers are concerned with individuals, but only as socially situated agents. This is part of a more strategic positioning that makes certain theoretical or philosophical assumptions about the social world; more specifically it is the connection between 'grand theory' and empirical social science, mediated through a further body of knowledge or set of assumptions that constitutes the substantive social science disciplines to which I referred above. Research on the economy will be motivated by a body of economic theory, which in turn will rest upon certain assumptions about humans as economic agents. Social research, though united by many principles, practices and techniques is nevertheless grounded in theoretical positions that often lie at the heart of substantive disciplines. It begins then from a set of theoretical, moral and political assumptions about human society which pose problems, or puzzles to be solved. A further important ingredient might be termed authenticity: are the conclusions we reach an honest answer to the problem we began with? Do we believe ourselves?

Social research, particularly that presented statistically, is sometimes derided as just political rhetoric, a cynical manipulation of data to produce conclusions conducive to a particular viewpoint. That this happens is certainly true, though more often than not such data have resulted from honest social research, but have been misused by politicians, journalists and policy-makers. Perhaps more common is 'weak' social research that draws unwarranted conclusions from its data. The first is certainly dishonest, the second maybe, but is just as likely to be the result of poor training and lack of rigour.

Honesty is, of course, a state of mind, but fortunately there are third party guarantees that the researcher has indeed been honest. Such guarantees come in a commitment to rigour in method and part of that rigour is a transparency about how the research has been conducted. The very best social research is rigorous and seeks an honest answer to the problem. This means that the methods themselves should be the best known practical means to tackle the research problem. In this book I will maintain the position that this inevitably leads to a methodological pluralism, that the problem will dictate the method and that each method will have advantages and limitations. A key skill of being a good researcher is to recognize these advantages and limitations and to select the best methodological approach, though of course like most skills this is one that is born of experience.

Methodological approaches

Some writers list many different types of social research (e.g. Sarantakos, 1998: 6) and this is quite legitimate but, for the purposes of clarity, to begin with I will speak of only two broad approaches, that is quantitative research and qualitative research. While these broad approaches can be sub-divided and thought of in numerous ways, the difference between these is underwritten by quite different assumptions about knowledge of the social world and how we go about research. Of course, like all categories these can be subverted and it can be shown that there are qualitative aspects to quantitative research and vice versa. But that is for later.

Quantitative research is about quantities. It is about measurement, saying how much of something there is, about explaining why something happened and perhaps predicting under what circumstances it might happen in the future. Most, though not all, quantitative research is conducted at a 'macro' level, that is, it is interested in explaining and predicting aggregate behaviour and characteristics. Quantitative research is rooted in the scientific tradition of studies of the social world and depends on statistical and mathematical techniques. The principal form of quantitative method is the social survey, though experiments and 'quasi experiments' are also used (see Chapter 5).

Qualitative research is conversely about the qualities things have. It mostly originates in a different tradition in the humanities (though many believe this does not preclude it being scientific, see Hammersley, 2000). The important characteristic of qualitative research is that it is about interpreting and coming to understand the social world at a micro-level. Research is usually with small groups or individuals and aims to understand intentions, meanings and actions. The techniques of this approach include unstructured in-depth interviewing, group interviewing and observation.

In the following chapters I will discuss the underlying thinking behind these methods, how they developed and what their strengths and limitations are. However, first, let me end this Introduction by saying something about how the book is organized and how you might use it.

The book: who should read it, what's in it and how to use it

In writing a book of this kind the author always wants the widest possible audience, if for no other reason than the desire for bigger royalty cheques! In this I am no different, but I do nevertheless believe that 'one size fits all' is not a good idea for methods books. The book is introductory, but it goes a bit further than some introductions and not so far as others. It is aimed at professionals who find that they are confronted with a need to do research and it is aimed at undergraduates and graduates for whom research methods will be a fairly significant part of their training. I have tried to write the book in a direct and accessible way, avoiding jargon as much as I can and because the publisher would not let me write a 200,000 word book, where I have only given a small amount of space to a topic, I try to direct the reader to more detailed texts.

Using this book

I would be delighted of course if the reader sat down in her favourite chair, with a favourite snack and maybe a glass of something and read this book cover to cover. But I know that, like me, most people rarely get a chance to do that kind of thing and are more likely to use text books as resources. Certainly more will be derived from this book if you are actively engaged in research, in which case you might need to dip into particular chapters just to get a feel for an issue of immediate concern. Nevertheless the order of the book pretty much mirrors the direction of the research process, with a couple of exceptions. Interpretive research (Chapter 3) may well come after survey research in multi-method studies and research design (Chapter 9) is intentionally later in the book for reasons explained there.

Structure of the book

Chapter 1 *Science and Commitment in Social Research:* The relationship of social research to science and commitment. The positivist–humanist debate and methodological pluralism. The role of values and an argument for objectivity.

Chapter 2 *From Question to Method:* Where research questions come from and their relationship to theory. Building and testing theories and their 'operationalization' into research. Realism and social research.

Chapter 3 *Research as Interpretation:* Qualitative approaches as interpretive method. The possibilities and limitations of interpretivism. Key approaches in field research, depth interviewing and focus groups.

Chapter 4 *Selecting and Sampling:* The principles of selecting and sampling. Probability and non-probability samples in survey research. Sampling and selecting in interpretivism.

Chapter 5 *Survey Research:* Types of survey and methods of data collection and principal methods of data collection. Quality issues in surveys.

Chapter 6 *Questionnaire Design:* Question context, content and appearance. Asking about attitudes, beliefs and behaviour. Question wording and layout, types of question. Piloting questionnaires.

Chapter 7 *Analysing Survey Data:* Cases and variables. Introduction to probability, measures of central tendency and dispersion. Analysis with one variable. Analysis with two variables, contingency tables and elaboration. Statistical significance and hypothesis testing. Correlation, regression and analysis with three or more variables.

Chapter 8 *The Ethics of Social Research:* Ethics and their importance in research. Decisions about what is ethical research. The avoidance of harm and deception. Issues of privacy and informed consent.

Chapter 9 *Designing Research:* Design decisions and strategies. Resources and research. Multi-method research and triangulation. Ten questions to ask when designing research.

Chapter 10 *Reporting Findings:* Disseminating research results. Audiences and ways of reporting research. Styles of presentation and what can and cannot be claimed.

I have tried to tread a path between the discursive and the illustrative throughout the book. Some things about social research can be communicated in a how to do or how not to do things. Social research *is* about doing, so there is a lot of that. But I also think that the discursive is important, because there is much in social research that is contentious. I, like every other writer on the subject, will not be giving you a neutral account, a workshop manual, but a personal view of what research is like and what is important. For this reason I have stuck to the traditional practice of concluding each chapter with a conclusion, but to help the reader with orientation and to make the book look nicer, I have also incorporated the following:

- Each chapter begins with a short summary of contents.
- In each chapter I've inserted brief research examples in boxes to illustrate the issues discussed in the text. These should be seen only as 'tasters' and it is recommended that where possible the original source is consulted. Indeed, in such short cameos it would be impossible to thoroughly describe all of the intentions, methods and results of the research.
- Each chapter ends with some discussion points, questions to consider or things to do. The ways these are done might vary from individual mental contemplation to group or 'workshop' exercises.
- Also at the end of each chapter there are a few recommended readings that carry the subject matter of the chapter a little further. These are very much personal recommendations and you may find other books that you consider more helpful.
- Finally, although I have explained most terms used either in the text or in chapter end notes, the reader may find it useful to acquire a copy of W. Paul Vogt's splendid *Dictionary of Statistics and Methodology* (1998).

Science and Commitment in Social Research

In this chapter:

- The difference between the natural and social world
- Science and art in social research
- Positivism and anti-positivism
- Methodological pluralism in research
- Normative and objective approaches
- Values and bias in social research

Social research, unlike natural science disciplines, investigates the activities, beliefs, values and situations of other human beings. Though natural science is also a human activity and its agenda and social relations are shaped by human concerns, its subject matter is not. Gravity discriminates against no one and its effects are not subject to human redefinition or opinion. Many of the things social researchers investigate are. They are socially constructed and subject to redefinition. What counts as poverty now is not the same as in the past and definitions of it will vary from place to place. This characteristic of the social world has produced a contentiousness about the purpose and possibility of social research that is absent in the natural sciences. Certainly there is plenty of debate about scientific method and the ethics of science in the latter, but few would seriously doubt the efficacy of science *per se* in investigating the natural world. In investigations of the social world it is different with, historically, two broad groupings: those who believe that a scientific approach to investigating the social world is just as appropriate as in investigations of the natural world. Second, those who believe scientific approaches are inappropriate and instead the methods of the arts or humanities should be used. Traditionally these groupings have mapped onto the two methodological approaches I mentioned in the Introduction with the 'scientists' favouring quantitative methods and the 'humanists' favouring qualitative methods. However, like so many things in life, it is not that simple, because many of the scientists use or advocate the use of qualitative methods as well, though few humanists advocate quantitative approaches. Moreover, as I hinted, there are many shades of opinion in each grouping and some who would deny the distinction altogether. Its sharpness here is intended to bring some initial conceptual clarity.

The difference extends beyond method to why we do social research at all. Again, two groupings which roughly map onto the scientific/humanist distinction, are those who believe that social research should be objective and serve no ideological or political master and those who see social research precisely as a tool to achieve ideological or political goals. There are, then, two big conceptual issues at the heart of social research, the question of science and the question of commitment.

The aim of this chapter is to help make sense of these issues and their ensuing distinctions and to show how social research is transcending them. But if they are being transcended, you may ask, why bore us with history? Three reasons: first, it helps in order to make sense of the reasoning (which has evolved historically) underlying quantitative and qualitative approaches. Second, if these divisions are being transcended, then what is it they are transcending? Third, any choice of method comes with some underlying assumptions which can make a difference to its usefulness in describing, explaining and understanding the social world. In this chapter I will proceed as follows.

In the first part I will discuss the uneasy relationship between scientific and non-scientific approaches and the possibilities for a social research that transcends these difficulties. In the second part I will consider the issue of objectivity. I will conclude that a rigorous effective social research requires both a commitment to a moderate view of science and a belief that social research can be objective.

Science and art in social research

In a pithy book about the relationship of science to art (and a justification for the utility of the former) Raymond Tallis (1995) provocatively entitled the first half of the book 'The Usefulness of Science' and the second 'The Uselessness of Art'. Now it is not the intention of Tallis to suggest that art has no value for human beings, nor indeed that they can always be sharply divided. Rather, Tallis wants to say that for the betterment of the human material condition (in health, nutrition, technology that makes life easier, etc.), art is of no use. Indeed, to make the benefits of art widely available we need science's emergent technology.

In studies of the social world things are not so clear-cut. I believe Tallis is still right if we regard studies of the social world as science, but it is not the case that all studies of the social world are science. Although some say none are, I think some are and some aren't and even those that are must make use of the techniques of art. Before I look at the historical perspective I will briefly try to separate out (in very rough terms) those kinds of studies that are art and those that are science (even though they may use techniques borrowed from art[1]).

Art can tell us much about what we like as individuals and about the human condition and it does so through music, literature and paintings. The statements of the artist are personal, but they are to be shared and perhaps (often unconsciously) they are statements that seek an empathy. Now perhaps this is a rather bland statement to make – of course, art is about the human condition, but how is it about investigation? There is an area between the humanities and what we might term social studies that is overtly about investigation. Often this is experimental art or literature, or historically an investigation of existing texts by scholars. Originally the latter work (in medieval times) was undertaken by scholars on biblical texts and aimed to uncover hidden meanings, to find a deeper interpretation of the texts. This was the art (or science – these things are never clear-cut!) of hermeneutics and its great champion in the study of human affairs was Giambattista Vico (1668–1744). Vico was especially interested in the study of history and main-tained that because 'nations' and their history were made by humans, then it was open to ways of understanding not available in the natural sciences. To study history is to seek the meanings of the actions of the people involved. To use the anthropologist Clifford Geertz's (1994) expression, the aim is to find 'thick description', in which layers of meaning are uncovered.

Since Vico, many have held that this can be the only way to study the social world (I will return to them presently), but we can certainly agree on two things. First, that the self-reflecting, self-constructing nature of human society makes it conceptually different to the physical world and, second, that at least some of this is about art. A great deal of what we know about the world comes from the pen, or the brush of the artist. In other words, artists interpret the world (and that's good!), but sometimes the point is to change it! Art changes the world, but it changes it at a subjective level, it is the world of caprice and emotion.

Yet while social research must call upon the artist's methods of interpreta-tion (and these I will discuss in Chapter 3), it needs also to be dependable and cannot therefore be art. We need more from social research. It needs to be able to give us information that will help the policy-maker resolve prob-lems such as crime, poverty and discrimination. We need data about popu-lation projections that will help us plan for health, education, social security, etc. and we need trustworthy reports of people's opinions if we are to provide the goods and services they require. Harold Kincaid makes a succinct plea for dependable social science in warning us of the alternative

> If no social science is possible, if the best social scientists can do is to give us many different kinds of literary 'thick' description of social reality, then social policy is groundless. Imagine that we could have no real knowledge about social processes. Government intervention in social and economic affairs would be inane. How could we evaluate educational programs, prison reform, economic policy and so on without having well-confirmed generalisations about the causes of the social phenomena? (Kincaid, 1996: 7)

Put like that, who could disagree? Certainly if we cannot aspire to these things then social research is indulgent, and if it cannot produce results, then who will be prepared to pay for it? The quotation from Kincaid comes early in a book mostly devoted to a defence of the position of scientific naturalism in social research – briefly, the perspective that the reasoning and methods of the natural sciences are just as much part of the social scientific project. In other words Kincaid's view is by no means without challenge. But what is it that is being challenged? Textbooks often tell us that it is something called positivism, so let us look at what is meant by the term and what are the objections to it.

Positivism

The term 'positivism' was coined by Auguste Comte (1798–1857) and later became associated with Emile Durkheim (1858–1917). Both have been influential in sociology, particularly the latter who combined analysis of numeric data with writings justifying the scientific approach to investigation, particularly emphasizing the importance of observation. However, despite their fame as positivists, a greater influence was that of logical positivism (sometimes called logical empiricism), a 'scientific' version of the philosophy of David Hume (1711–76). Hume's version of empiricism has two strands important to us here: the centrality of sense data (and therefore observation) and a scepticism towards knowledge claims that could not be grounded in observation. Hume's influence had been important throughout the nineteenth century, but in its logical positivist form dominated philosophical thinking about natural and social science in the first half of the twentieth century[2].

The influence on social research was not usually direct, but much more via the importance attached to statistical evidence and the consequent prioritization of statistical data for policy-making, particularly in the United States (see Platt, 1996). Social research was dominated by a profession 'trained in statistical methods, with mutually reinforcing motivations to win promotion and produce the "facts" needed by mayors, presidents and corporations' (Manicas, 1987: 226). The methods of this period were primarily the social survey, in which standardized data were collected from identified groups in the population on a range of topics as diverse as political polling and army life. What became known and accepted as positivism was never in this period any kind of unified approach (though a few such as George Lundberg (1939, 1947), tried to make it so). It was certainly a commitment to scientific social research, but a particular form of scientific social research. In other words, positivism does not exhaust the ways in which social research can be scientific. There are a number of very good books written on positivism, in particular, *Positivism and Sociology*, by Peter Halfpenny (1982) is to be commended and many authors have summed up what positivism consists of (see Phillips, 1987: Chapter 4; Bryman, 1988: 18–19; Williams, 2000a: 20–2). It is important not to conflate scientific method with positivist method, so what I will do here (in Table 1.1) is to list some key characteristics of science (as I see them) and some characteristics of positivism. Positivism believes in the characteristics of both columns, whereas the methodologist committed to scientific method need only align themselves with the items in the first

Table 1.1 Key characteristics of science and positivism

Scientific Method	Positivism[3]
Explanatory	Prioritizes observation
Predictive	Verificatory (procedures should show whether a statement is true or false)
Evidence based	Value free (moral values have no part in science)
Seeks truth	Operationalist (scientists can only deal in those things which are measurable).
Objective	
Logical	
Parsimonious	
Numerative	

column and may (if she is a realist, critical rationalist, etc.) substitute other items for those in the second column.

I will refer, to varying extent, to all of the items in column one in further chapters (but particularly in the next chapter), but first what happened to positivism?

Well, it got itself killed off by a philosopher called Karl Popper (1989, Chapter 11). Though he took quite a lot of his long career to say it, his refutation of logical positivism is simple and elegant. Positivists believed that all propositions about the world are only meaningful if we can show how they can be *verified*. Now this was stronger than saying scientists have to produce evidence, it meant that scientists must have two sets of statements: theoretical statements and *observation* statements. If you have a theory that children from one-parent families under-achieve, then you need to say what will count as under-achievement and the children will be seen to have underachieved, if and only if that under-achievement can be measured. Priority is placed upon measurement rather than a prior articulation of the concept. Now we all know that terms like 'achievement' are subject to definition and redefinition, but it took Popper to point this out. Popper was not talking about one-parent families of course, but about complex ideas in physics. The problem for social science was the followers of logical positivism (for example, the above-mentioned Lundberg) believed that there could be unproblematic observation statements in the social world about such matters as class, alienation, etc.[4] The second (and most famous) part of Popper's refutation was to do with observation itself. The logical positivists believed observation could show a theory to be wrong and the theory should be discarded, but if instead it was verified, then it stood as knowledge. Positivists, then, believed in facts. These were the result of rigorous observation. Popper raised an objection that had actually been pointed out by Hume, but ignored, mainly on the grounds of the observational success of science since. The objection was, how can you know that all of your sightings of X fully describe all Xs? He illustrates this with the neat example of swans. Until European settlers travelled to Australia all swans sighted were white, so it was therefore believed all swans were white. The first white settlers in Australia soon discovered that in Australia there were black swans. Thus the statement 'all swans are white' was falsified.

However much observational evidence you have can never prove anything; indeed, said Popper, science (or at least good science) does not proceed in this way. Instead it proceeds through criticism, through setting out to falsify a theory, rather than proving it.

There's a lot more to Popper's argument than the brief summary I have given and it has been subject to a lot of critical debate since (see, for example, Lakatos and Musgrave, 1970), but nevertheless it did cause the logical positivists to lose heart rather and positivism withered on the vine, eventually to be replaced by much more sophisticated versions of empiricism in natural science (see van Frassen, 1980). Despite this, if we are to believe the many, many textbooks on social science method, positivism is alive and well in social science. It isn't, it's dead (see Phillips, 1987 for a full discussion of its passing). Indeed, the reason for the brief excursus into Popper was to show why this is the case. Its continued ghostly existence is due to two things.

First, quite a lot of social research (particularly surveys) exhibits a kind of naïve empiricism (Williams, 1998: 14), whereby it is implicitly accepted that the measurements devised measure the reality as theorized. Now this is pretty much what the positivists believed, except they believed we could only talk of *sensations*, not realities. Take the example of homelessness. What I characterize as naïve empiricism is the belief that when you measure or describe homelessness, in a social survey, you are directly describing or measuring a reality of homelessness. It is more complex than that. First, it is very difficult to produce a definition of homelessness that will capture the many forms it takes and, second, respondents who may experience the same objective housing conditions may well interpret or define their experiences in different ways. The 'reality' of homelessness is heterogeneous and dynamic (Williams and Cheal, 2001).

Critics are right to a point when they claim to discern a continuing positivism within the social survey, though the naïve empiricism I describe is not absent in interpretive research (see Bryman, 1988: 119). The second reason why many think positivism is still alive is much more to do with the ideological success of anti-science in social science. In this view positivism and science are interchangeable (see Guba and Lincoln, 1982; Denzin, 1983). Now there is much in (let's call it) humanism that is of value and some of its intellectual pedigree is impeccable, but it is sometimes hard to separate out the rhetoric from the sound methodological points.

Humanism

There are two important strands to humanism: ideological and methodological. Though the first is important in the history of the social and natural sciences, I shall discuss this only briefly (but see Williams, 2000a Chapter 4 for a full discussion) and spend a little more time on the methodological.

Ideological strand: only the mad, or those of great vision, questioned science up until Hiroshima and then ironically they were often scientists themselves (Sagan, 1996). The real opposition to science only got going in the 1960s. Disillusionment with the arms race, the inability of science to feed the world and the horror of Vietnam produced a counter-culture that simultaneously looked to alternative non-Western philosophies for inspiration and to humanistic Marxism (Roszak, 1995 [1968]). The latter in particular emphasized the ideological nature of power, thus science was powerful, but was the product of a bourgeois hegemony. It followed that if there was to be revolution, then bourgeois science must be likewise overthrown.

The specific ideological criticism of science gained credence from the writings of Thomas Kuhn ([1962] 1970) who claimed that science was not simply a triumphal progress toward truth, but in fact what counted as truth and progress were often contained within an overall 'paradigm' which consisted not just of 'verified' discoveries, but also social and psychological assumptions about what counted as legitimate knowledge. Kuhn's critique, though often only half-understood, was actually much more influential on social science than Popper's.

All of these things contributed to a widespread (as Gerald Holton put it) 'delegitimation of science' (Holton, 1993). This took a while, especially in the United States where through the 1960s it was pretty much business as usual (Platt, 1996). Up until then social theory had been strongly influenced by the work of Talcott Parsons and political economy by the Keynsians, both emphasizing scientific method, and both came to be seen as apologists for capitalism. In both the United States and Great Britain government social research remained dominated by statisticians, mostly trained in the heyday of positivism. By the end of the 1960s social science as 'science' was being challenged in Europe and the United States. It was accused of being cold, impersonal and most of all in the service of the ruling class. The period of social revolution, in the late 1960s, coincided both with the elevation of young people as important consumers and citizens (as opposed to the comparatively subservient youth of the 1940s and 1950s), but also the expansion of higher education in the USA and Western Europe. This expansion favoured the social sciences and humanities and the new cohort of graduates had very different views on the purpose and method of social science to their predecessors. Though survey research was still favoured by government and market research, the shift to interpretation was marked in academic social science, especially sociology and anthropology and the reaction against it was muted (Goldthorpe, 2000: 65–6). The rise of postmodernism and post-structuralism in the 1980s provided further impetus and at the time of writing there is evidence to suggest that this approach still dominates British academic sociology.[5]

Methodological strand: the social sciences expanded rapidly in the 1960s, both in numbers of graduates, but also in terms of intellectual production. The implications for method were enormous, but can be summed up as marking a shift from explanation to interpretation, from number to language. This was combined with a specific commitment to social change, rather than simply describing social life.[6] What was at issue was whether study of the social world should be nomothetic or ideographic. The nomothetic is equated with *abstract* generalizable law like statements, and the ideographic can be equated with specific instances or moments. The best known champion of interpretivist method, Max Weber, held that social science should be both (Weber, 1975). Unfortunately rigorous attempts to resolve the dispute in Weber and later in the work of Herbert Blumer (Hammersley, 1989) were forgotten and the complex issues became rather simplified in the revolution against 'positivism'. Positivism became a mythical beast that had to be ritually slain in print at every opportunity.

As with the positivist case, which was far from being all bad, the anti-positivist humanist case was based on some sound reasoning. An important figure in this was Peter Winch, who in 1958 published a groundbreaking little book called *The Idea of a Social Science* (Winch [1958] 1990).

Winch argued that the social world was not law-governed, so the search for causes was mistaken. What the 'positivists' had taken to be laws were in fact rules, and, as we know, the defining characteristic of a rule is that it can be broken. Moreover, rules only apply locally. They can be seen as local grammars, which we must come to learn and, when we are proficient, are capable of changing. Until we are proficient we cannot understand, or we misunderstand a rule when seen from the outside. Rules themselves are often literally grammars and are expressed through language, therefore many of the mistakes we make are linguistic ones, which carry social consequences. The British comedian Jasper Carrot tells an apocryphal story of when a traffic cop pulled him over during a visit to the United States. The cop asked for his licence and noticed it had two 'endorsements'. 'Say, you must be a very good driver', says the cop 'your licence has been endorsed twice.' In Britain a licence endorsement is the accretion of penalty points for bad driving! On a rather similar note of cultural difference between the USA and Britain, few men called Randall use the diminutive in the latter country.

At the risk of bowdlerizing Winch's complex work, the argument runs like this. Social life is rule-governed, rules are linguistic and languages, or the use, or the nuances of languages are local. To know the local, you must be a local. Winch's conclusion is pessimistic about studying social life at all, but the followers of Winch took the linguistic point seriously and many embraced epistemological relativism – the belief that in interpreting other cultures there are no truths universal to all cultures. Nevertheless, most assumed that some kind of interpretation was possible, but it had to be an interpretation that was faithful to the culture being interpreted. It should not be the researcher, but the voices of the researched we hear.

Now this is a long way from hypothesis-driven surveys, where the researcher tries to find out how many people have characteristics X or believe Y and possibly goes on to produce mathematical models to explain characteristics, or behaviour. For many new to studies of the social world, what has been termed the 'linguistic turn' seemed altogether a more liberating method for both the researched and the researcher. Indeed, most of us have experienced a frustration when faced with a choice of a, b or c on a questionnaire, none of which fit our views or circumstances. 'Shall I put you down as a "don't know"?', says the interviewer. Such practices distort our view of social life, say the interpretivists; we must learn to understand the meanings people hold for what they do, or say. We must learn about social life in context.

The experience of interpretive methods in anthropology, particularly the use of the techniques of 'participant observation' or 'unstructured interviewing', has fed back into the work of sociologists and policy researchers. Participant observation requires the investigator to partially, or wholly, immerse herself in the culture of those he or she investigates. This might be within an 'alien' culture, such as that investigated by anthropologists (see, for example, Geertz, 1979) or more 'familiar' cultures such as the inner city (see, for example, Whyte, 1955 [1943]; Suttles, 1968; Spradley, 1970; Hobbs, 1988). The participant comes to understand (it is claimed) the culture from the point of view of a person from that culture. There are no firm prescriptions for the collection of data, or what kind of data are collected. The investigator uses whatever is best or possible (notebook, tape recorder, or just memory) and records those things that help to build a coherent picture of the culture that faithfully captures the meanings of its participants. Likewise the unstructured interview (confusingly sometimes called the focused interview), though often guided initially by some questions from the interviewer, is intended to allow those investigated to develop their perspective (Bryman, 1988: 47). No hypothesis is being tested, standardization of the interview (questions, format, etc.) is unnecessary, the aim simply being 'to make sense of an object of study' (Taylor, 1994: 181).

Now this sounds very plausible and many feel it is a better way of doing things than an impersonal survey. Unfortunately the above approach and Kincaid's strictures do not go well together, or at least interpretive method comes at a price.

The first problem is the one that Winch identified. If only a member of a community, knowing the rules of that community, can really know that community, how can an outsider ever achieve accurate knowledge? Now Winch meant this in respect of very different cultures to ours, though it can be a problem even within our own Western culture (see the Jasper Carrot story above). How can the researcher know that the interpretations he or she makes are the 'valid' ones of those interpreted? Alan Bryman (1988: 74) discusses this in relation to school studies, where to an extent all adults are strangers!

While it is generally acknowledged among interpretivists that some kind of solution, either at the philosophical or technical level, is possible to the above problem of internal validity, the problem of external validity is both more difficult and more contentious.

Survey research is based upon the well-established statistical principles of sampling. That is when we have an identified population of people or things, it is possible to devise procedures whereby a sample taken will reflect the characteristics of the wider population (see Chapter 4). For all sorts of reasons this is not a strategy open to the interpretivist. As we will see in

Chapter 4, interpretivist researchers do attempt to select, even sample, but groups investigated cannot be sampled in a conventional sense for a number of methodological reasons: for example, because they are elusive, rare, the research must be covert or a large enough sample is unachievable.

If there can be no systematic approach to sampling, then the researcher cannot know whether the findings are typical, or simply confined to the group being researched (Williams, 2000b). However rich the descriptions are, however sophisticated the interpretation of meaning, the researcher does not really know the likelihood of this being a one off.[7]

There are other associated methodological problems, which I will discuss in more detail in Chapter 3, but briefly, the advantage of the unstructured interview is that it allows respondents to prioritize or choose categories appropriate to them, but this also means that any standardization of procedure is limited. There are no questionnaires, often no predesigned questions (though there will usually be lists of topics) and consequently many of the questions that are asked in interviews, or the scenes recorded during observations, are not repeatable (or at least are not repeated). Finally, although the aim of interpretivism is to conduct research in 'natural' surroundings, the researcher can never know to what extent he or she has changed the nature of the surroundings by being there at all. Added together these problems inevitably lead to the question of whether interpretivists can ever know if they have got it right or wrong. There are no criteria of external validation (Jones, 1998).

It is not just the critics of the ideographic approach who have realized these problems; they are recognized by many interpretivists themselves. Broadly, there are two responses to this. There is the relativist approach embraced by postmodernists, which simply sees all accounts as epistemologically equal and not to be privileged one over another (Rosenau, 1991: Chapter 7). In its extreme this approach is art and art in the romantic tradition and represents precisely the kind of 'research' Kincaid complained of. I will return to this below in the context of values. Conversely there is an opposite approach of moderate realist ethnography, often influenced by the Chicago School of research (more about them in Chapter 3). It is represented in the methodological writings of Martyn Hammersley (1989; 1998; 2000) and embraces the view that while interpretivism has inherited a great many methodological problems, technical and philosophical solutions are possible and must be sought in order to preserve the great utility of the method. As no doubt you will have discerned, my own sympathies are very much closer to Hammersley than the postmodernists, though I recognize that between the two positions there are a host of others that have at least some methodological value.

Methodological pluralism

In the foregoing I have outlined two extremes, which have been for the most part abandoned by mainstream social research. Nevertheless there are postmodernists out there still fighting the good fight against positivism (see Denzin and Lincoln, 1994, for examples) and a few unreconstructed mathematical junkies wanting to explain the social world solely through statistical algorithms. Most researchers have embraced what are sometimes termed post-positivist positions on methodology, believing that the principal objections to positivism and interpretivism can be overcome within a methodological pluralism. The spectrum of post-positivist methodologies is wide and embraces (for example) critical theory, some forms of feminism, critical rationalism, realism and a number of hybrids of these. I shall say no more about these because this is a methods book and not intended to be an extensive discussion of philosophical and theoretical issues underlying research (though see further readings recommended at the end of this chapter),[8] but I think we can identify and summarize a middle ground which overcomes some of the more serious difficulties I discussed above.

THE LIMITATIONS AND POSSIBILITIES OF SCIENTIFIC METHOD   All science begins with theoretical constructions which are turned into testable hypotheses. After Popper and Kuhn we know these are social constructions, but to a point they are testable, though we may need different methods to test different kinds of theories and hypotheses. The answers we get are not final, but subject to further redefinition and testing. We may hypothesize that Community A is more 'religious' than Community B and we may test this through measuring formal public religious worship in a survey. However, it is likely we will decide that formal public worship may only measure one aspect of religion and to fully develop the concept and the survey questions we may have to use interpretive methods to find out what counts as 'religious' in each community.

THE LIMITATIONS AND POSSIBILITIES OF INTERPRETIVISM   Two big problems exist for interpretivism. The first is, how can a stranger come to know society S; the second is how can we know whether the features of S are unique, or common to other societies? To continue with the hypothetical example of religion. First, in trying to understand a religion there are almost certainly characteristics that will be present in all religious observance, for example a belief in some form of superhuman existence and engagement in worship or contemplation. These kinds of things provide initial identifiers for the researcher and they are unlikely to exist in a cultural setting that is without any other kinds of referents to other cultures. Winch described extreme examples rarely found nowadays and there will usually be some kind of cultural consistency and continuum. This does not mean that we can know whether a particular feature is general or specific, say, a particular kind of religious ceremony, but as with the survey, the limits of this method can be transcended by using other methods.

Methodological pluralism is not necessarily the view that we must use multi-method approaches (though I will discuss these things in relation to research design in Chapter 9), but it is a perspective which maintains that social science needs a particular methodological approach that can combine scientific reasoning with methods suitable to social investigation. This means recognizing both the potential and the limits of each methodological approach. The critique of positivism and the counter-critique of interpretive methods did much to clarify the potential and limitations of these methods and paved the way to methodological pluralism. How this might be brought about in the context of a social *science* will be discussed in subsequent chapters, but I turn now from the question of science to the question of objectivity and commitment in social research.

Social research and commitment

I, like so many others, did not become a social researcher through methodological commitment. The motivation was social commitment: I wanted to learn about social science, so that I could use that knowledge to make the world better. This remains the case, but I also have come to realize that the causes in which we believe are best served by truth. This, however, is not always a simple matter. Natural and social scientists alike now mostly accept that the activity of each is socially situated, that 'value freedom' is no longer tenable. In social research it has become almost a cliché to say that values enter the process at every stage. When people speak of values they usually mean moral values, but the word value can have a broader meaning encompassing both utility and measurement. To say something measures 3 degrees and not 4 degrees is to make a mathematical and logical distinction between two states. To say something is 'good' is to make a similar logical contrast between a desired and not desired state. These different uses of the word value are less distinct that would first appear, as Steven Shapin (1979) has shown in the story of phrenology and cranial topography. Though the former was motivated by now discredited moral values, much of what we know of the latter was due to measurements undertaken by nineteenth-century phrenologists. A second example can be found in the story of the *t* tests, widely used in social statistics. Here we have to thank beer drinkers for its existence. William Gosset was a research chemist working for the Guinness brewery in Dublin in the early twentieth century when he worked out the *t* distribution. He was not allowed to publish under his own name and used the pseudonym 'student' – hence the 'student's *t* test' (Clegg, 1982: 87). Though in the second case there was more of a commercial desire to sell beer than moral prescription, but what both of these examples tell us is that even measurement values have a social history.

Some go further than this claiming that measurement itself is a moral value, born of particular cultures. Prominent in this view are some forms of standpoint feminism which hold that the attempts at the language of value neutrality in science disguise deeply held masculine social values. Most standpoint feminists are not intentionally anti-science, but believe the whole scientific project needs rescuing from androcentricity. I will return to this below.

Social science has not been immune to such criticisms. The anti-positivist movement of the 1960s and 1970s was not just methodologically radical, but it was also radical in terms of values. The above mentioned Thomas Kuhn claimed that there was an 'incommensurability' between paradigms. This was not just the way of doing science, but what counted as discovery or the resolution of a problem – truth itself. Though Kuhn never intended it to be the case, his claim led to a conclusion of epistemological relativism among some philosophers of science and social scientists. This means that the truths of one culture are not the truths of another, nor are they translatable into each other. No overall, encompassing truth is available. The relativist conclusion was therefore not the same as that of the standpoint feminists. The latter accepted the claim about the moral basis of values, but drew the conclusion that the problem could be transcended.[9]

The acceptance of the value-laden view leads to three broad positions on values and commitment. These positions have not just moral implications for social research, but methodological ones to do with bias as well.

Relativism

Epistemological relativism is the starting point of postmodernist and many poststructuralist accounts of the social world. For the reason I set out at the beginning of this chapter, that research should be dependable, I do not think these accounts qualify as research at all and I only mention them because of their prominence in the (mainly) anthropological and sociological literature in the past 15 years. The absence of any acultural standards of truth about the way the world is leads to a comparative method of alternative 'interpretations' of aspects of the social world in which no interpretation can claim any privilege. It follows from this relativism about what is, that a similar position about what ought to be, is held: 'that no cultural tradition can analytically encompass the discourse of another cultural tradition' (Tyler, 1986: 328).[10] The plea is instead for multiple voices to be heard, but none to be privileged – a sort of moral agnosticism. In a curious way this extreme scepticism has come full circle to meet the value freedom of the positivists in that neither claim any prior moral commitment. For examples of relativist accounts in anthropology see Clifford and Marcus (1986), and for a powerful critique of these positions see Jones (1998).

Normative approaches

What I term 'normative' approaches are all committed to a moral view of what is right or wrong, desirable or undesirable in the social world. The best known of these is Marxism. There are fewer Marxist researchers around now than there used to be (presumably because they've paid off their mortgages) and Marxism is perhaps more interesting in the positions on values it has influenced, in particular feminism and critical theory.

There are many strands of Marxism, but central to them all is the view that no one occupies a politically neutral position. All are members of one or other class and this will determine one's political perspective. Neutrality in social science occupies a similar position to equality before the law: it is a bourgeois myth. Therefore social research will reflect its own class bias and if you are a Marxist then you should orientate what and how you research to the interests of the proletariat. This does not stop you being objective as a researcher, but objectivity is grounded in a particular class agenda (see Wright, 1997).

Similarly, critical theorists insist that knowledge is obtained from a perspective. Also, like Marxism (from which critical theory originated), there is a commitment to emancipation. The role of research is in the furtherance of that emancipation. However, the difference between this perspective and a Marxist one is that critical theory is first and foremost committed to social science as critique, or as Nancy Fraser puts it: 'A critical social theory frames its research programmes and its conceptual framework with an eye to the aims and activities of those oppositional social movements with which it has a partisan, though not uncritical, identification' (1989: 113).

Later versions of critical theory have placed emphasis on the role of self-reflection in the research process (May, 1998a) and the importance of the provisional nature of knowledge (Fay, 1996).

A third example of the normative perspective is that of feminism, particularly the standpoint feminism I mentioned above (see, for example, Rose, 1983; Harding, 1986; Hartsock, 1987; Harding, 1996). As with critical theory, emancipation is the aim, the difference being that a particular emphasis is placed on producing objective accounts of reality. This is a very different kind of objectivity to the traditional scientific view (and the one to which I'll refer below). Science, including social science, is seen as a gendered activity that simply reflects a patriarchal value system. The view that science can be objective under these circumstances is itself a patriarchal myth. Such myths distort science and its results. A more objective view of the world must be grounded in women's experience, an experience shaped by patriarchal subjugation. The particular importance of the feminist perspective lies in the methods adopted, which begin from the express position of women and their subjective experiences. This often leads to alternative methods such as autobiography and diaries (see Ribbens and Edwards, 1998).

The justification for most normative positions is that researchers cannot be neutral observers and in the case of the 'strong' positions I have outlined, have a duty to take a stance on values if they wish to be agents of change. Moreover, it is often held, the whole project of social science is itself a normative one, not just about explaining or understanding the social world, but about changing it.

The difficulty with all normative positions is that of agreeing what the goals of the ideological or political project shall be. There are substantial differences within critical theory or feminism about how emancipation shall be achieved, or indeed about what counts as emancipation. Second, when truth is seen as subject to context, then a change of context can change what is seen as truth (see Hammersley, 2000: Chapter 6, for a discussion of this). This can make a difference even in respect of the methods adopted. Feminisms and critical theory have mostly eschewed survey methods, in the former case because they are seen to embrace the very androcentric values of science that had subjugated women for so long. The need for non-hierarchical methods was argued for by Anne Oakley (1981) as a result of her research on motherhood. The richness of her data was seen (by her) as resulting from a personal engagement with the mothers she interviewed. However, 19 years later things had changed and Oakley was arguing that the gendering of methods had produced an unhelpful ideological reaction (Oakley, 2000). Things had gone too far.

Objectivity

In my view normative positions throw up as many difficulties for the researcher as that of value freedom, especially as at a pragmatic level the adoption of particular ideological positions about research outcomes tends to make the research less believable to those who do not hold such positions. If I am conducting research on homelessness I do not want to be believed only by those who see homelessness as an unacceptable consequence of the commodification of housing, I want also to be believed by those doing the commodifying and those who have no position.

This view might be seen as a successor to both that of positivistic value freedom and normative positions. It is accepted that values permeate the entire research process and that value freedom is unobtainable. Indeed, as I have shown, it is the case that non-moral values, such as measurement values, themselves often have moral antecedents. However, to abandon objectivity is to abandon any kind of dependability in research with the possible consequence that there is no difference between the believability of research findings and fiction. An unfortunate consequence of anti-positivism is that it has left a legacy of conflation between value freedom and objectivity, leaving normativism as the only value position (as opposed to relativism) to occupy.

What I have termed the position of 'objectivity' has a history traceable to Max Weber (Weber [1925] 1978). Rather confusingly, (though in keeping with the time in which it was written) Weber's version of objectivity in sociology is described as 'value free', though it is quite different to that advocated by the positivists. Instead Weber says that the sociologist must *begin* from a position of values. He regarded values as a defining characteristic of human beings. Nevertheless he also recognized (Albrow, 1990: 243) that if we accept that all values are subjective or culturally contingent, then this leads inexorably to relativism. Instead Weber believed that only by embracing values wholeheartedly can a scientist achieve value freedom. Moreover, he also recognized that science itself is founded on values such as truth, rigour and clarity.

Weber's position rests on the acceptance that in science in general and specifically in sociology, there will be a debate about 'ends', about what policy should achieve and therefore what research should be done (Weber, 1974: 75). It does not follow from this, however, that the investigation itself need be biased by those values. For example, interpretive methods allow us to know the meaning of social practices for the people we investigate, but it does not mean we have to take sides on the values they hold. One does not have to be a Fascist to understand Mussolini and why he took Italy into World War II; one does not have to be deviant to understand deviance. In sociology Weber's objectivity is to make the subjective values of those investigated the subject matter of the discipline, to show how their values guided their actions. Objectivity does not imply neutrality, as the positivists believed. Alfred Tauber (1997: 30) cites Robert Proctor's distinction between the two. Neutrality implies that science does not take a stand, whereas objectivity is about whether science is dependable. Proctor uses the term reliable.[11] Particular sciences may be completely objective, but may serve economic or political interests.

A lot of good social science has followed this dictum of Weber's. Yet leaving one's values behind is not always as straightforward as it seems. Feminists are not wholly wrong when they claim that the methods of science are themselves culturally influenced (see, for example, Harding, 1996). The development of scientific social science was less to do with its perceived methodological efficacy in its own right and much more to do with the success of scientific method in investigating nature. Despite this, and here all would agree, science (and social science) need methods of some kind and moreover some kinds of method do seem effective in obtaining data. A recent thinker to recognize this is Helen Longino (1990), herself a feminist. She speaks of science having both constitutive values that are internal to it (things such as accuracy, reliability, etc.) and contextual values, those external things which shape what it is science is about, or what particular sciences should strive for. This position is similar to Weber's, but she goes further and says that contextual values do and should inform constitutive values. The history of both natural and social science would bear out that this is indeed so. Developments in methodology have nearly always been linked to contextual goals. The rapid industrialization of the United States in the first half of the twentieth century coincided with the growth of scientific sociology, both survey method and experiment (Madge, 1963; Platt, 1996). Likewise it was not just idle curiosity that led to the development of urban ethnography by the Chicago School, but the perception that the poverty that grew out of urbanization was a serious social problem. The context of the slum shaped the ethnography itself. Longino's resolution of the conflicts of interest this might entail is to redefine objectivity as (what she calls) 'transformative interrogation'. The values are acknowledged, but they are examined communally, so that, unlike Weber, she does not believe the decision about objectivity is a burden an individual should carry.

The idea of a critical community of social or natural scientists seems splendid, but does it follow from this that objectivity would indeed emerge, or would it be the case that consensus, whether or not such consensus was right, would prevail?

Objectivity cannot be a matter of democracy or consensus, for it leaves no room for the maverick and may well punish innovation. Yet objectivity can be a public good that we strive for, but it must be a good we also strive for individually. It is possible to accept that objectivity is indeed a social value, but one which has the unusual property of helping us get a little closer to the truth. Proctor's redefinition of objectivity as reliability seems useful to me. Two social scientists could, for example, disagree on what ends a research programme should serve and may disagree on the theoretical motivation for the research, but they could nevertheless come to agree upon the objectivity of statistical testing, of scaling within a survey question, or about good and bad technique in participant observation. Objectivity as reliability is a striving to make research as dependable as possible by eliminating as much error as possible. Box 1.1 shows the values in social research.

Box 1.1 Values in social research

Moral or political values can enter into social research at a number of stages. Here are some of the principal ones:

- What to research: the first and most fundamental entry of values is why, who and how decisions to research X or Y are made. In the UK the Economic and Social Research Council (ESRC) (http://www.esrc.ac.uk) is the major conduit for government funding of social science and although nominally independent, it must continue to demonstrate to government that the research it funds is useful and relevant. Views on usefulness and relevance are likely to change with governments.[12] Very little research these days is 'resource free', those resources have to come from somewhere and will usually come with some control over what is researched. The researcher has some control over which funds or jobs to apply for, but this will be constrained by what can be funded. In social research, as natural science research, political and societal values will influence what research is sponsored.
- Values of the researcher: even though many of the strategic decisions about what kinds of things will be researched are external to the researcher, the values of the researcher will play a major role. Obviously he or she must make the decision as to whether to work on a project or not, but researchers are citizens too and will be more motivated by one thing than another. This might be purely academic interest. Most famous sociological and anthropological studies, such as Goffman's study of asylums (Goffman, 1961), Malinowski's study of the Trobriand Islands (Malinowski, 1937), or Lynd's study of an American small town (Lynd and Lynd, 1929) are such, but even here the choice of studying a particular topic in a particular place is the expression of a value. Most research is conducted as a result of a particular concern about a problem, whether that problem is

articulated in a specific way, such as particular instances of inner city deprivation, or a more widespread societal concern about the changing nature of urban community.

- Choice of method: this does not sound like a candidate for a question of moral values, but, a decision to use unstructured interviews, for example, will give a much more individual perspective on a question than that of a large-scale survey, which may emphasize structural features. Choice of method will therefore make a difference to outcome.

- Theory choice: more than one theory can be used to explain our data. A Parsonian functionalist, for example, and a Marxist would explain differences in the amount of days lost to strike action from quite different perspectives.

- What to analyse and how to analyse: every research project will yield far more data than can be analysed (this applies to all methodological approaches). Some data may support our hypotheses (see Chapter 2) and some may refute it. In practice, firm confirmation or firm refutation are unusual. Secondary analyses of data using different theoretical assumptions or statistical techniques may produce quite different answers to those originally obtained (Dale et al., 1988: 54–5).

- What to report: even the most honest researcher must decide which findings he or she will prioritise and just how much credence he or she will give to a confirmation or refutation of a hypothesis. I will return to this question in Chapter 10.

Values and bias in social research

How do values enter social research and how do they relate to 'bias'? Traditionally bias has been seen as pejorative in science, a distortion of method or findings. However, with the discrediting of the positivist value-free position, things are not so clear-cut. Indeed, as Martyn Hammersley and Roger Gomm note, the term bias is used in many different ways in social research (2000: 155). Where one stands in terms of values will make a difference to whether one sees bias as something to be avoided, reluctantly accepted, or celebrated. Moreover, much depends on the point at which bias enters. A standpoint might be seen as a bias, for example, and a deliberate and necessary one, though whether one consciously adopts a standpoint or comes to occupy it is contended (Harding, 1986: 136–51). A later version of the feminist standpoint, Harding's 'strong objectivity' (Harding, 1996) is a deliberate attempt to prioritize and examine those social distortions that may reduce objectivity. This strategy is often called reflexivity (and I will discuss this further in Chapter 3) and in various forms has been advocated by interpretivists for a long while and to a varying degree of introspection and deconstruction (Seale, 1999: Chapter 11). As a form of personal auditing and accounting this is valuable, though the problem is knowing to what extent the researcher can really know what kind of values he or she holds and which of these might bias her research.

Box 1.1 shows some of the ways and the points at which values enter research. From the position of objectivity I advocate, some of these are legitimate, even desirable – they are Longino's 'contextual values', which will underlie the kind of research we do and our values as citizens and researchers. For example, we may not agree with the particular funding priorities of the ESRC or SSRC, but we would have to agree that funding councils would have to make decisions about what to fund. These things may be bias, but they are not error. Error can lead to bias, but the reverse is not always true. Hammersley and Gomm (2000: 162), though taking a slightly different position to this, helpfully focus on the many different ways error can enter and influence research. Some error is to do with outcomes. Error may be systematic or haphazard. It may be culpable or non-culpable. An important facet of error and bias in social researcher is that the researcher does not simply read off accounts of the social world with differing degrees of competence or accuracy, but instead is active in creating those accounts. For example, a great deal of feminist interpretivism has been an active engagement in helping women to gain a 'voice', to make public those things that would have otherwise been private and unknown; see, for example, Melanie Mauthner's account of sister relationships (1998).

What might be see as culpable on non-culpable error is not clear-cut in terms of this kind of engagement and this is particularly the case in interpretive research. Fortunately there are areas of research where things are a bit simpler. Some kinds of bias are obvious and culpable. For example, deliberate selection of respondents who will confirm one's views, or the prioritization of convenient findings over inconvenient ones. However, some kinds of error are unintentional and lead to a form of bias about which there is widespread agreement. These are, for example, sampling bias, bias in question design or choice of analysis strategies. I will return to these in subsequent chapters.

Conclusion: art and science, objectivity and subjectivity

Social research requires commitment. It requires moral commitment, a motivation to change the world or to know our humanity a little better. Without this kind of commitment we lose sight of the difference between the social and the physical world. The latter is morally inert, though often changed by, or imbued with human values. The former is morally active and our investigation is itself a moral act. We could not be uncommitted even if we tried, therefore our commitment is a matter of reflection (May, 1998b).

All of this would lead to a narcissistic introspection unless we hold on to the value of objectivity, the cornerstone of any kind of investigation. To be objective is to be transparent but to aim to get as close as possible to the truth. The truth may not always be clear and, like the rainbow's end, we will never fully possess it (and if we did, how would we know?). This in turn must commit us to following the best method toward our investigative goals.

In the chapters that follow this translates into a pluralism and a pragmatism about method, though never losing sight of the importance of the deeper methodological implications of choosing one approach or technique over another. In the next chapter I will consider how we begin to take the first steps from the commitment to a research goal, and methods to achieve it.

Questions for reflection and discussion

Seek out two or three research projects that interest you and ask the following of them:

1 Who funded the research and why?
2 Did the research claim to be 'scientific', or use 'scientific methods'?
3 Who would benefit from the research?

Suggested further reading

The issues I have discussed are complex and more nuanced than could possibly be captured in one chapter. There is a very large literature on the methodological themes I have discussed.

Some of the issues in this chapter are developed further in my own *Science and Social Science* (2000a). A perennially useful book on methodological issues raised by the quantitative/qualitative divide is Alan Bryman's *Quantity and Quality in Social Research* (1988). The issue of values in social research is considered in depth in Martyn Hammersley's *Taking Sides in Social Research* (2000). Fiona Devine and Sue Heath's edited collection *Sociological Research Methods in Context* (1999) considers many of the issues raised in this chapter and others in later ones. A thoughtful and sometimes provocative book is John Goldthorpe's *On Sociology: Numbers, Narratives and the Integration of Research and Theory* (2000).

Notes

1 Actually I think it goes further than that. There is a great deal of 'art' in science, even natural science. One only has to look at the beautiful equations of the great mathematicians and physicists to realize this. There is more in common between Einstein and Bach, or Hilbert and Sisley than is often allowed (but see Tallis, 1995).

2 There was plenty of opposition to logical positivism, even in the USA, particularly from R.S. Lynd and C. Wright Mills (Horowitz. 1983), but opposition usually took the form of a debate with positivism.

3 I discuss the definitional issues of positivism in more detail in Williams (2000a).

4 Lundberg and later Blalock favoured a doctrine called operationalism. This was the view that what counted as alienation, achievement, etc., was what could be measured as such (see Blalock and Blalock, 1971; Williams, 1998).

5 This claim is based on current research being conducted with Geoff Payne and Suzanne Chamberlain. The research is a documentary analysis of key characteristics (method, topics, authors, universities, etc.) of articles published in three generic and one specialist British sociology journals in 1999–2000. Only 14 per cent of the papers in the generic journals used quantitative methods. Thus 40.6 per cent used qualitative methods and 7.4 per cent used mixed methods, while 37.7 per cent were non-empirical.

6 The methodological debate in social science, from the 1960s onwards, was a re-run of the *Methodenstreit* (battle of methods) dispute at the end of the nineteenth century. In the earlier dispute traditionalists favoured a value-free scientific approach to political economy, that science was 'pure' and investigations could and should be free of moral (social and political) values. In opposition there was the 'historical' school of Gustave Schmoller (Manicas, 1987: 124) who maintained that the social equivalent of natural laws could not be established and that economy should be studied in historical context as only one part of social life.

7 For many anti-positivists taking 'randomly selected samples of human experience' (Denzin, 1983: 133) is not a legitimate strategy because there is a rejection that research should be 'generalizing' from individuals or groups to wider society in the first place. It is held that there is too much cultural variability for sampling and generalization in social life.

8 Though in the next chapter I will briefly discuss and advocate a broadly realist approach to research.

9 Though it is often claimed that 'standpoints' lead eventually to either essentialism (for instance, that women come to occupy standpoints because of particular defining characteristic), or it leads to relativism where there are many competing standpoints (Halberg, 1989).

10 As Hammersley (2000: 157n) points out, we should not conflate epistemological relativism (as described above) with cultural relativism, the view that there can be multiple cultural perspectives in the social world. It is quite legitimate to be a cultural relativist (as most social scientists presumably would be) without any commitment to epistemological relativism.

11 Proctor is using this in a somewhat different sense to its use in survey research (see Chapter 5).

12 In the USA the funding regime is slightly different. The Social Science Research Council (SSRC) http://www.ssrc.org/ is independent of government and at the time of writing was even actively sponsoring academic contacts between the USA and Cuba, an anathema to the US government. In the USA and the UK there is also a great deal of direct government funding, through departments, of specific research projects.

From Question to Method

In this chapter:

- Research questions and theory
- Grand, middle range and experiential theory
- Building and testing theories
- Operationalization in survey research
- Dependent and independent variables
- Measures, indicators, values
- Levels of measurement
- Realism and social context

All research begins with a question. We want to know what something is like, why it is like it is, how much or how many. The problem is how to go about it. In this chapter I will describe a procedure from the conception of the question to the act of conducting the research. The first part of this chapter describes the relationship between theory and method; the second part how theory can be translated into measurable concepts in survey research. In the following chapter I will consider how research questions might be translated into qualitative methods.

It is important to remember that the procedure I describe here, even with the variations I discuss, will rarely be precisely the procedure that takes place in actual research projects. There will be resource and technical constraints, or the research question will have features that require different procedures. One cannot learn social research (or any other kind for that matter) simply through following recipes; experience counts. Similarly, certain approaches, or disciplines will have their own methodological prescriptions, for example psychologists will tend to use experiments more than other disciplines and anthropologists will use quantitative methods hardly at all.

The research question and its relationship to theory

The research question is simply a statement of what it is we want to know. For example, does social class make a difference to educational attainment;

why do people vote for the extreme right; what are people's attitudes to out-of-town shopping. Usually it can be expressed in a couple of sentences, or a short paragraph. However, sometimes the question itself is tied up with deeper meanings or definitions grounded in abstract or contested theory. Box 2.1 illustrates this in an example of research on the concept of 'trust' in voluntary organizations. The success of a research project is usually linked to our ability to answer this question, though the act of carrying out the research may lead to new questions that are as important, or more so.

Box 2.1 Trust, confidence and voluntary organizations

Tonkiss and Passey (1999) investigated the nature of 'trust' in British voluntary organizations. Their research was sponsored by the voluntary sector (National Council for Voluntary Organizations) and used focus group interviews to investigate whether and how people distinguish between trust and confidence in charities. Though on the face of it the research question is straightforward, issues of what people understand by concepts such as 'trust' are fundamental in such research. For example, one could trust the goodness of a cause served by a charity, but have little confidence in its efficiency (1999: 262). 'Trust' is an altogether deeper concept and can be seen as a basis for voluntary association itself, it can underpin public goodwill or it can lend legitimation (ibid.: 262–3). Research such as this is inevitably deeply theoretical and the fieldwork itself was informed by the debate concerning the nature and conditions for civil society, in the writings of theorists such as Gellner, Fukuyama, Seligman and Eisenstadt. It was then research which moves from an abstract theoretical dimension in social theory, to an operationalization in topics to be discussed by members of the public. For the authors the ensuing data helped to sharpen the issues and their conclusion was itself a retrospective argument 'that a primary means of understanding these processes is in terms of a movement away from trust to confidence relations between voluntary organizations and their various "stakeholders", through institutional and contractual means' (ibid.: 272).

Though researchers seek truth, it is often not a matter of truth about the way things actually are, but instead the truth of how people see them. Quite often there is no 'right' answer and often we are simply interested in views and attitudes. Researchers who investigate public perceptions of why people become homeless, for example, are interested only in the perceptions, not the 'real' reasons for homelessness (Furnham, 1996).[1] Similarly, interpretive research seeks out the meanings people have for their actions or situations.

The researcher of religious practices does not attempt to discredit the practices of those he or she investigates, however mad or bad they may appear (see, for example, Barker, 1982; Bruce, 1994).

Research questions can arise in a number of ways. In academic research they may have arisen as a result of prior research or theorizing on a topic. A particular theoretical writing may suggest issues that might be investigated by research, or previous research may throw up questions or anomalies requiring further work. For many graduate or undergraduate students this is often where research begins. However, a researcher may well, of course, be drawn to the topic itself through the kinds of moral commitment I spoke of in the previous chapter. The first example of research, in Box 2.1, though typical of a growing number of research partnerships between the public or voluntary sector and academia (Tonkiss and Passey, 1999) is actually quite a 'theoretical' piece of research, which begins from a debate in social theory about the nature of civil society. However, while the research question is embedded in abstract theory, it is clear that the topic is very relevant to policy issues in the public and voluntary sector.

Box 2.2 Homeless young people and the Children Act

The UK Children Act of 1989 covers much of the law relating to the care and upbringing of children, including the responsibilities of statutory bodies such as local social services departments. The Nuffield Foundation funded the housing campaign for single people, CHAR, to carry out an investigation of how the law was working in relation to young 16–17 year olds who were homeless. The research reported in McCluskey (1993) is typical of a well-structured research report intended for a wide audience of legislators, local government officials and voluntary sector workers. The approach is pragmatic and sets out what the Act is meant to have achieved and how it has succeeded or failed, according to the findings of the research. The theory being tested is that social services departments are failing to implement the Act in relation to this particular group. This was indeed the case in most departments and reasons for this (lack of finance, homelessness seen as an insufficient criterion of 'need', lack of knowledge, poor record keeping, lack of liaison with housing departments, etc). The section on methods consists of just one page in a 58-page report. This is not a failing, but reflects the anticipated concerns of the audience. Sometimes a separate technical report (see Chapter 10) will be produced, giving a detailed breakdown of methods and providing copies of questionnaires, etc. In this particular research, the methods were fairly straightforward and consisted of a postal questionnaire to all 116 social services departments in England and Wales.

Outside of academia research questions often appear to be straight-forward and usually address a problem of a lack of knowledge in an area. The acquisition of that knowledge will then be used to guide future actions. This kind of research question is probably the commonest and the basis for most market research and policy research in the public sector. The example in Box 2.2 concerns the question of how national legislation affects a disadvantaged group – in this case, homeless young people. It might at first seem that the kind of *ad hoc* investigation conducted in market research, the voluntary or the public sector, has little or nothing to do with theory. In one sense this is true – a discussion of Bourdieu's 'habitus and field' (Bourdieu and Wacquant, 1992) will be of limited use to the market researcher trying to find out who eats Pot Noodles. However, this will depend on what you mean by theory: all research implies theoretical assumptions, but good research sets out by making those assumptions clear. Before we can look at how theory informs research, it will be useful to look at different types of theory. Before that I will briefly clarify what exactly a theory is.

What is a theory?

A 'theory' is a logical proposition, or set of propositions about relationships between phenomena. It proposes that something is, or isn't the case. It may be about the very big – that the universe began with the 'big bang' – or it may be trivial, perhaps that the stain on my shirt is chocolate. In virtually all cases the postulation of a theory has implications, certain things follow. In particular if a theory is true it implies that the world must be or act in certain ways. Durkheim's theory of suicide (1952) has the implication that not all suicides are of the same kind and that suicide, though finally resting on an individual decision, has social antecedents.

To use scientific jargon, a theory should have testable consequences. In other words it should predict or forbid certain things to happen and that these predictions should lead to measurements (our ability to say whether or not something is the case, or how much or how many of something). Popper's falsification version of this (see Chapter 1) says a theory should clearly specify the criteria of what should *not* be the case. For example, had Durkheim (1952) found no measurable differences between countries, or over time, in suicide rates, his theory would have been shown to be wrong, or falsified. When a theory predicts something is the case and this turns out not to be so, then we can make a *deduction* that the theory was wrong. However, the instances in social science of a theory of the magnitude of Durkheim's being shown to be wrong are probably non-existent. Indeed, outright falsification of natural science theories is also very rare and few scientists wholeheartedly embrace such an approach (see, for example, Lakatos, 1978; Chalmers, 1990; Evans and Over, 1996). Often bits of a theory are shown to be wrong and the critical spirit of 'falsification' is valuable in science (Williams, 2000a: 145), but for the most part social scientists (and natural scientists) are happy that the evidence generally supports the theory – though this may be a provisional conclusion. This approach to gathering data supportive of a theory is called *induction* (see Chalmers, 1999: Chapter 1).[2] Yet how we actually test theories, especially in social science, is a bit more complex than either trying to prove them wrong, or prove them right. I will return to this question.

Grand theory

Sometimes called 'macro-level' theory, such theory focuses on society (or large parts of society) as whole. It is very often grounded in philosophical assumptions or reasoning, or some cases it might be prescriptive as well as explanatory. All theories, if shown to be correct, *explain* something through what they claim. Lévi-Strauss's structural anthropology makes the theoretical claim that collective phenomena have an unconscious nature, Giddens' social theory explains social life through a duality of action and structure and Marx explains social relations with reference to the economic basis of a society (see Skinner, 1985, for examples of some contemporary grand theory). The problem with grand theory is that its sweep is often just too grand! It is both very easy and extraordinarily difficult to explain high levels of youth vandalism in small towns, with reference to Marx's theory of alienation. Maybe we can tell a plausible story about how the young people in Poppleton are separated from their species being through tedious and mundane work, but equally we could recruit Freud to say that their indulgence in vandalism is a failure of the superego to overcome the id!

It is often quite hard to know what would count as success (or failure) of a grand theory at least partly, because while it might be simply specified as an ensemble, any particular theory implies a whole group of interrelated theories. Marxism is a good example of this and although it is unlikely that anyone will come up with a means to show how historical materialism is wholly right, or wrong, the general approach can be taken as a set of working assumptions which provide a backdrop to the development and testing of certain parts of the theory. Though less fashionable now, a great deal of 'Marxist' research was conducted in the past, in which certain features of 'grand' theory were extrapolated to inform investigations of specific phenomenon (see Westergaard and Resler, 1975; Cockburn, 1977, for example). This has likewise been the case more recently in feminism and it might be argued that a comparison of 'grand ' theory in Marxism and feminism will show that the latter better explains the specific material circumstances of women than the former (see, for example, Evans, 1995: Chapter 8).

Finally, certain kinds of grand theory, for example critical theory (see Chapter 1) can provide a procedural backdrop for research and some, such as critical realism (Bhaskar, 1978, 1998; Archer, 1995) offer quite a lot of methodological potential, though as yet unrealized. We can conclude that it is hard, though not impossible, to link grand theory to research. This was realized by Robert Merton (1968, Part 1) when he conceived of 'middle range theory' to describe the theoretical propositions that lie between grand theory and low level, or experiential theory.

Middle range theory

The idea of middle range theory started life in sociology, in the work of Robert Merton,[3] but it is applicable across all social science disciplines. Merton first advanced his ideas at the time when the very abstract and complex theoretical work of Talcott Parsons was influential. Parsons' functionalism (Parsons and Shils, 1951; Parsons, 1968 [1937]), though logically elegant (that is, the concepts fitted together and did not contradict each other) was too abstract to be much use in empirical research. Conversely the positivist approaches associated with people such George Lundberg led to a naïve matching of observation to concept (Lundberg, 1939) and was substantively indistinguishable from experiential theory, see below). Middle range theory started life as a translation mechanism between grand theory and 'operationalizable' concepts. For example, Merton's concept of manifest and latent function allows the production of testable concepts that avoided the circularity of functionalist arguments.

Many of the theoretical concepts we use in social research (and the ones I refer to in this book) are middle range ones: deviance, counter-urbanization, urban poverty, gender and mathematics, etc. However, connections to grand theory are often absent and deemed unnecessary or impossible. Where they do exist, they may be tangential or 'sensitizing'. This is often not the fault of the researcher, but is due to the methodologically untranslatable nature of grand theory and is more of an indictment of the theory than the research (see Mouzelis, 1995). More important for much of social research is that middle range theory describes the relationship between variables (more about this below) we can measure. For example, how rates of suicide will vary according to the level of social integration of a community, or how electoral participation might vary according to class.

Tonkiss and Passey's research (described in Box 2.1) exemplifies a fairly typical research – theory relationship. The theoreticians' work they call upon is somewhere between grand and middle range theory. In my interpretation the concept of civil society veers toward grand theory, but 'trust' and 'confidence' are middle range concepts from which testable propositions can be derived and, once tested, can allow the researcher to test the adequacy of the theory. Now this sounds straightforward, but as John Skvoretz warns, 'Theories cannot be tested by simply "reading off" the results directly from the facts' (1998: 239), but need the development of theoretical models. In its simplest form a theoretical model is a set of variables that arise as a consequence of a theory and imply logical relations between the theory and the world.

A simple example from population geography: counter-urbanization (Berry, 1976; Cloke, 1985) is the (middle range) theory that attempts to explain the population 'turnaround' in rural areas, in Western countries.

Prior to the 1960s such areas lost population to the cities, but this has been reversed ever since. To what extent is this attributable to economic or lifestyle conditions or motivations? How much does the countryside 'pull' and how much does the city 'push'? This is translatable into a model which first of all tests economic status (income, class, housing, etc.) prior to moving to the country and then after moving. Evidence for economic factors would be either an actual improvement in performance on these variables, or the prior perception that such a move would improve performance (Williams and Champion, 1998). Lifestyle can be likewise specified (as before and after) in a model, which might predict the actuality or perception of a cleaner environment, shorter commuting distances, proximity to friends/family (Perry et al., 1986). The problem for counter-urbanization is that a model of economic factors derived from a theory is not mutually exclusive of one lifestyle factor and may vary from place to place, but such a problem is unfortunately typical of the research–theory relationship in any discipline. Nevertheless, Skvoretz is right: a translation mechanism from theory to measurement, in the form of a model which will predict certain measurement outcomes, is possibly the most rigorous way to test a theory.

Experiential theory

What I have called 'experiential theory' (because it is suggested by our direct experiences of the world) crops up in several places in research. First, it might appear as a hunch about something. One might, for example, have a hunch that fear of death is an important factor in people becoming religious. Now it would be very arrogant to believe that one was the first to have such a hunch, so we would assume that the hunch would take us into the psychology and sociology of religion to find out how this had been theorized and how this had subsequently been turned into research.

Nevertheless such theory is logically indistinguishable from hypotheses – actually all theories and hypotheses are logically equivalent as propositional statements, but their status varies in what they purport to tell us about the world. It is a statement of prediction that can be tested: for example, that boys aged between 10 and 14 shower or bath less regularly than girls. Of itself it doesn't say much, but such statements expressed as hypotheses are crucial if research is to be about specifics. This kind of theorizing is the kind we use in everyday life, which should come as no surprise, because social research investigates everyday life and it is also often the point from which research begins.

The research – theory relationship

The message of the foregoing is that theory and research are inseparable. It is perhaps true that the more complex or 'grand' the theory is, the more complex and sophisticated the research is likely to be. Nevertheless McCluskey's research (Box 2.2) is not devoid of theory, but emerges as a statement, derived from experiential perceptions, that legislation is not working. In this case that the number of homeless 16–17 year olds, far from decreasing, had apparently increased (or at least more were being reported by voluntary organizations). This led to a clear hypothesis and some fairly straight-forward research.

Building and testing theories

Because theories exist at different levels, from the hunch to grand theory, the research question is never devoid of theory. The possible theorizing in terms of fairly straightforward policy research is potentially very complex. Yet the development of theory is not just a device to lend academic legitimacy to research, but a powerful explanatory tool. Consider the analogy of the detective who is called on to investigate the murder of a local big-time gangster. Suppose the murderer is easily apprehended and turns out to be a man with only a minor criminal record. Does the detective leave it there? Probably not; the death of a big-time gangster may imply only a personal matter between him and his murderer, but it might imply the beginning of a gang war and many more deaths. The detective then, will attempt to build up a body of theory, which he or she will test. This is what good researchers do also.

Theory building and testing are interactive. Every matter implies some theory, however low level, and the lower the level, the less explanatory power the theory will have. However, bigger theory and greater explanatory power come at a cost and that is whether the theory is testable. This, as we have seen, is the problem with a lot of grand theory: it does not produce testable consequences. To make it testable, the researcher has to build theory downwards. By theory building we usually mean either the generation of new theory or building on existing theory (Layder, 1993: 32–4).

To generate new theory we always begin with some experiential theory, the very topic of interest implies some view or other, but this may be very limited in scope. Theory generation can occur through the use of surveys, but unless this is serendipitous, it is unlikely because the construct of the survey questions themselves implies theoretical perspectives (I will return to this issue in Chapter 9). Therefore theory building often begins with inter-pretive research, frequently in the form of a pilot study.

One of the most rigorous approaches to theory building is that of grounded theory (Glaser and Strauss, 1967). In this approach the researcher first develops conceptual categories from the data gathered from observa-tions or interviews and then conducts further exploratory research to develop these categories (Bryman, 1988: 83–4). I will discuss this further in the next chapter. In truth very little exploratory research is about developing theories from scratch. Even most pilot studies have at least a loose theoreti-cal framework which can be later tightened.

Then comes building and testing theory. Very little research is about devel-oping brand new theory and typically only research conducted in academia is consciously about theory building. The aim is usually to further develop, sharpen, or clarify an existing body of theory, or theoretical propositions. A somewhat idealized sequences runs like this, where T = theory and H = hypothesis:

T1 (H1, H2, H3) → Research → T2 (H1, H2, H4, H5) → Research

In this sequence the hypotheses derived from the theory are tested. Only two are confirmed, but this and the falsification of the third hypothesis lead to a new theory, from which amended hypotheses are derived. This in turn leads to further research (though not necessarily by the same researcher). Implicit in building new theory is the testing of the old and even when we are not consciously trying to build a body of theory, this inevitably happens to an extent, because by confirming or falsifying all, or part, of a theory we add to a stock of knowledge in that particular domain.

If only it were that simple! The research – theory relationship rarely proceeds so smoothly and for every confirmation, or falsification of even part of a theory there will usually be challenges. This is well illustrated in the debate over what defines popular culture in South America. Nestor Garcia Canclini (1992) refers to two quite different starting points for research: *deductivist*, those who begin with structural features such as the mode of production, class, etc. and from this theorize the types of popular culture found; and the *inductivists* who begin by assuming the existence of certain properties in 'subordinate classes' (ibid.: 20). In the first theory, changes in structure should influence the way culture is manifested or reproduced and in the second, this should make no difference. Each of these is a broad approach and actually the result of a re-definition by Canclini himself, who proposes a third theoretical framework which prioritizes the interactions between the opposing structural factors of modernity and tradition, the role of transactions in political resistance and an analysis of reception and consumption.

It is fair to say that in social science theorizing and research are often seen as two separate activities (Pawson, 2000: 283). The word 'theory' does not enter into a lot of social research, while theory producers remain prolific as ever. Despite the latter, researchers often find that their data is not explained by any of the (plethora) of theory. Assuming that we are not developing theory from nothing, other than experiential theory, how does the researcher (especially the novice researcher) decide on which theory to test, or having conducted the research, which theory is confirmed or falsified? This problem, you might be relieved to hear, also confronts the natural scientist and is termed the 'underdetermination of theory' (Newton-Smith, 1981: 40).

So what makes a good theory? Very little is said in social science about what counts as a good theory. Although undocumented, one gets the impression that a lot of research is carried out on the basis of experiential theory and is matched later to grand, or middle range theory, which is not quite the same as using theory to make sense of the data. How the latter might be done well has been a preoccupation of philosophers of the natural sciences for a long while. The ideal state is one where there is a clear deductive link between a theory and data. William Newton-Smith (1981: 226–32) suggests some characteristics of good theory. He, of course, is writing about the natural sciences and even here what he suggests is an ideal state. Nevertheless I think that these characteristics do offer some guidelines and, with imagination, can be adapted to social science. I have phrased Newton-Smith's 'good making' characteristics of theory in the form of a possible theory of counter-urbanization.

Let us suppose that we have developed a theory that the apparent economic motivations for urban to rural migration are the outcomes of lifestyle decisions, that economic factors are used to justify the preference for living a particular way (I'm not saying this is correct, but it's plausible). First, the new theory would have to explain more things in the data. For example, the old economic theory explained those moves where there was economic benefits for the migrants, but not those where there was not. The new theory should explain both and should have more explanatory power than any other theory on offer (Stinchcombe, 1968: 20).

Second, our new 'lifestyle' theory should be capable of explaining a wide range of urban – rural migration and not just those moves within a particular study area. The longer it is able to go on explaining such migration, the more valuable the theory becomes. The old classical economic model (Jackson, 1986) worked very well, for as long as migration was rural to urban.

Third, our new theory should be compatible with other theories of socio-economic behaviour. For example, if there was no evidence at all that lifestyle decisions required economic justifications in other areas, the new theory would have to show why it explains one area of social life in a quite opposite way to how other theories explain related or adjacent areas.

Fourth, and related to this, one should avoid introducing auxiliary hypotheses, that is explaining those things that cannot be explained by reference to new hypotheses that are untestable with the current data. This is a tall order and rarely achieved even in that most macho of natural sciences, physics (see Chalmers, 1999).

Fifth, the theory itself should be logically consistent. If, for example, my theory postulated lifestyle motivations for economic decision-making, this would either have to apply to urban – rural migration and rural – urban migration, or show which third variable might permit an opposite explanation for each.

In the natural sciences, Newton-Smith suggests that the theory should be compatible with well-grounded beliefs in science about the way the world generally is, or, if not, show why those beliefs are wrong. The equivalent in social science is compatibility with grand theory, but as we have seen there are quite serious difficulties there.

Finally, the theory should be as simple as possible. One of the difficulties of the grand theory of, say, Parsons or Giddens is that it is extraordinarily complex. Next time you are on a long train journey try this game. Try to devise a grand sociological, political, economic, psychological theory to explain Western civilization. You will be surprised how easy, but just how convoluted it gets. It's not much use, however, because its very complexity renders it untestable. Abstract theorizing is great fun and very profitable financially for some theorists, but it's not always useful to researchers.

Operationalization in survey research: descending the ladder of abstraction

In the move from the theoretical to the measurable it is sometimes said we are 'descending the ladder of abstraction', quite simply, we are moving from the abstract to the concrete. The procedure is termed 'operationalization': we are developing the operations that will result in observations of the social world, the empirical test of our theories. We do this in stages, because we cannot simply 'read off' theories into measurements. It would not be a good test, for example, of embourgeoisement[4] theory just to go into the local shopping centre and ask people what class they are – though it would tell you what class they *think* they are, which might be interesting in itself.

Operationalization is a process and a key part of the design of research. Usually we think of it as applying to survey research, but although less formalized, it is still necessary to define and refine one's concepts, even in interpretive research, but that is a topic I will consider in the next chapter.

To recap, we begin with the *research question*, the overall interrogative framework for the research. The research question will usually be embedded in, or informed by, an existing (usually middle range) body of theory. Suppose that we wish to explain the tendency toward a lower percentage of people voting in local government elections. First, we must clarify the status of the phenomena. For example, how long has this been happening, is it unique to one country, how many elections has this been recorded over? The research question itself should be clear, specific and answerable. Assuming the first two criteria are met, can the question be answered?

Second, the phenomenon will not exist in isolation of other social factors and it is knowledge of these that will provide the theoretical basis for developing hypotheses. In this particular case there are several explanatory theories, but for the purposes of illustration let us just take three.

Those who do not vote will be members of particular social groups and not voting is simply evidence of a wider alienation from civil society. There is evidence that such alienation is concentrated in people under 25, in ethnic minorities and those from manual classes (Rallings and Thrasher, 1994). The hypotheses derived for not voting will then be a test of a wider theory to explain alienation from civil society.

Disillusionment with political parties or the political process may also be a reason. This might turn out to be part of the 'alienation' theory, or in some cases it might stand on its own. Some groups who are less likely to vote may be active participants in civil society, especially in New Social Movements (Sutton, 2000).

Local effects – certain events in particular countries may serve to increase or decrease voter participation. In the UK, for example, the Poll Tax in the late 1980s was an important factor in reducing voter registration in precisely those groups said to be more widely alienated and a source of concern ever since (Rallings et al., 1996).

Each of the theoretical explanations has explanatory antecedents at higher and more abstract levels of theory and will connect to grand theory, and the second and third may well be explicable as a subset of the first. From the outset, then, the researcher must decide what the parameters of the explanation sought are to be. In the above one could trace a chain of explanation back to, say, Marxism or functionalism, but the further and deeper one goes in this direction, the more difficult operationalization becomes. Research in the public or voluntary sector would not go 'back' very far at all (see the McCluskey example above) and only as far as where an explanation might permit a useful intervention or initiative. In academic research, papers describing the results may refer to deeper explanations, but these will, of course, not have been tested in the present research.

In terms of the practicality of the research, this leads to a further problem. The wider ranging the research question, the more levels and types of explanation it implies. If, for example, the research question had been a prior one which simply asked whether it was the case that fewer people were voting in local government elections, then this would have simply required definitional and measurement decisions and no 'deeper' theoretical explanation. We may be burning to ask a research question 'why is there poverty in the United States?', but we would need an awful lot of resources to attempt its answer. If instead we asked the question 'Why is there poverty in South Chicago?', we may call upon theoretical explanations that claim to explain poverty nationally, but we will test them locally (and this would not entitle us to make claims about poverty nationally) and we may call upon specific local explanations. Even then, such a project would be a large one (see Wilson, 1997, for such an example in the USA).

For the most part (and this is certainly the case if you are a student), the research question will be a modest one and its operationalization will not attempt to go too deep into theory. How then could we 'sharpen up' the question about voting in local government elections?

The first explanation is very wide-ranging and in practical terms a very large project, or possibly even several projects. The second and third are more manageable and would actually allow us to test hypotheses that relate positively or negatively to the first 'alienation' explanation anyway. Let us take the second theoretical explanation and use this to produce a shaper research question, thus: 'Low voter participation is explained by a negative public image of political parties'.

There are three possible outcomes here: this will be falsified (shown to be wrong), confirmed (shown to be right), but much more likely in social research it will prove to be a partial explanation. Rarely can social researchers 'prove' something to be wholly right or wrong. For example, in this case, a survey may establish that for small number of people this was the

Table 2.1 Key variables

Variable	Definition
Voting behaviour	Participation/non-participation in local government elections
Elector	Person registered to vote in local government elections
Public image	Attitudes toward political parties
Political parties	Those registered political parties participating in the elections in which the 'voter' did, or did not vote

case all of the time and for many more, some of the time. In which case this would lead to further research questions.

As I noted above, theories and hypotheses are logically equivalent, so if you are thinking 'The difference between "theories", "research questions" and "hypotheses" is just a matter of degree', you wouldn't be wholly wrong, the difference being simply the level of abstraction. In sharpening the research question you are actually producing a hypothesis. The question itself might, however, consist of several hypotheses. Some writers on social research methods, for example Sotirios Sarantakos (1998: 134–6), see the development of hypotheses as coming after the identification of variables. This is not wrong; the formation of hypotheses is always an ongoing process, and, as he goes on to say, hypotheses are of different kinds and occur in various places in the research process. The research question itself will produce a number of working hypotheses that allow us to name variables, but once these have been operationalized, we return to further hypothesizing during the analysis stage of the research (see Chapter 7).

The operationalization of our 'sharper' research question is not without its difficulties for it requires us to obtain data from the very people whose absence we wish to explain. Those who do not vote may be unlikely to participate in surveys either (especially if the first explanation, which we are not testing, is correct). In the first step of defining our concepts and key variables, we may want to take this into account. For the purposes of the study our concept of a voter (and this will make a difference for sampling, see Chapter 4) is someone registered to vote in local government elections. Key variables might be defined as follows in Table 2.1.

This does not exhaust our list of variables. For example, we may not just want to ask whether a person voted, but about their attitudes in general to voting at local government (or other) elections. We may not only be interested in their views on political parties, but on other organizations too. To record disillusionment with a political party will tell us that disillusionment with organizations is present, but it will not tell us whether or not that disillusionment stops with political parties. Conversely, some people do vote, but may still hold negative views of political parties. We therefore need more information about attitudes toward many other issues and information about the voters themselves. Much of the latter is typically collected in what is often called 'face sheet' information on variables such as age, sex and social class, but may also include education, ethnicity, marital status, housing tenure, etc., (see also Chapter 6). In the particular example we would almost certainly want to collect information on each of these. Indeed, in a survey it is always a good idea to think carefully about the variables you wish to collect data on. If, for example, you cannot see an immediate need for data on income, be absolutely sure you will not need it later. If in doubt and resources permit, then collect the data.

Dependent and independent variables

The social world is usually too complex to be able to specify simple cause–effect relationships, as the above example shows. Nevertheless it is sometimes useful to think in terms of what kind of things bring about effects in other things, even though they may just be statistically associated (I will say more about this in Chapter 7). It is a useful strategy then to specify the clearly the variable that will be affected by other variables. In this case voting behaviour is the dependent variable (because it 'depends' on other variables) and the independent variables are those things which 'cause' such behaviour (in actuality associated with such behaviour). As you can imagine, researchers usually specify a lot more independent variables than dependent ones.

A third type of variable you will encounter I will mention here but return to in Chapter 7. Control variables are usually specified in the procedure of analysing data, but as with dependent and independent, it is important to think of what they might be and how they should be specified at the design stage. Suppose, then, we hypothesized that failure to vote was 'caused' by disaffection with political parties, this would almost certainly be conditional on a whole range of other variables such as age, class, ethnicity, housing tenure, education, etc.

Measures, indicators and values

Having specified our variables, we need to find reliable ways to measure them – indicators of the presence or absence, or the extent of, of the phenomenon. The aim of operationalization is to produce reliable tests of our theoretical propositions. Now this means that measurements must measure that which they purport to measure. Even something as apparently straightforward as voter participation in local government elections would require a specification of which level of local government (in the UK, depending where you live this could be one, two, or three levels) and which election – the last one, the last two? An indicator of voter participation must be clear on these things and might actually require more than one question in a questionnaire.

Some variables, such as class, are notoriously difficult to measure and there is still no universal agreement about what counts as a good measure of class (Kirby, 1999). For many years social class was measured by establishing the occupation of the head of household, or chief wage earner. Up to about the 1960s this worked relatively well, except that it was in practice a measure of the class of men. A woman may have had a first class degree from Cambridge, but if she was married to a road sweeper then her husband's occupation[5] determined her social class. As traditional divisions of labour and occupation became unravelled, occupational measures of class became less useful and some researchers now use broader definitions of class which require a battery of questions to determine class, including occupation, household goods, education, etc. Nevertheless, occupation remains the basis for determining class in government surveys in Britain. In recent years a new schema has been tested which replaces the old 'occupational class' measure with a new measure based on socio-economic classification (Rose and O'Reilly, 1997). The two are contrasted in Box 2.3.

Box 2.3   Class and classification

Social Class		Socio-Economic Classification	
I	Professional Occupations	1	Higher professionals/senior managers
II	Managerial and technical	2	Associate professionals/junior managers
IIIN	Skilled Non Manual	3	Other administrative and clerical workers
IIIM	Skilled Manual	4	Own account non-professional
IV	Partly skilled	5	Supervisors, technicians and related workers
V	Unskilled	6	Intermediate workers
		7	Other workers
		8	Never worked/inactive

The SEC requires that survey data be collected on (i) occupation; (ii) size of employing establishment (if any); (iii) employment status (employer, employee, self-employed, not active (see Aldridge and Levine, 2001: 39).

Attitudes and opinions also require sophisticated treatment. One is unlikely to measure disillusionment with political parties by asking 'Are you disillusioned with political parties? Yes/No/Don't Know'. It is more likely that one would use various attitude statements and/or measures of behaviour (e.g. party membership) to measure this (though fairly direct attitude statements would not be ruled out).

Levels of measurement

Finally, indicators are not just about absence or presence, but about how much, or how little, how big how small, how old, etc. Indicators imply values, even if these are just dichotomous (yes/no). Often they require a range of values and thus decisions about how those values can be represented. Although the aim of the survey researcher (or experimenter) is to represent measurements numerically, this requires some concept of the difference of the kinds of measurement we must make. Social researchers speak of different levels of measurement. These depend on how a thing is conceptualized and measured. All variables are either discrete or continuous. The former consist of distinct categories, which may or may not have some form of ranking (e.g. ethnicity or social class), whereas the latter have an infinite number of values along a continuum. Continuous variables can be turned into discrete ones, but not the other way around. For example, age, measured in years, could be divided into 'young', 'middle aged' and 'elder', but the conversion could not be made the other way. Discrete and continuous variables are further divided into levels of measurement.

- Nominal. Sometimes this level is called categorical, for it simply measures categories without any ranking at all. Ethnicity, for example, might be measured through six categories plus an 'other' category, but being a member of one ethnic group does not imply any mathematical value in relation to another, but simply a different category.
- Ordinal. There remains a level of ranking here, but the differences between the ranks need not be equal. We may wish to measure levels of educational achievement by asking the respondent to specify level of qualification attained. A Master's degree is not twice the value of a Bachelor's degree, for example.
- Interval. Interval level measurement is often used to measure characteristics of the physical world, such as temperature measured as Celsius or Fahrenheit. Interval data have no true zero, though the points on the scale must be equidistant. Though both of these scales have a point called zero, it is not a true zero, as anyone who had been to Siberia in the winter would tell you.
- Ratio. Ratio scales are scales which begin from a true zero, but in which adjoining values are the same distance apart. Income, for example, can begin from zero dollars or pounds and rise to whatever you wish to measure. Scores on a ratio scale may be multiplied and divided, but those on an interval scale can only be added and subtracted.

I will return to levels of measurement in Chapter 6 on questionnaire design and in Chapter 7 on quantitative data analysis.

The distinction between these levels of measurement becomes important in analysis, because different levels of measurement require different statistical measures. But here I am straying into questions more properly dealt with in Chapter 6, which deals with analysis and the technical dimension of developing questions and questionnaires. However, in order for us to develop the kinds of models Skvoretz advocates there is a need to consider an external dimension of the relationships between variables and the processes they represent.

Social context and social reality

In measuring social life we are not simply measuring the once and for all existence, absence or extent of phenomena. We are instead measuring the relationships between variables in order to make inferences about dynamic social processes. The procedure of operationalization tends to artificially 'fix' the definition of a variable as measured. For a long time and in most research methods books, this was simply regarded as a technical issue of validity (see Chapter 5). How valid are the concepts we measure – to the respondents themselves, to the research question, the theory and its wider applicability, and so on? However, in recent years and since the discrediting of positivism, there has been a concern with the relationship of measurement to social 'reality'.

Positivists held the view that science could only speak of those things which it could measure. A theory specified that certain things should happen, or be the case. The researcher turned these things into measurements and said whether this was, or was not the case. Indeed, so far, none of what I have said about theory has precluded this. But the problem is that this assumes, as I noted above, some kind of direct relationship between what is measured and the theory. Theoretical models and middle range theory[6] are not enough, they are simply translation mechanisms from the abstract to the concrete. Let me provide a hypothetical example.

Suppose that we conduct a survey and find that in town A only 40 per cent of people registered, as patients, with a dentist, but in town B this figure was 60 per cent. The population of each of the towns is approximately the same and the number of dentists practising in A is only slightly less than in B. The number of dentists practising would not sufficiently explain the lower registration in A. Assuming that in the survey we had collected data on a range of different characteristics, we could using the analysis strategy of elaboration (which I will discuss in Chapter 7) test to see which variables combined with which others produced the best explanations. There are even ways in which we could test for the effect of several of these variables together to see how important each was. This is the strategy of multivariate analysis, but the problem is that even this only takes into account those bits of the world measured by the research. It ignores the fact that the social world is an enormously complex place and interactions between individuals and the social world are continually changing each other.[7] In other words, the reality of the lived experience of people may not coincide with the theories of the research.

To accept this is to accept a minimal, or moderate, form of realism, i.e. that there is a level of reality beyond that of experience. Positivists and empiricists in general do not deny that this is the case, but simply maintain that if we cannot access it, then it is pointless talking about it. However, despite this apparently down-to-earth response, history and common sense are on the side of realism. In our everyday lives new levels of reality reveal themselves to us. Processes that have been going on beneath the surface become known to us in their effects. We get made redundant, we find that our house is in the way of a new motorway – each outcomes of deeper social processes

(Williams, 1998). Now realists accept that we can only know effects directly, but the good researcher will be aware that these are evidence of deeper processes. Some forms of realism (such as that of Roy Bhaskar, 1986; 1998) are both politically radical and very abstract, but the moderate realism that many social researchers adopt now aims to make a difference to how we approach our research, analyse it and understand the results. In particular, it shifts much more emphasis onto theory as an explanatory device and suggests a constant interplay between theory and research. Ray Pawson (1989: 213) has suggested a simple way of conceptualizing this. Any outcome, such as a statistical relationship, which we want to explain will result from a mechanism which has generated those things which are observable. The 'mechanism',[8] in the case of my hypothetical example, might be series of different factors which each partially explain the lower registration in town A, but to make any sense of this, says Pawson, we have to understand the context. The context might be lots of things we did not measure, such as press coverage suggesting a dentist shortage, changes in local practices amongst dentists, and so on. Finally, there will be intervening factors in each and every case that will determine whether a person registers. Some of these intervening factors would have been measured, some not, and some of those that were not become part of the context.

In practical terms a one-shot survey is just a snapshot (as would be a focus group, or in-depth interviews) and may not measure much of what I have termed context. This then implies two things: first, that research is a constantly interactive process, never final and always subject to error. Second, it implies the methodological pluralism I spoke of in the previous chapter. Envisage the example like this: the initial survey produced only partial explanations of low dentist registration, but the researcher goes back and conducts in-depth interviews with patients who have and haven't registered (in both towns), with dentists, with health officials etc. Gradually more of the context is measured and some tentative explanations should begin to emerge which, funds permitting, would permit a further survey. Gradually the mechanisms that lead to the effects become clearer, but these mechanisms interconnect with and are embedded in further mechanisms which require further exploration of contexts. The researcher's job is never done!

If we take the earlier example of research on the impact of the Children Act on young homeless people and dig a little deeper, context and mechanism reveal themselves a little. Take just one of the findings: that local authorities did not have the financial resources to deal with the issue of homelessness in the 16–17 year olds in their areas. This implies a mechanism of local government funding which ends up having an effect on quite a different mechanism, the implementation of the Children Act. Both mechanisms have to be understood in the context of the Thatcherite regime of the time, which capped local government funding as part of a monetarist policy to keep the Public Spending Borrowing Requirement (PSBR) as low as possible (Butcher, 1990). One could also speak of the wider contexts, such as the ideology of Thatcherism and possibly moral panics about child welfare, that led to the Act.

The research in question only sought to show one kind of relationship (in terms of absence or presence), that between the legislation and young homeless people an the context and mechanisms are simply hinted at in the report. However, several years on, research might be undertaken which shows important differences in how local authorities deal with the young homeless. In order to explain this we would have to refer to the comparative contexts and mechanisms operating then and now, to particular changes in government, in ideology and the impact of further legislation.

Conclusion

In this chapter I have summarized the translation procedure in the move from theory to empirical research and set this in the context of a realist approach to researching the social world. What I have described should not be read as a recipe that should be followed, but rather as a description of a process that evolves in a slightly different way in every research project. Moreover, the process of operationalization has been described here only as it relates to survey research. In practice and in the pluralist approach I advocate, the translation from abstract theory to survey research, would involve an intervening qualitative element that would suggest the nature of the mechanism or process underlying the variables to be measured. In some instances, case study research, or single case evaluations for example, a quantitative element may not follow – I will discuss this further in Chapter 9. Finally, there are areas of the social world that are not amenable to survey research and can only be explored qualitatively, though interpretation. In the next chapter I will examine the process and methods of the interpretive approach to research.

Try this

Consider the following scenario: the University of Poppleton is situated in a satellite town of a large conurbation. The latter has experienced mixed economic fortunes in the last few years and although there are affluent suburbs and Poppleton itself is quite prosperous, there are large numbers of people living in poverty in the conurbation. A key strategy locally and one adopted by the university has been to attempt to widen participation amongst poorer local residents. It has failed badly and less than 20 per cent of its students come from working-class backgrounds.

1. Can you think of any 'grand theories' that might offer a useful explanatory framework?
2. If so, can any testable middle range theories be derived? If not, how might we begin to theorize the situation?
3. Consider the process of how these theories might be operationalized into research that might help the university solve its participation problem.

Suggested further reading

Derek Layder's *New Strategies in Social Research* (1993) covers much of the ground of this chapter in depth and attempts to bridge the theory – research gap. This too is the topic of the May and Williams collection, *Knowing the Social World* (1998) in which philosophers, theorists and methodologists show how each is informed by the other. Daniel Little has written a very clear book *Varieties of Social Explanation* (1991), which focuses on different forms explanation of the social world can take. Often these are mutually exclusive and demonstrate that the research answer you get will depend on where you start from theoretically. Ray Pawson's *A Measure for Measures* (1989) is a sophisticated but accessible introduction to, and argument for, a realist quantitative social science. Sadly, it is out of print, but much of the argument can be found his and Nick Tilley's *Realistic Evaluation* (1997).

Notes

1 Though of course those perceptions could well be correct, but such studies are usually conducted to establish what public attitudes to homelessness are.

2 Note also that an inductive process is used in theory building. See the section on analytic induction in Chapter 3.

3 For a very clear discussion of the relationship between research and theory building/ testing, using theories of the middle range, see Layder 1993, especially pp 19–37.

4 Embourgeoisement theories concern the adoption bourgeois aspirations, standards and lifestyles among working-class people (see Goldthorpe et al., 1969).

5 Or father's occupation if she still lived in the parental home. This method of measuring class is a further example of the social basis of measurement, in this case ideological assumptions about gender relationships.

6 Nevertheless middle range theory is entirely compatible and some, notably Ray Pawson (2000), would say that it was indispensable.

7 There is a huge literature in social theory on how this happens. See, for example, Giddens (1984); Layder (1990); Archer (1995).

8 I prefer the word 'process' to suggest a dynamic heterogeneity in the social world rather than the more deterministically sounding 'mechanism'; however, for the purpose of the discussion of Pawson's approach I use his term.

3

Research as Interpretation

In this chapter:

Methodological issues

- Interpretivist and survey method compared
- Realist and relativist approaches to interpretation
- Reflexivity and internal validity
- Understanding and interpretation
- Generalization and its limits
- Reliability

Doing interpretivist research

- Theory building and post hoc clarification
- Field research
- Interviewing
- Focus groups
- Analysing interpretive data

This chapter is concerned with the range of methods variously referred to as 'qualitative', 'ethnographic' or 'interpretive'. The principal methods used are field research (often called participant observation), depth, or focused interviews and focus groups. In the first of these the researcher participates wholly or partly in the activities of a social group, learning about the group through observation and conversation. Depth interviews may be conducted within field research, but they also constitute a quite separate method. Focus groups are currently a popular form of research in evaluation studies and market research. In this method group interviews will be conducted by a 'moderator' with several people, on a specific topic or range of topics. Each of these methods prioritizes the interpretation of actions, conversations or context and for this reason I will refer to the overall approach as interpretivism.

The Concise Oxford Dictionary offers the definition of 'interpret' as 'to elucidate or bring out the meaning', or to 'explain or understand behaviour'. In our everyday encounters in the social world this is pretty much what we do and that we have the resources to do this successfully (most of the time) marks out our competence as social actors. Though the act of interpretation is an individual one and logically each individual interpretation of the same social situation could be different, in everyday life there is enough cultural continuity in the things we know (what Alfred Schutz called 'typifications') to facilitate the elucidation of meaning, or to understand behaviour. Max Weber (Albrow, 1990: Chapter 10) believed this could be accounted for by shared forms of rationality, which did not mean that what was rational was the same everywhere, or that people always acted rationally, but that given some knowledge of rational behaviour in any social setting, it was possible for the social scientist to interpret what was going on.

The need to interpret at all presupposes that social life is not transparent and indeed social science operates on two opposite, but equally true particulars: that some things in the life world of people are known better to them than the outsider and that the outsider is often in a position to better know other things. In order for the social scientist to be in a position to know the latter, it is often crucial to obtain insights of the former. The use of survey method does not preclude this, but for three main reasons survey method is inappropriate in many situations.

First, if a researcher knows very little about a social group, then it is often not possible to formulate standardized questions that will get at the important aspects of that social group that are hidden. Even if standardized questions can be formulated, usually there is a limited range of responses a respondent can make. A question about why a person moved to a location might be categorized into job reasons, lifestyle reasons, to be near family, friends, etc., and the respondent may answer to more than one category (Perry et al., 1986), but the job reasons may be complex and the circumstances of family relationships or friendships multi-layered and heterogeneous.

Second, surveys collect data on previously identified variables and offer only limited conceptual flexibility. A conversation or a depth interview will often throw up a range of concepts, views or circumstances that lead the researcher to re-think the original question.

Third, for ethical or cultural reasons, a survey would not succeed. Surveys are an artefact of Western society and require, for their success, a shared set of meanings between researcher and researched. The anthropologist in a non-Western society has to develop those shared meanings on the terms of those he or she researches (Okely, 1994). Even within Western society the investigation of some groups precludes any form of overt method. Many groups or organizations, such as religious sects, political groups or deviant sub-cultures do not welcome the attentions of the researcher and covert (or semi-covert) methods are required. See, for example, Wallis' study of the scientology sect (Wallis, 1976), Fielding's study of the British National Front (Fielding, 1981) or Polsky's study of the underworld and 'hustlers' associated with American pool (Polsky, 1969).

It is perhaps becoming apparent that there is no algorithm for interpretation. Each interpretation is unique to its setting. In this respect it *is* more like art than science, which poses a difficulty for the researcher wishing to produce reliable[1] accounts. How can art be reliable? More specifically, how can one develop a methodology of interpretivism and then, having conducted interpretive research, what is the status of one's findings? A formulaic answer to these questions would offend the spirit of interpretation; however, in this chapter I will try to set out some of the methodological issues which should assist the reader in deciding just how reliable interpretive methods or findings can be. In the second part of the chapter I will describe some of the principal methods of interpretivism.

Methodological issues

Survey research has plenty of methodological controversies, but there is no doubt that most survey researchers could agree on some of the key characteristics of a good survey. With minor exceptions standards of research design, sampling, questionnaire construction and analysis are quite settled, but the same is hardly true of interpretive research (Oakley, 2000: 57). What unites survey research is a logic of inference, 'a logic of relating evidence and argument' (Goldthorpe, 2000: 67), essentially within the kinds of methodological structures I have described in the previous chapters. While some researchers maintain that such a logic is equally appropriate in interpretivist research, others insist that the latter is a form of art and inappropriate.

At the risk of over-simplifying the issues, a useful way to characterize the situation is to view positions on interpretive method as ranging on a continuum from realist to relativist. I make no secret of my own position as being very much nearer the realist end of the continuum. But is this just a doctrinal dispute which makes little difference to how one carries out interpretive research? No – it is important because what is disputed is fundamental and concerns issues of how one should conduct the research, what and how much one can claim and the whole *raison d'être* of research in the first place. What I have termed the 'realist' (see Chapter 2) and 'relativist' views owe allegiance to very different philosophical and methodological traditions.

Realism and relativism in interpretive research

The first can trace its roots to the scientific tradition of social science (Williams, 2000a: Chapter 3), through the anthropology of Malinowski and Radcliffe Brown, Weber and the Chicago School (Hammersley, 1989). Relativism arises from the quite opposite anti-scientific tradition of nineteenth-century humanism (Tallis, 1995: Chapter 2), is influenced by the philosophy of Hegel, Nietzsche and more recently postmodernism and post-structuralism.

REALISM   The realist view is an ontological commitment to a social reality that is not always apparent and obvious, but nevertheless shapes individuals and that they in turn can shape it, though the consequences of individual action is not always intended or known (see Chapter 2). The epistemological commitment is to the pursuance of truth in a world that is knowable, at least in part. The aim, at least, is to produce verifiable knowledge that will be of social use to policy-makers, academics, particular communities, etc. The moral position is that research and ideological commitment make uneasy bed fellows, that (after Weber, 1974) although one can choose to work on an issue that one has an ideological commitment to, this should not blind the researcher to seek out the truth of the matter (Hammersley, 2000; Williams, 2000c) even if this is inconvenient or contrary to one's ideological position.

The realist position in interpretivism shares common goals with survey research and indeed, in some variants, emerged from the same positivist tradition (Seale, 1999). While it seeks to explain social life, usually through micro-level studies, it aims to make generalizing statements about social life. This approach was typified by the Chicago School of sociology, associated with Robert Park, Ernest Burgess and Herbert Blumer (see Bulmer, 1984). Its subject matter was mostly urban social processes and its method observational and direct. It is summed up by Robert Park's famous exhortation to

> Go and sit in the lounges of the luxury hotels and on the doorsteps of the flop houses; sit on the Gold Coast settees and on the slum shakedowns; sit in the Orchestra Hall and in the Star and Garter Burlesque. In short, go get the seats of your pants dirty in real research. (Quote from McKinney, 1966: 71)

Chicago sociology was about linking the subjective and objective 'to learn to see the world from the perspectives of those under study, but at the same time this subjective point of view was to be located within an objective scientific account of the world' (Hammersley, 1989: 69). This goal produced (and continues to produce) philosophical and methodological tensions in realist interpretivism. Specifically, how is one to be objective about subjectivity? Surely there is a tension in immersing oneself in everyday lives and remaining objective? Moreover, this is assuming that when one makes the decision to study the rich of the Gold Coast, or the poor of South Chicago, this decision and all that follows remain free of observational, psychological or ideological influence.

RELATIVISM   The relativist begins from the position of a denial of this objectivity. Since the 1960s and the 'anti-positivist revolution' of Popper, Kuhn and Feyerabend (Chalmers, 1999), there has been a gradual dismantling of traditional criteria of trust, reliability and objectivity, in much of interpretive sociology and anthropology (Jones, 1998). It has been a move away from science toward the humanities and the very different values of enquiry embodied in the latter. The reasoning for this approach is quite compelling. If it is the case that we wish to interpret the subjectivity of social life and we acknowledge that those interpretations themselves cannot ever be a 'view from nowhere', then we are acknowledging that enquiry itself is subjective and this is precisely what the artist and writer do.

An important contributory factor in this dismantling came with the insights of Marxists and feminists, that knowledge and its pursuance, and indeed the values of science themselves, are products of class and gender positions (Harding, 1986). Yet since the mid-1970s the critiques of Marxism and feminism have themselves come under attack as *grand narratives* and in what Norman Denzin and Yvonna Lincoln call the 'fifth moment' (1998: 29–30) (to indicate a fifth stage in the development of interpretive research):

> Poststructuralists and postmodernists have contributed to the understanding that there is no clear window into the inner life of the individual. Any gaze is always filtered through the lenses of language, gender, social class, race and ethnicity. There are no objective observations only observations socially situated in the world of the observer and the observed. Subjects or individuals, are seldom able to give full explanations of their actions or intentions; all they can offer are accounts, or stories, about what they did and why. (Denzin and Lincoln, 1998: 24)

The consequences of this are epistemological and moral relativism. In the first case, because there can be no objective or verifiable account, each account must have equal status as knowledge, stories about stories or travellers' tales. In the second, as Clive Seale describes, the anti-positivist scepticism that has resulted from 'critical perspectives' has ended up de-legitimising research as an activity (1999: 14), though there is an attempt to try to rescue this through a denial of moral relativism in favour of a commitment to the politics of liberation (ibid.: 46). Seale cites Guba and Lincoln's current (and influential) position as a belief that studying the world from the position of an interacting individual, one can uncover ideological, political and economic oppression. Though as Oakley (2000: 72) counters, 'in-depth interviewing and ethnographic observation may well only bring us nearer to the truths that flourish inside researchers' heads.'

The philosophical and methodological gap between the utmost expressions of realism and of relativism seem pretty well unbridgeable. The realist would (quite rightly) point out that the logical outcome of relativism is an abandonment of any attempt at dispassionate or reliable research, whereas the relativist would counter that despite 'post-positivist' concessions to the subjectivity of enquiry, there remains a hankering for deterministic truth and political or ideological control. Thus any attempt to overcome methodological impasse will almost certainly be interpreted as favouring one side or the other.

My own view, outlined in Chapter 1, is that social research does indeed begin from moral commitment, but that such commitment is best served by objective research. Whilst it is absolutely right to maintain that research will always be influenced by the psychological dispositions and social location of the researcher, it does not follow from this that the researcher should abandon attempts to be objective and rigorous, no more than medical researchers should abandon the search for a cure, because cures cannot always be found. If we take this position, then we can perhaps view methodological issues as productive tension, a compromise between good practice and constraint. Let me briefly consider some of these tensions.

Reflexivity and internal validity

Interpretation requires reflexivity, a self-awareness and a realization of one's own position in relation to those being researched. What effect will my presence have upon those I research?[2] This is both an ethical–political question and a methodological one.

An example of some of the practical difficulties entailed by positioning are illustrated by Dick Hobbs' reflections on researching the entrepreneurial culture among petty criminals in his native East End of London (Hobbs, 1988). How far does one need to shed academic identity in order to attain credibility and thus obtain the data sought? How far is it desirable to 'go native' – as Hobbs so memorably put it, after long evening sessions in the pub, the following morning presented the dilemma of 'whether to write it up or bring it up' (Hobbs, 1988: 16).[3] Ultimately the decision one makes is personal and a balance between obtaining and presenting the world of those being researched from their viewpoint and being able to see it only from their viewpoint.

For Tim May (1998a; 1998b; 2000) reflexivity is about social positioning, but he emphasizes the importance of separating out the positioning of the researcher and the researched (though they can overlap). What he terms endogenous reflexivity refers to the knowledge we have of our immediate social surroundings, how we reflect upon this and how it consequently informs our actions. It follows from this that the social researcher in the community of social research is also engaged in endogenous reflexivity. However, the social scientist investigates others and in doing this must deploy a different kind of reflexivity, one that May describes as referential and 'refers to the knowledge which is gained via an encounter with ways of life and ways of viewing the social world that are different from our own' (1998b: 158). The researcher must be aware of not just of his or her own biography through endogenous reflexivity, but also be aware the effects the actions of his or her research will have on the researched and the wider community.

Quite apart from the ethical and political effects on those researched, there is the question of how valid are our findings as an account of the people we are studying. Specifically, what is the effect of our presence upon the context and how will this affect our results? This is the issue of internal validity and it is closely bound up with the kind of reflexive accounting we undertake.

It is often assumed that better internal validity can be achieved in field research, where the researcher becomes a full or partial participant in the social group he or she is researching, than in-depth interviews or focus groups. Obviously the more 'natural' the setting is, the less the researcher interferes, but it does not always follow that insider observation and conversation will produce the most valid findings. Sometimes the anonymous stranger (the researcher) is less of a risk to confide in than someone more intimate. As Ferdinand Zweig remarked of his experience of depth interviews: 'I made many friends, and some of them paid me a visit afterwards or expressed a wish to keep in touch with me, and I often heard the remark "Strangely enough I have never talked about that to anyone else,"' (Quoted in Burgess, 1984: 103).

Sometimes intimacy can bring us closer to the lives of respondents, but sometimes ironically distance and the perspective of the role of the outsider can bring useful results (Payne, 1996: 25–6). If we are reflexive in our research we can come to appreciate that our own identities as men, women, members of one ethnic group or another will have an effect on those we research, leading to particular ethical and methodological consequences. It does not follow from that, however, that one must always be an insider to do research, or that being an outsider is necessarily harmful to those we research.

Understanding and interpretation

The impression I have perhaps given so far is that interpretivism is 'deep', about the unlocking of dark secrets, or tapping into complex subjectivities. Many of those studies regarded as 'classics' fit this description, but really the subject matter and the level of engagement can vary from field research in which one becomes an active, or partially active participant in the lifeworld of the researched, to relatively straightforward depth interviews, or focus groups, of the kind used by market researchers about preferences in goods and services. Even with field research, not everything requires a deep or empathic engagement.

For much of the time no great depth of interpretation is required, because often the researcher shares many aspects of the same social world as the researched, calling upon the same referential resources (which is why endogenous and referential reflexivity overlap). Indeed, to be reflexive is not just about accounting for one's position as a stranger, but sometimes as an insider. The latter requires the researcher to stand back and treat the world as 'anthropologically strange'. Simon Holdaway's research on police culture (1982) was conducted while he was a serving police officer. Unlike other studies of police culture where the researcher was an outsider, attached to a police force in some capacity (see Bittner, 1967, for example), Holdaway had to carry out his day-to-day policing duties, while keeping enough 'distance' to reflect upon his role and that of his fellow officers.

Though Holdaway's research held quite different reflexive challenges to those of, say, an anthropologist researching non-Western cultures, he at least shared referential resources that were located in a shared rationality of policing. As I noted above, Weber's method depends crucially on the existence of such shared rationality. Given this, Weber distinguishes between descriptive understanding (*actuelles Verstehen*) where one understands what is happening (for example, someone is digging with a shovel) and explanatory understanding (*erklärendes Verstehen*) where one comes to know why (to plant potatoes) (Weber, 1978). The level at which one moves from *actuelles* to *erklärendes Verstehen* will depend on the shared cultural resources, but the principle remains the same: the researcher needs to *understand*.

Reflexivity, understanding and interpretation are interwoven. To understand how, or why something is like it is requires an act of interpretation, but the 'depth' of interpretation will itself depend on the question asked and the extent of the social resources held in common by researcher and researched.

Generalization and its limits

It has often been said that one cannot generalize from the findings of inter- pretive research because there is too much variability of meaning and action in the setting one researches (Denzin, 1983; Taylor, 1994), but if this is the case, it begs the question, why do the research in the first place? In Clifford Geertz's words, 'we want to say something of something' (1979: 222). Virtually all research is intended as a statement about the kinds of things one can expect in a similar context to that researched. Now as we will see in Chapter 4, this is less of problem for the survey researcher for he or she begins with a represen- tative sample (usually a random or quota sample – see Chapter 4), the charac- teristics of which can then be generalized to the population. The interpretivist is not so fortunate, for he or she can never be sure whether the characteristics of 'sample' go beyond that sample. In one sense they do not, because, as Denzin and others claim, the variability of micro-level interactions is far too great. Each situation is unique, yet it is not that hopeless. First, generalization is not a monolithic concept. It can refer to the kinds of deterministic generali- zation one can make about the laws of nature, of the kinds of statistical gener- alizations survey researchers (and other scientists) make, or it may refer to *moderatum* generalization, whereby the cultural consistency generated by shared norms, values, rationality and similar physical situations will produce replications (Williams, 2000b; 2002). Indeed, this is just the kind of cultural consistency we depend on every day to make sense of our lives.

Sue Fisher (1993), for example, carried out a study of young people's playing strategies in a gaming arcade in Devon. The research had important social policy implications (for example, on the problem of young people and gambling) and unless one could generalize from the context, then the research would be no more than an interesting traveller's tale. But of course one can. A gaming arcade in Devon will share many of the physical characteristics of one in Durham or Detroit and the children using it will have been subject to many of the same cultural influences, from similar street slang to the Simpsons.

Nevertheless these are *moderatum* generalizations and mark the limit to what is possible in interpretive research (Williams, 2000b). They are, within their own frame of reference, testable or perhaps more importantly they are testable as part of a pluralist methodological approach. This may imply a linking to quantitative methods in which very specific hypotheses are tested through surveys or experiments, or it might imply comparative case studies between locations and groups.

Reliability

For the quantitative researcher reliability can be construed as trusting the results obtained. Such trust is grounded in methodological procedures such as replication, representative sampling and testing. These procedures are either absent or take a different form in interpretivism. For the relativists, reliability is seen simply as exercises in promoting an artificial consensus about general truths (Seale, 1999: 42), whereas realists, because they believe in a reality that has some social consistency, aim to produce accounts that are more or less in agreement. Failure to do so is not seen as a failure of interpretivism *per se*, but a failure of the specific instance. In survey research, reliability is indeed demonstrated by the replicability of the whole study, or parts of it such as specific questions (see Chapter 5), but interpretivist studies are rarely replicated, because replication (except in the very broadest sense) would impose a rigidity quite alien to the approach.

Just how much can we trust interpretive accounts of research? Among those I characterize as 'relativists' there has been scepticism about the appropriateness of scientific methods and the findings produced by such methods, but this scepticism often does not extend to those of interpretivism, where often the researcher presents findings that are personal interpretations, unlike survey results, not open to external scrutiny. As Hobbs recalls: 'I noticed that a male audience was less likely to question the feasibility of a woman speaker presenting a paper on rape or domestic violence, and that white audiences appeared reluctant to interrogate black speakers on subjects such as police harassment or racism in schools' (Hobbs and May, 49).

Reliability as trust must take a different form. Seale suggests an approach that is informed in spirit by the Karl Popper's falsificationist approach (Seale, 1999: 74–8) (see Chapter 2), a systematic search for negative instances. In interpretivism this can take the form of asking what other interpretations could be placed on findings, or are the findings themselves (to use Howard Becker's words) 'deviant'? Obviously there is a danger of an infinite regress here where alternative interpretations themselves must be subject to scrutiny, lest they take on an authority greater than that of the original or first one. Yet there are strategies in data collection that can help. Research I participated in on family responsibilities in the resolution of housing needs (Buck et al., 1993) employed a 'dual interview' method, where two researchers used simultaneous depth interviews to explore versions of events and attitudes held by different household members. Differences in views about what *ought* to be could not be seen as inconsistent, but differences in stories of what *was* could be compared. If respondent A says the family provided housing help to X and respondent B says the opposite, then one can immediately see the problem of reliability that arises if only A or B had been interviewed.[4] The method of dual interviewing of couples was pioneered by Rhona and Robert Rapoport in the 1960s (Rapoport and Rapoport, 1971) in their research on professional dual career couples. This research went much further and the couples were invited to comment on the research when it was written up, first, as their 'case study' as a couple and then again prior to publication. The researchers used this method both as means of conducting open and ethical research, but also in the belief that their perceptions and those of couples together would produce a more valid approximation to the truth.

An approach that elevates the search for data deviance into a central plank of method is that of Analytic Induction, a method first suggested by Florian Znaniecki (1934). The method was developed by several sociologists between the 1940s and the 1970s (Lindesmith, [1947] 1968; Cressey 1950; Bloor 1978), but as a formal method it has somewhat fallen into disuse probably because of its strongly positivist character. The method proceeds as follows: first, the problem is specified in quite general terms and a hypothesis is constructed. A single case is first examined to see if it supports the hypothesis. If it doesn't, the researcher then either reconstructs the hypothesis, or redefines the initial problem. This is repeated on further cases until all of the deviance disappears and there is a 'run' of confirming cases. The method was adopted to study drug use by Lindesmith, by Cressey on financial trust and Bloor in surgeons' decision-making. After known deviance is 'eliminated', confirming instances are seen as unproblematic, but we can only really ever know about those cases observed and cannot really know if unobserved deviance remains.

Falsificationist approaches and analytic induction far from exhaust specific strategies aimed at improving reliability, however, much can be done to increase the trust in the reliability of a particular research project through methodological openness. This means providing an account of how respondents were recruited, or entry to the field was gained, how data were recorded and analysed, or what kinds of things intervened that might have affected the results. How many interviews were conducted, or how long was the researcher 'in the field' and what was his or her status? See Devine and Heath (1999) for a discussion of these issues.

Doing interpretivist research

In the last chapter I discussed the process by which we move from theory to operationalization in the social survey. While the development and testing of theory are equally relevant within interpretivism, there are some important differences. First, in interpretivism, the process of operationalization is very much more flexible (indeed the term is hardly used there) and the specification of fixed measures, indicators or values is absent. Theory testing in interpretive research is both more 'holistic' (variables are 'fuzzier') and more heterogeneous.

Second, a great deal of interpretive research is not about theory testing, but theory building and it is to this I now turn.

Theory building and post hoc *clarification*

Although research always begins with what Malinowski referred to as 'foreshadowed problems' (Hammersley and Atkinson, 1995: 25), often researchers will initially know very little about a topic area and will need to 'build theory' (see Chapter 2 and Chapter 9), particularly in the case of anthropological fieldwork (Okely, 1994: 19). This process is often quite informal and the findings may play only a small role in final outcomes. They help the researcher to ask the right questions, either in a general sense, or the specific sense of survey questions, or they will sensitize the field researcher to the kind of things he or she should be looking for. Some approaches to theory building are more formal, such as those used in grounded theory (Glaser and Strauss, 1967) (see Box 3.1). This approach was intended, like analytic induction, to be a method of doing interpretive research, for like the former method it relies on an inductive logic of concept construction rather than deductive theory testing. The researcher begins by making sensitizing observations (or interviews) and then begins to develop 'categories' that fit and clarify these. The categories are 'saturated' by gathering further instances of them until the researcher believes these are what are relevant and necessary to the study. More formal categories are proposed and in further stages these are developed and relationships to other relevant factors of the setting are developed. The method is rigorous and has been used in a variety of settings, in particular socio-medical ones (see Strauss and Corbin (1997) for a range of examples), but as a method of research in its own right it has attracted criticism. Martin Bulmer, for example (1979), has questioned whether it is possible for a researcher to suspend judgement on existing theories until quite late in the research process. Nevertheless, as a way of conducting exploratory research it has the advantages of allowing the researcher to develop a framework to cope with the messiness and unstructured reality of the social world and allows the development of categories or theories which are relevant and meaningful to those being researched (Bryman, 1998: 84).

In practice, most theory building is very much less structured than this and a great deal of initial research is rather informal and exploratory, often aimed at producing a testable theory that links what I termed 'experiential theory' (see Chapter 2) with middle range theory. Many larger studies begin with pilot interviews to gain basic information, or test variables prior to developing survey or field research.

Conversely, focus groups and depth interviews are also commonly used to 'tease out' meanings, or contradictory results from survey research, to 'flesh out' the findings. (Mitchell, 1999).

Field research

Field research, as I have noted, is often called participant observation and describes a range of interventions from complete participant to complete observer. The extent to which one participates is in principle independent of whether one's identity as a researcher is unconcealed, partly concealed or wholly concealed, though in practice the more covert one is, the more one is forced into one of the two extremes.

Box 3.1   Grounded theory in European integration research

Grounded theory has been used for theory building in exploratory research in a wide range of situations. In international relations Howell examined the limits of European integration using this method. European integration is a rapidly changing landscape and current explanatory theories were seen as inadequate, while earlier theories required reassessment. A specific study area, the regulation of life assurance across the European Union was investigated. First, 'open coding' (comparing and categorizing) was undertaken on the use of key concepts. Surveys of life assurance companies, of European Parliament members/officials and interest groups were then conducted. The emerging matrix of categories was then fitted to the 'core' concept of European integration. Here, 'axial' coding was used to provide a framework of concepts to which earlier categories could be fitted. These were:

- membership of the European Union
- creation of the Single European Market and legislation to create regulatory environments
- the European decision-making process
- the harmonization of market conditions (with reference to the life assurance industry)
- interactions between member states and decision-making bodies.
- outcomes: the creation of a single market in the life assurance sector as an example of a move toward European integration (Howell, 2000: 33).

Grounded theory develops theory, but there must be either informal theories (experiential theory) or assumptions arising from earlier grand or middle range theories to begin with. In this case there is an assumption that in convergence and integration actors will aim to maximize their self-interest.

Examples of the use of grounded theory in management research can be found in Locke (2001) and in medicine in Strauss and Corbin (1997).

Let me deal with the role of the complete observer first. Here one's presence is completely unnoticed and the research may literally be 'one of the crowd'. The strategy is more used in social psychology for passive studies of behaviour and the extent of interpretation is very much limited to that of observation (see Box 3.2).

Box 3.2   Unobtrusive observation

Observation is not just about observing people, it can be about observing their artefacts, or what they leave behind. Eugene Webb and his colleagues used some ingenious methods to obtain hard to research phenomena (Webb et al., [1966] 1981). For example, how could we tell which museum exhibits were most popular? The standard method would be to ask people, but respondents may tell the interviewer what they think he or she wishes to hear. The researcher could stand next to exhibits and count the number of people looking at them, but the presence of the researcher may well be noticed, or become off-putting. Webb and his colleagues instead suggested that wear and tear on the floor could be used as an indicator of popularity!

Much more common are studies where there is at least some minimum social interaction between the researcher and the researched. For example, some years ago I conducted a passive observation of clients in an open plan local council office, recording and classifying their reasons for visiting the office. To the clients I was all but 'invisible', just another council worker sitting at his desk, but to the council staff my identity as a researcher was known (Burns and Williams, 1989). Mostly, however, the level of interaction with the group of interest is much higher.

As a participant the researcher may enter and leave the field on an intermittent basis (as in the case of Hobbs above), or may remain constantly in the community he or she is researching. This kind of approach is common in anthropology. Sometimes researchers, as in the case of Holdaway (above) are already doing a job and take on the role of researcher after being in the job some time, while in others, the researcher takes on a job or role for a period of weeks or months. This is fairly typical approach to field research.

In several sociological studies of 'deviancy' researchers have not revealed their identity at all and have adopted a cover story. Such research requires great skill to maintain the story and at least some *a priori* knowledge of the group to be researched. Such studies are also often ethically controversial (see Chapter 8) and can place great stress upon the participant. Box 3.3 describes the experiences of a researcher in one such study.

The researcher will not always attempt to blend in and may negotiate a shifting role between outsider and insider. That the person is a researcher is known, but their involvement with the community may change. In the studies described above both Dick Hobbs and Nigel Fielding were both 'open', but in different ways and to a different extent. Hobbs is an Eastender and though he made no secret of his research role, this was often forgotten because his

---

Box 3.3 The nine o'clock story

It is not just that when researching deviant groups that the researcher may be in danger (though that is certainly sometimes the case), but as Hammersley and Atkinson describe in respect of Mitchell's research on survivalists, it is what one has to do or say to maintain the role.

The 'nine o'clock' story concerns Mitchell's volunteering to take on the role of a guard at Christian Patriots Survivalist Conference. In the quiet of the evening (at nine o'clock) Mitchell found himself sharing violent and racist stories with his fellow guards. These included Ku Klux Klan members and one man on the FBI's 'Ten Most Wanted' list. Mitchell had to invent stories in order to demonstrate his own commitment to their beliefs and maintain his role. The necessity of this subterfuge, that on the basis of what he had said, members of the group had regarded him as one of their own, left him distressed.

> If there are researchers who can participate in such business without feel-
> ing I am not one of them, nor do I ever hope to be. What I do hope is some-
> day to forget, forget those unmistakable sounds, my own voice, my own
> words, telling that Nine O'clock Story. (quoted in Hammersley and Atkinson,
> 1995: 119–120)

---

persona was first and foremost that of a 'native', whereas Fielding partially revealed his identity as an academic, while giving the impression of sympathy toward the National Front.

All research is different and there are lots of variations on these models as well as the extent to which the 'real' identity of the researcher is known. This brings us to the question of deception and the extent to which this is justified. I will talk about the ethical issues of deception in Chapter 8, but for the moment let us consider methodological issues. As I noted above, though 'blending in' can increase internal validity, it does not always follow that it does. Assuming an identity that is not your own is both difficult and stressful to maintain (Fielding, 1993: 151) and might even be dangerous (see the Mitchell example above). Often it is necessary to have some command of the vocabulary and culture of the group researched, but the more of this one tries to adopt as an outsider, the more likely one's cover is to be blown. One of the most dramatic examples of this was the research conducted by Howard Griffin (1977) in the 'deep south' of the United States in the 1950s. Griffin's research was intended as a scientific study of the 'Negro in the south', but ended up as a personal account of his experiences. Griffin, as a white man, could not blend in any black community, so he became black himself through a course of medication. What happened to him while he was 'black' is a fascinating story, but the dangers of exposure became particularly acute when the medication began to wear off and he began to recover his white pigmentation. Griffin's work is certainly a methodological oddity (and ethically controversial – see Homan, 1991: 99), but nevertheless maintaining a false identity in an 'alien' community requires quite a lot of prior knowledge of the cultural context and social grammars.

The decision to do field research at all should not be taken lightly. It is usually time-consuming (and therefore costly). Paul Siu's study of Chinese laundry workers took 20 years to complete (Siu, 1987), but field studies will rarely take less than weeks or months. Nevertheless valuable experience can be gained through doing 'practice' mini-studies of a day or so. One of the ironies of academic field research (except in anthropology), is that for most researchers the only period when they will have the time and resources to conduct this kind of research is when they are graduate students, which is also when they are least experienced. In most social sciences funding for pro-tracted field research is not that easy to find.

Field research presents a number of particular problems, which I will just touch on. First, one has to get access to the field. Posing in a particular role, in covert research, may require a confidant who is in a position to 'hire' the researcher temporarily and this may not be the same person who can act as a gatekeeper to other members of the group. Gatekeepers are those persons (uaually in an organization) who have the power to grant or withhold the researcher access. Often they are 'in charge', or a person of authority, but not always (Burgess, 1984: 48). In overt research the identity of the researcher is usually known to the gatekeeper, who must decide whether or not to grant access. Nigel Fielding (1993: 158–9) warns that gatekeepers may well want to know what benefit your research can bring to the organization (or group) and this needs to be taken into account when deciding what information to provide.

The researcher in the field not only has little control over the rate and extent of stimuli that he or she will be exposed to, but must also learn to distinguish useful data from ephemera, suggesting that at least some organizing theory (if only experiential) is necessary. Having learnt to know what counts as 'data', he or she must then find ways of recording or remembering it. For the most part tape recorders or video cameras are unusable (or unethical, see Chapter 8) and even note taking would be impractical – which does make one wonder how it can be that some of the classical field research studies of the 1940s and 1950s managed to have quotes, sometimes up to one page long, from key informants. Either the researchers had incredible memories, or they lugged tape recorders, then the size of one-armed bandits, around with them. For most field researchers, who are able to conduct interviews, notes written up assiduously at the end of the day or the session is about the best that can be done. It is often said that field researchers may find it useful to suffer from a weak bladder! The writing up may be a descriptive 'diary' style, or may make use of formal identification categories for people or events (for a detailed discussion of this see Burgess, 1984: Chapter 8). The diary also has a secondary role as a confessional and means of letting off steam for the researcher.

One of my favourite examples of 'diary research' shades into literature. *Wellington Road*, by Margaret Lassell (1962) is a rich account of the domestic life of a working-class family and their social milieu in the early 1960s. Lassell lodged with 'Mary and Joe Johnson' in their house on the outskirts of an English industrial town and kept a diary which (in the book) is presented in almost the style of a novel or a soap opera. For example:

> Joe and Mary are feeling increasingly irritated by Maureen. She can now do nothing right in their eyes – if she doesn't offer to make the tea she is lazy and selfish; if she makes it it is too strong and too sweet; if by any chance it is just right, they say how changed she is, and are sure it won't last. (Lassell 1962: 95)

An issue often mentioned in respect of field research is that of 'going native'. To go native is to adopt the culture and world-view of those we research. Some models of research, particularly action research, where the researcher has an advocacy role and is an 'agent of change' perhaps hold the greatest danger. Alison Lurie's novel *Imaginary Friends* (1967) is an absorbing demonstration of how some members of a research team investigating a religious sect gradually get drawn in to becoming members themselves. The problem with going native is that a lot of the time one is unaware that it is happening!

Going native is not just about losing oneself in the milieu being studied; it can even extend to the conclusions drawn from the research. This is precisely the criticism Martyn Hammersley makes of Paul Willis's study of working-class boys (1977). Willis's study used the categorization of his respondents to divide the boys into 'lads' (the group he researched) and 'ear'oles', the boys who take on school values. 'Lads', Willis maintained, got working-class jobs, rather than middle-class ones, because their counter-culture fits in well with the culture of the manual workplace.

However, Hammersley sees Willis as having an 'over-rapport' with his respondents, taking on their values when they accorded with his own and, second, seeing the 'lads' as representative of working-class culture, while the conformists (those characterized by the lads as 'ear'oles') were equally working class. In Hammersley's view the book becomes a celebration of the 'lads' (Hammersley, 1995: 111–12).

Despite these challenges field research is exciting, rewarding and has produced some of the richest social science data we have. Probably the best advice one can give to researchers contemplating this kind of research is to read others' accounts and to practise first with simple observation studies – to see without being seen. Hobbs (Hobbs and May, 45) quotes William Burroughs, who recommended to his students to take a walk in a street and try to see everyone on the street, before they see you. If you do this, generally you won't be noticed, but if you realize you have been noticed, then try to work out why!

Interviewing

Interviewing may take place in a field setting, but probably for most interpretive studies interviews will be the principal means of data collection. In

Chapter 5 I will talk about interview schedules, structured documents with which the interviewer 'teaches' the respondent to reply according to a standardized format. In other books one will read of the 'ethnographic interview', suggesting these two modes are quite different approaches to data collection. Actually they can be represented along a continuum of increasing – decreasing structure. Interviews will have varying amounts of 'structure' and even the so-called 'unstructured interview' will contain some standardization of recording, such as a description of the respondent. In practice every interview has some structure and although what are sometimes called 'focused interviews' permit respondents to set the topic agenda to what is of importance to them, usually the researcher will at least have a list of topics he or she wishes to explore. Indeed, if the interview is felt to 'drift' too much, then the researcher will 'bring back' the respondent to the topic areas in which he or she is interested.

Interviews are sometimes semi-structured, that is part of the interview consists of standardized questions (or observations). The respondent may be encouraged to expand on the standardized answers, or the interview may be allowed to 'evolve' into a focused one. The amount of structure and the extent to which the respondent are prompted into particular replies are often proportional to the amount of prior knowledge the researcher has.

As in any conversation all interviews require a rapport between the parties, but this is particularly so in focused interviews where respondents are very often being encouraged to talk openly about issues which they may find sensitive or difficult. Furthermore in order to elicit such openness, the researcher must strike up a rapport between himself or herself and the respondent, yet not lose sight of the need to produce an objective account.

How can this be done?

Although all interviews are conversations, interpretive interviews (whether semi-structured or focused) are much more like a natural conversation than an interview schedule. This has advantages and disadvantages. The respondent is not just being given categories to choose, but asked to talk, in their own words, about their lives and opinions. This can be both liberating and threatening. In order to get the best out of an interview there must be 'ontological security' as Anthony Giddens puts it (1984: 50). The respondent should feel safe in their environment and comfortable about doing the interview. The interviewer can help through sympathetic body language and eye contact. As a student I recall learning the importance of these things, but in my first interviews (with local politicians) I was more scared than they were and had they not been politicians, my nervousness itself might well have damaged their ontological security!

Going native is rarely seen as a problem outside of field research, yet it is certainly possible to feel so drawn to the respondent that the investigative role of the research is lost. Even in a focused interview, the researcher should avoid 'leading' the respondent. For example, far better to say "So what did you say to him…", than "So did you say XXXX to him?" In this respect the word 'yes' can be deployed in many ways from the strongly affirmatory to the weakly permissive. The language one uses in questions is a useful tool in achieving a balance between empathy and objectivity. Nigel Fielding (1993: 141) suggests several 'probes' one may use (in increasing order of imperativeness):

- an expectant glance
- uh, hm, mm, or yes, followed by an expectant silence
- what else?
- what other reason?
- please tell me more about that
- I'm interested in *all* your reasons.

He goes on to suggest that, as a rule of thumb, whenever a statement appears ambiguous, the researcher should probe, much as one would in an ordinary conversation.

As with most things in interpretivist research there is no foolproof recipe for interviewing and no real substitute for trying it. Whereas in field research it is usually best to 'blend in', in an interview one can never blend in. There is always a power relationship between interviewer and respondent (see Oakley, 1981), but it does not follow that it is always the interviewer who is powerful, nor whether, if he or she is, it is any bad thing. Reflexive accounting can assist us in our own positioning in relation to those being researched and can help us to understand what effects interviewers could potentially have. Whether this means only black women can interview black women, gay men gay men and how far we must go in producing cultural matches is a vexed question.

A practical issue is how to record the data. At one level this will depend on what you are using the interview for. If it is merely exploratory, aimed at clarifying some issues or processes, for example, how an organization works, then making notes and writing these up more fully afterwards will suffice. If on the other hand a 'deeper' analysis of the content is needed (perhaps using a computer application – see below), then the data need to be capable of transcription and tape recording is necessary. In most interviews tape recording, if it can be done unobtrusively, is advisable. Even if you don't transcribe, you still have the tapes to listen to. Of course researchers should never secretly tape interviews (see Chapter 8 on ethical issues). In my experience the worst problem with taping an interview is not unwillingness on the part of the interviewee (they usually forget it's on), but that the juicy bits are often imparted to the researcher after the tape recorder is switched off! One last practical piece of advice is that whether you record or not, if you are conducting two or more interviews on the same occasion try to make summary notes in between so that you have an overall picture of what went on in each interview. After the first two or three they begin to blur!

Focus groups

Focus groups have become so popular among opinion formers and 'spin doctors', that it was rumoured that the British Labour Party, in 1999, commissioned focus groups to explore why the public was fed up with them. An apocryphal tale maybe, but it is probably true that focus groups have become a quick and dirty substitute for other forms of research. This is a pity, because used for the right ends, focus groups are a powerful research tool (see Barbour and Kitzinger, 1999). What are focus groups and when should they be used?

Focus groups, or group interviews, are used to generate interactions that can produce discursive data that is unlikely to be obtained from individual interviews, though often a combination of individual and group interviews can be used, one to validate the other. In a well-conducted focus group the whole becomes greater than the sum of its parts, the group interaction itself is part of the method (Smithson, 2000), though there is some debate as to whether a focus group is an artificial performance or a natural discussion. In my own experience the worst groups can be wooden, or formal with interaction forced, or even one group member dominating. In the best groups the interaction is so good the moderator plays only a minimal role.

As with focused interviews there are no hard and fast rules for setting up or running a focus group, though there are a few things that can help. First, unless the research is very exploratory indeed, then several groups will be needed in order to capture a range of interactions. The composition of the groups is usually varied by social characteristics, gender or age. In mixed sex groups, unfortunately men will often dominate the discussion, so at least one group consisting only of women is usually a good idea.

How directed should the group interviews be? A balance is needed between the moderator dominating with his or her agenda and completely free-ranging discussion tangential to the issues that interest the researcher. In order to have a fruitful discussion the group needs some 'tools'. These are some questions to answer, topics to discuss and at least some knowledge of the matter in hand. This might mean showing a short video, or giving a brief introductory talk (see Box 3.4). One of the commonest problems in any focus group is the dominant member, usually counterposed with the shy retiring one. The moderator can intervene by directly asking the 'quiet' person about the issue at hand (Smithson, 2000: 108), though the problem in either case is that these are individual voices and not 'interacting' ones. The aim, then, is a near spontaneous discussion that nevertheless remains focused on the topic of interest.

Finally, how does the researcher record the interview? In focus groups there should be some kind of audio-visual recording, as notes (even taken by a moderator's assistant) are not really sufficient. The ideal is an unobtrusive video camera, though care must be taken to keep such recordings confidential and usually they should be destroyed after analysis. Where group members do not wish to be individually visually identified, it is often possible to set up the video camera behind a semi-circle of discussants.

Box 3.4　The use of video in focus groups

Sylvie Gomez (Gomez et al., 1999) used focus groups to explore young people's views on the setting up of a local Youth Foyer. Youth Foyers aim to tackle the linked problems of homelessness, unemployment and lack of training opportunities among young people. Although the primary role of the foyers is to provide accommodation while young people find work or embark on training, they are also a community resource for the non-homeless and most have other facilities such as cafés or crèches. The problem for Gomez was that local youngsters did not know what a foyer was and could therefore hardly provide opinions. To resolve this, a short information video about foyers was shown at the beginning of each group and the groups themselves were videoed. Reactions to the infor-mation video were thus videoed, though the most useful aspect of videoing the groups was to identify who said what and what were the non-verbal reactions from other group members. Several groups were conducted and content analysis of verbal and non-verbal data was undertaken. Some respondents did not wish to be identified on camera and in these circumstances the camera was set up behind them.

Analysing interpretive data

It is possibly only when the analysis of interpretive data is considered that the real differences in the approach to that of the social survey (or experiment) are realized. The analyst of survey data must 'interpret' what the relationship between his or her categories means and indeed must interpret the research question in order to know which categories to exam-ine. Yet the categories are there, they have identifiable quantitative char-acteristics and moreover, their analysis is after the event – the trail has gone cold.

The interpretivist, in effect, begins analysis as soon as he or she begins the research (Hammersley and Atkinson, 1995: 205). Reflexive interpretation begins with the identification of concepts and continues while in the field through a selecting and interpreting of what is seen and heard. Indeed, as we have seen, grounded theory uses exactly this approach to refine and develop theoretical concepts. The importance of reflexivity in selecting particular data cannot be over-emphasized, for how else can the researcher make any sense of the sensations that he or she will encounter in fieldwork, or the views and personal constructions of events that will constitute interviews? The reflexivity in this case is to start with a battery of concepts, but to allow these to be challenged by what one encounters. Indeed, we cannot help doing the first bit, but the second is harder, because all of that which we come to know through our senses must be interpreted according to the con-ceptual resources we have. To treat the world as anthropologically strange is to be able to marshal those resources in new ways. In field research the 'funnel approach' is often used (Agar, 1980), whereby the researcher begins with an open-ended approach to the setting and people within it, allowing the people themselves to 'shape' the research. Clearly in such a holistic approach there is no sharp divide between data gathering and data analysis.

Interpretivism is not then about data raids, grabbing loads of sense impressions and bringing them home to the researcher's lair. Specifically, if interviews are the chosen method, then it is probably bad practice to do all of the interviews and then start transcribing and analysing. These are not standardized interviews and the researcher is not aiming to see how many people think x is the case compared to y, but to explain what they understand by x or y. Reflexive interviewing means the researcher will carefully examine the data from the first interview and see how these can assist in the next and so on.

No interpretive analysis will either fully exhaust or provide a correct understanding of what was going on. This does not imply a slide to relativism, but a realization that analysis is an ongoing enterprise in which (like any other scientific analysis) we try to move to better accounts. The reflexivity continues with further analysis. Judith Okely, reflecting on her fieldwork with gypsies, observes: 'Thus the seemingly trivial description of domestic objects, trailer interiors, and stray remarks volunteered in conversation, all meticulously noted, assumed massive significance when scrutinized and sifted, months and sometimes years later' (1994: 24).

Ian Dey has described the analysis of interpretive[5] data analysis as 'a series of spirals as we loop back and forth through various phases within the broader progress of the analysis' (1993: 264). Yet all of this begins to sound like a mysterious process, which if we persist with long enough, will produce categories and understandings like images in a crystal ball. There is certainly a skill in such analysis that cannot be expressed through an algorithm and will only be acquired with some experience (though that is not so different to any other form of analysis in the social or natural sciences), yet interpretive analysis is principally taxonomic. Even when interpretations require empathic understanding, analysis still requires the researcher to select and categorize. In recent years there has been a move toward the development of sophisticated computer software, such as NUD*IST and NVivo, able to search and categorize transcribed data. Providing we remember to be reflexive, such forms of analysis can at least take the pain from taxonomy.

Whether or not we are using computer software, some kind of category grouping needs to take place and this might be accomplished through many different schema. These might be spatial, social relational, physical objects, etc. The reflexivity in the analysis lies in the ingenuity of the researcher to know which categorical schema to use. In this respect, computer software is a useful aid to help the researcher look for members of those category groups.

Burgess (1984: 177–8) discusses Macintyre's procedure for classifying her data from a field research study of single pregnant women:

Stage 1   A list of problems, concepts and indices was constructed before entering the field. These were sub-divided into conceptual, socio-demographic categories, etc. A computerized index system was used for this.

Stage 2   Coding of that which can be coded took place throughout the research (here she followed a grounded theory approach).

Stage 3   The remaining material was coded and data re-read. The various data sources (field notes, transcripts, documents) were brought together.

Stage 4   The ways in which the data could be analysed and presented were considered, for example, through detailed case studies and at different time points to compare what was happening to each of the women or the comparison of the accounts of the different actors, such as professionals, clients, etc. She finally settled for an analysis of conceptual categories (e.g. 'moral character', 'bargaining in encounters', etc.).

Stage 5   The topics having been identified could be retrieved using the index.

Stage 6   A fairly simple quantification and interrelationships analysis was conducted.

Stage 7   The relationships between the major topics were examined.

The brief summary gives an indication of the different stages of analysis, though such a procedure does not prevent the researcher retracing her steps and conducting the analysis in different ways. Note also at Stage 6 that quantification is employed. This is less to do with making generalizations, but understanding the logical and hierarchical relationships between categories.

Conclusion

A lot of my own research has been through the use of secondary analysis of survey data, but in every frequency distribution there are what are known as 'outliers', those characteristics that deviate from the 'mean' or the 'norm'. These are the markers for the heterogeneity of social life that can so often be lost in the generalizations of the survey. Someone once said to me that in one or more respects each of us is an 'outlier'. Interpretive research is about finding out what it is that makes us different, or indeed the same. The 'celebration' of that difference and the multiple perspectives on reality that exist in social life has led to an undermining of the belief that we could make any kind of explanatory statement about the social world. The corollary of this is that there can only be interpretations and maybe interpretations of these, but in none is there any epistemological or moral authority.

As a citizen I like these values in my music and my food, but I think they are pernicious when we need to make decisions about social programmes. So whilst I recognize the limits of survey research in helping us to understand why or how, the methods we use need both to be sensitive to the social and moral ecology of that which we research, and also to produce explanations that are reliable. In this chapter I have tried to show, first, the limits and possibilities that are entailed by such an ambition and then (all too briefly) to consider ways of turning this into method. There are two kinds of limits to interpretive research. The first is to do with what we are like as human beings. Our taxonomic and conceptual skills are always limited, even when we use aids such as computers, so our understanding will only ever be partial, partly because there would be too much to understand and partly because by the time we think we have understood something the world moves on. This is also true of survey research, but the latter is conceptually 'closed' in terms of logical outcomes, whereas interpretivism is open and heterogeneous. Nevertheless, though never complete, as Paul Rock said: 'The most authentic appreciation of the world is lodged in an immediate confrontation with it' (1979: 70).

The second limitation is, just how big can our explanation be? How much can we generalize from one setting to another? Obviously if we could do this in detail, surveys would be obsolete, but we can do it in terms of generalities and in respect of some detail. Fisher's gaming arcades showed types of behaviour presumably recognizable to psychologists in different contexts and some of the detail, such as the design of the machines, will enable and constrain behaviour in any location where such a design can be found.

Reliability within method helps us to transcend those limitations and the very best interpretive research does not ask what is it that helps me to confirm what I think, but what challenges it. What are the possible meanings of X and how can I use what I know to make more sense of it? And when this has been done as rigorously as possible, then all the researcher can do is to hope that this will then lead to someone else producing a better explanation!

Questions for reflection and discussion

1   What are the strengths and weaknesses of interpretivist methods?
2   How far can we generalize from interpretive data?
3   How would you maximize the objectivity of field research?

Try this

Ask a colleague (or divide into pairs if you are in a group) and find out what the other person's hobby or main leisure interest is. Then, through a depth interview of around 20 minutes, try to find out what you can about the hobby/interest, what attracted your colleague to it and how important it is in his or her life. You should then consider, through a discussion, how *successful this method was and especially the 'quality' of the data you obtained.*

Suggested further reading

The literature on interpretive/qualitative research is enormous and some of it is quite specialized and technical. Two very good introductory and general texts are (in my view) Martyn Hammersley and Paul Atkinson's *Ethnography: Principles in Practice* (1995) and Jennifer Mason's *Qualitative Researching* (1996). Clive Seale discusses with clarity and depth many of the methodological issues raized above in *The Quality of Qualitative Research* (1999). Tim May's collected volume *Qualitative Research in Action* (2002) is a wide-ranging examination of methodological and technical issues in interpretive research. With the advent of computer-based analysis of interpretive data, there are a number of new books on the horizon. A well-established collection that discusses principles and practice is Alan Bryman and Roger Burgess's *Analysing Qualitative Data* (1994) though a visit to the Scolari website (http://www.scolari.co.uk) will give an overview of current analysis applications available.

Notes

1 I use the term 'reliable' (and reliability) in the sense meant by Robert Proctor (see Chapter 1) as being dependable research; discussions of reliability in interpretive research often contrast it with its use in surveys.

2 In older literature this is sometimes discussed under the heading 'reactivity', however I think this term fails to capture fully the dynamic nature of the encounter. In my view its eclipse by the concept of reflexivity is a methodological advance.

3 Jake Arnott's novel *The Long Firm* is a semi-fictional account of the same London criminal culture Hobbs researches. In the novel, a central character, also a sociologist, does indeed go native.

4 There was actually a large amount of agreement about such 'matters of fact', but where difference arose was in the importance or emphasis placed on particulars by different family members.

5 He uses the term qualitative.

Selecting and Sampling

In this chapter:

- Selecting, sampling and typicality
- Sampling in social surveys
- Censuses
- Probability samples
- Sample size
- Non-probability sampling
- Selecting and sampling in interpretive research

Selecting, sampling and typicality

Issues of sampling are so often seen as a matter for survey research, but this is to lose sight of the wider issue of selection in all approaches. The decision about what to research is very often closely tied to decisions about who to research and this is equally the case in interpretive research.

All research makes claims about the way the social world is. This may be anthropological claims about what a social group or society is like, or it may be that researchers wish to explain a phenomenon in society, or make some kinds of predictions about, say, the results of elections, the popularity of a product or wider public attitudes towards an issue. The kind of selections or sampling made has crucial implications for generalization, specifically with the confidence we have in those generalizations. Now just as there are different levels of generalization,[1] there are different levels of selection. Statistical generalization cannot (or at least should not) be made from *ad hoc*, or opportunistic selections, though *moderatum* generalizations may be possible (see Chapter 3). Holdaway's choice of the particular police force to research was 'opportunistic', in that it was the one he was a member of and the only one he could covertly observe (see Chapter 3). However, because there would be many cultural continuities between British police forces, or indeed in some respects police forces in other countries, he was entitled to make *moderatum* generalizations. Strictly speaking, Holdaway and other ethnographers who carry out such research are not sampling, but they are selecting. Sampling is a more formal process of selection, though at what point we should talk of sampling, as opposed to merely selecting, is not clear-cut.

Sampling is a search for typicality. A sample of a larger aggregation is an attempt to represent the latter in miniature, whereas a selection just implies the most suitable choice, for whatever purpose. Although sampling is more usually associated with quantitative methods, it is also an important issue in interpretive methods, even though the term is used less often there. However, even when a selection is made on grounds other than typicality, it is usually the case that some generalizing claims will be made and it is therefore not unreasonable to ask *post hoc*, how typical was the selection that was made? In this chapter I will begin with survey sampling, the most overt attempt to find typicality through a sample. Although I will then discuss sampling and selection in interpretive research, the issue should not be seen as a dichotomy, but more of a continuum from statistical dependability to weak generalization.

Sampling in social surveys

In the social survey the best kind of sample is not a sample at all, but a census – at least in theory. In a census data are gathered from every member of a given population, as in national censuses (see Dale and Marsh, 1993), though in practice this is rarely achieved (see Box 4.1). Perhaps more importantly, censuses are usually impractical on resource grounds. A census of all students in a university or all of the adults in a given town would be costly in terms of time, labour power and materials. Mostly, then, survey researchers use samples to represent a population.

The term population does not necessarily have to apply to the human population of a given geographical location, but is a statistical term that refers to a collection of persons, groups, events or things about which we wish to generalize. Our population might be all of the people, or all of the adults living in Springfield. It could be the households, it could be all of the police officers, or it could be the fire hydrants. In selecting a sample from a population, the intention is that the sample should be representative. Therefore if 25 per cent of the population of Springfield are people over 65, then the sample itself should consist of 25 per cent of people over 65. There are several ways representativeness can be achieved, though there only two broad types of sample: a probability sample and a non-probability sample. Generally speaking, when one wishes to obtain the most representative sample the aim should be to construct a probability sample, though for reasons I will discuss below, this is not always possible.

Box 4.1   Are censuses better than samples?

A census counts everyone, right? Wrong! Most national censuses suffer from undercount. Certain groups in the population are not reached, or do not want to be reached by the census enumerators. In the 1991 UK Census this was around 2 per cent (around 1 million people). Those not enumerated are more likely to be those aged 18–30; men; the elderly; or those who live in inner cities (Diamond, 1999: 17). Sophisticated and often controversial methods of sampling or imputation are used to make good the missing data (Darga, 1999). In the USA particularly there is a direct link between the allocation of federal funds and the numbers of people present. Consequently when the poor are undercounted, they are also likely to be under-funded in welfare programmes, etc.

Micro-level censuses, while virtually unavoidable in small populations (say, of just a few hundred) suffer disproportionately from non-response difficulties. In a population of several thousand a sample of a few hundred can be representative and (especially in self-completion surveys), researchers can 'over-sample' to compensate for non-response. In groups likely to be under-represented additional 'booster samples' can be taken. In a small census there is not a lot that can be done about non-response, which may be concentrated in particular groups. If in, say, a census of 160 people with no responses from 18–30 year olds, there is nothing you can say about 18–30 year olds! Hopefully in a large enough sample at least *some* 18–30 year olds would respond. The problem of non-response is discussed in Chapter 5 and that of missing data in Chapter 7.

Probability samples

In a probability sample (often called a random sample) each member of the population has an equal chance of being selected. Therefore providing data can be collected from every member that is sampled, it would not be necessary to know that 25 per cent of the population of Springfield were over 65, because about 25 per cent of the sample would turn out to be over 65 anyway. However, in life things are rarely straightforward and there will always be a margin of error in a sample – that is, the sample may not exactly replicate the population. Fortunately it is possible to know what the margin of error is, but before I discuss this, let us turn to questions of how to select a sample, the size of the sample and the different types of probability sample that may be used.

In order to select the sample we need certain information. We need a list of all of the members of the population, or at least the best possible list of those members. This is called a sampling frame. In practice there are few lists which contain an entry for every member of the population. For example, a sampling frame that has often been used for telephone surveys is the telephone directory. However, even in Western countries a small proportion of the population do not have phones[2] and a larger proportion choose not to have their names included. The latter group is growing as a result of increase in the number of telephone companies and lack of a common directory in many countries. In some US urban areas as many as 60 per cent of all telephone numbers are unlisted (Frey and Oishi, 1995: 15). Many research organizations who undertake telephone surveys, now use Random Digit Dialling (RDD) (see Box 4.2). One of the problems of RDD is that many numbers will not be in use or will be commercial numbers and consequently there may be low 'hit rate'. A variation on RDD, used by market research companies, is 'directory plus one' in which a sample is first drawn from the telephone directory and then one is added to each number drawn to produce a list of numbers which are then dialled (Thomas and Purdon, 1994). A increasingly important difficulty for telephone sampling is the growth in ownership of mobile phones. Here no directories exist and there are important ethical problems. Respondents may not be in a 'safe' location when they answer, or they may be children.

There are a number of lists one might use as sampling frames, for example, the electoral roll in the UK or lists of registered voters in the USA. The electoral roll is a public document containing the names and addresses of all voters, yet although registration is compulsory, a proportion of the population is absent for various reasons. Also in the UK the Postcode Address File (PAF), the list of addresses the Post Office deliver mail too, is commonly used. Very few sampling frames will be a complete record of a population and official lists of the kind I have mentioned are often too blunt an instrument to use as a sampling frame. Those missing from the electoral roll are more likely to belong to manual classes, to be young or to be transient. Although selection in the PAF can be made to avoid business premises and select only private addresses, this is not always successful.

A sampling frame can be any comprehensive list of the population of interest and many samples are of smaller populations with particular characteristics. If the population of interest was nurses, then lists of nurses employed by hospitals or health services would constitute the sampling frame, though in some countries access to lists held by organizations or statutory bodies is controlled by the law (in the UK this is the Data Protection Act).

Having chosen the best possible sampling frame the next step is to allocate a consecutive number to each member of the population. The sampling units (those selected from the population) can be chosen by selecting numbers from a random number table, or (more usually now) getting the computer to generate a series of random numbers. Suppose, then, numbers started at 01 and ended at 744, the computer would tell us to pick (for example) 04, 07, 22, 39, 41 and so on. Now in relatively small populations this simple probability sampling works well, but such a sample may not be sensitive to all of the characteristics that are of interest, or would be too costly and time-consuming in a large population. Imagine you wanted to conduct a survey on view of Australian voters towards constitutional change. A simple probability sample would require you to have a list of all of the voters in the country and then to make a selection from the list. But the task of selection, yet alone the survey that followed, would be formidable. Fortunately this is unnecessary and most probability samples are systematic, stratified, or clustered.

Systematic samples are, strictly speaking, still a simple random sample, but this method uses a different approach to selection. First, the size of the sample is determined and turned into a sampling fraction. If in a population of one thousand our sample is one hundred, then the sampling fraction is 1/10. The sample is selected by then choosing every tenth person from the sampling frame. This is usually begun with a 'random start', that is a number randomly selected as a starting point. An important weakness of this is the problem of 'periodicity', that is when a sampling frame is so structured that to choose every nth number yields certain characteristics. A certain London local authority once carried out a survey of resident's attitudes to their accommodation by selecting every fourth flat in several identical blocks. The principal dissatisfaction was noisy lifts, but this was found to be an artefact of choosing every fourth flat starting at n – every fourth flat was next to the lift! (May, 2001: 94).

Stratified samples divide a population into strata (or sub-groups). These are categories that the researcher knows something about beforehand. For example, suppose that we wished to conduct research on the opinions of university students on welfare issues. It is hypothesized that the type and quality of welfare provision are different in its faculties and that women, men and mature students have different welfare experiences. The 'strata' chosen will then be the faculties, men, women and mature students, with the appropriate proportion relative to the size of the strata. If we had used a simple random sample, chance may well have produced under-representation of some of these groups and an over-representation of others. Once strata have been identified, simple random or systematic sampling can be used.

Finally, cluster sampling uses naturally occurring 'clusters'. Often these are geographical and resolve the problem of representativeness across countries or large regions. For example, a polling organization that wished to research satisfaction with the Scottish Assembly might first select a probability sampling of voting constituencies across Scotland and then select a sample of voters from within those constituencies. Some care is needed in this approach when the number of clusters is not large. In the example given it is possible that the constituencies chosen might be mostly urban, or mostly rural.[3]

Box 4.2   How Gallup get their samples

Gallup is one of the largest polling organizations in the world. Since the 1980s it has predominantly used telephone interviewing. Their national sampling frame is not the adult population of continental United States, but all adults over 18 living in households with telephones. This excludes college students living on campuses, armed forces personnel living on military bases, prisoners, hospital patients and other residents of institutions. While telephone coverage is around 95 per cent, around 30 per cent of households are ex-directory, thus rendering the telephone directory unusable. Instead a two-stage sampling process is used.

First, a computerized list of all telephone exchanges is obtained along with an estimate of the number of phones attached to them. Next a computer programme uses this information to select a probability sample and perform random digit dialling (RDD).

See: Newport et al. (1997) and the Gallup website at http://www.gallup.com

---

Sample size

It is a function of the law of large numbers that unlike other areas of life, in sampling size *is* important! Selected carefully, a small sample of a large population can be more representative than a large sample of a small population. A sample size of 400 out of several thousand will usually be more accurate than a sample of 10 from a population of 50. This is because the more sampling units you have, the more likely the variation in population characteristics will be represented. However, the representativeness will also depend on the amount of variation that exists (or at least is measured).

The accuracy of sample is assessed through the relationship between the confidence level and the amount of error. Sampling error is the inaccuracy in inferences about a population. How does this come about? Suppose we filled a tub with 1000 balls, one-third blue, one-third yellow and one-third red, and we then decided to take a random sample of 99 balls, it is unlikely we would pick out exactly 33 balls of each colour, there would be some 'error' in our sample. Fortunately statistical techniques are available to help us calculate what the error is likely to be and how confident we can be in knowing this. We must therefore set a confidence level. This is not arbitrary and in social research it is usually set at 95 per cent (in natural science it is often 99 per cent or even up to 99.9 per cent)[4] (for a full description of confidence level and sampling error see Fink, 1995: Chapter 2). A sampling 'error' of 3 per cent and a 95 per cent confidence level means that we can be 95 per cent confident that the population would resemble the sample, plus or minus the

Table 4.1 Sample error and sample size
assuming a 95 per cent confidence level

Sample error (%)	Sample Size
10	100
7.1	200
5.8	300
5	400
4.5	500
4.1	600
3.8	700
3.5	800
3.2	1000
2.2	2000

3 per cent sampling error. For example, if a national opinion poll showed that 48 per cent of the sample said they would vote for the Labour Party candidate in a forthcoming election, then we could say that for 95 out of 100 cases in the electorate this would be accurate to plus or minus 3 per cent.[5]

Sampling error is crucial and is the small print of opinion polling. In the closely fought US Presidential Election of 2000 both candidates (Al Gore and George W. Bush) took around 48 per cent of the vote. In the days leading up to the election various polling organizations had variously predicted a 1 to 2 per cent lead for each candidate, suggesting at first that pollsters were not that good at their job, but in each case these results depended on a sampling error of 2 or 3 per cent. In the 1996 elections the Gallup polling and the final results differed by 1.7 per cent for Bill Clinton and 0.4 per cent for Bob Dole.

In an ideal world the researcher would choose the largest possible sample; in an ideal world we wouldn't be sampling at all, but would have data from every population member. The reason we sample is usually down to resources, so the size of a sample will also be a balance between available resources and the level of 'error' we are prepared to accept. Table 4.1 shows the sampling error (at a 95 per cent confidence interval) for different sizes of sample. So, while increasing the sample from 100 to just over 200 will decrease error from 10 per cent to 7 per cent, an increase from 4500 to 10,000 will only improve things by 0.5 per cent. The resources required to increase a sample from 4500 to 10,000 is likely to be too big an investment for the slight improvement in accuracy.

Table 4.1 assumes a 'binomial' distribution: that is on any given variable there is a split with 50 per cent of respondents having one characteristic (or answering one way) and 50 per cent another. If the split was, say, 80/20 a smaller sample could be used. Unfortunately we do not usually have information on how people will answer, or their characteristics, beforehand and this may differ between variables. Usually researchers play safe and decide the sample size on the basis of the variable which it is believed will show the greatest divergence (see Newton and Rudestam, 1999: 121–3).

Second researchers usually want to analyse sub-sets of data. For example, the opinion poll may show that 48 per cent of the electorate say they'll vote Democrat, but we may want to know if this is true of Hispanic people, or whether there are any differences between rural and urban voters. These analyses would shrink our sample size and increase the amount of error. The size of the sample should therefore reflect the heterogeneity of the population and the likely need to work with sub-samples (this incidentally is why sometimes researchers 'over-sample' certain groups). The mathematics of the detailed procedures are beyond the scope of this book (but see Fink, 1995, for a clear discussion), however, a good rule of thumb is that the smallest sub-group (e.g. sex, age, class, etc.) should consist of no less than 50 cases (de Vaus, 1996: 73).

Non-probability sampling

Sometimes probability sampling is not possible, or cost-effective. The most important non-probability sampling method used is that of quota sampling. Quota sampling is popular with market research companies in surveys of known populations. A quota sample requires the researcher to know how many people (or groups, etc.) there are in a given population with the characteristics of interest. Often the basis for this prior knowledge comes from national censuses, or other population measures. In any given town or city (in the UK, the USA and most other Western countries) we can know how many men and women there are, how many fall into each age group, how many live in public housing, have access to cars, etc. Consequently we can design a sample with a quota proportionate to the number of people with that characteristic in the population. Many believe this approach to be statistically as good as probability sampling, though it does have some drawbacks. For example, while an interviewer (the interviewer actually makes the selection according to the quota) can quickly fulfil a quota in a busy shopping centre (on the basis of age, sex, social class, etc.), there may be peculiarities about such people not specified in the quota characteristics. For example, though eventually you might fulfil your quota of those people in manual social classes, it may well be that the shopping centre chosen is too expensive to attract many people from those classes, which means those you eventually sampled may be atypical.

Second, some characteristics, especially age, depend on an initial observation selection. If you need five people between 40 and 50 years of age, it's quicker to go for those who 'look' about 45. I know, I've done this!

Some populations are rare or elusive. For example, probability or quota sampling would take far too long to locate members of small religious or ethnic groups in a population. Sometimes members of such populations, for example, those defined by illegal or deviant activity, are hidden. Obviously where a sampling frame does exist you can select simply from available lists and use a probability sample, but often no such lists exist and it is necessary to use *convenience* or *snowball* sampling. The former simply recruits respondents where it is possible (convenient) to do so and the second uses contacts to lead to other contacts. Neither produce statistically generalizable results in the strict sense, but might be said to at least produce some results that can give insights into a population, see Box 4.3 for an example of how not to do this.

Box 4.3 Can poor sampling inflame racial tensions?

After the World Trade Center attack in New York, in September 2001, there was a great deal of political concern in the USA and the UK about relations between Muslims and non-Muslims. There had been several attacks on Muslims and arson attacks on mosques. Unsurprisingly there was great concern when in early November *The Sunday Times* declared that as many as 4 in 10 British Muslims believed that Osama Bin Laden had reasons to mount a war against the USA.

What was the sample? How was the poll conducted? *The Sunday Times* reporters stood outside mosques questioning worshippers as they left! Only 20 per cent of British Muslims attend mosques and because they are likely to be the most devout, they are, it has been argued, also more likely to sympathise with fundamentalism. Even if the selecting and interviewing strategy of this group had been sound, the most *The Sunday Times* could have claimed (on the basis of their own figures) was that 4 per cent of Muslims supported Bin Laden.

(Hari, 2001)

Selecting and sampling in interpretive research

As I have suggested above, sampling and generalization are inextricably linked. In order to make generalizations we need to sample 'miniature' versions of the population. However, the status of sampling in interpretive research is much less clear than in survey research for two reasons. First, as I discussed in Chapter 3, many interpretivists deny that one should even try to generalize from interpretive findings and, second, even if one wishes to draw representative samples of a population, this is not always possible or even desirable. In the history of interpretive research this denial is a relatively recent development, dating to the 'anti-positivism' of the 1960s onwards. Unfortunately its legacy has led, at least in practice, to a low priority being given to sampling and selecting. A great deal of interpretive research simply selects a group of people or setting of interest, without much discussion of why this group, or why the setting (Williams, 2002).

Despite this there is history of a sophisticated approach to sampling and selection in interpretivism, particularly in grounded theory or analytic induction, where emphasis is placed (in the former) on concept construction or (in the latter) case-by-case inductive testing (see Chapter 3). It is in interpretive research where issues of selection are often prioritized over statistical representativeness. Therefore individuals, settings, etc. are selected not necessarily because they are typical of a larger population, but because they have characteristics which are of interest to the researcher in specific ways. However, as Hammersley and Atkinson (1995: 36) note, the issue of selection does not arise when the researcher chooses to research the setting he or she is in, or as I noted above, when this is the only setting within which the research can be conducted.

One possible distinction between selections that are samples and selections which are not, is the extent to which the selection is deliberately made to provide some kind of typicality. In cases of research where there is no choice and the selection is opportunistic, it may be possible to make later *moderatum* generalizations. Whenever one wishes to claim typicality, then it is important to remember that the typicality must be based on known characteristics. If I say my cat is a 'typical cat' , you would be entitled to ask me in which ways is she typical. Her shape, her colour, her habits and, if so, which? Characteristics, it will be recalled from Chapter 2, become variables in social research. As Jennifer Mason (1996: 88) has pointed out, the prior identification of variables is often an anathema to interpretive researchers, because this is pre-judging the interpretations to be made. While this might be a legitimate issue occasionally, where very little is known at all about the people, events, time, etc. that is to be researched, to deny selection is to make selection by default, thus introducing factors which can crucially influence the research. For example, if I say I am going to conduct research on Welsh language communities and just pick any old Welsh-speaking community I can never know whether factors such as the proportion of non-Welsh in migrants, the nature of the economy, local dialect, etc., made a difference or not. If, on the other hand, I base my selection on comparative instance of different levels of in-migration to communities, different economic arrangements and different dialects, I can have some idea of whether these made a difference. The interpretive nature of the research is unaffected, because these kinds of selection characteristics are already known and do not need to emerge through interpretation (though of course their form and influence in the community might).

The only good reason for not making some kind of *a priori* sampling decisions, in interpretive research, is when this is not possible, or it is simply not relevant. Sometimes one's choice of a community or setting is determined by one's position within it, for example, Geoff Payne's study of 'Fearnbeg' would not have taken place had Payne not gone to live there (1996), or when it is the only one of its kind, for example Roy Wallis's study of Scientology (1976) or Fielding's study of the National Front (1981). Nevertheless even in such cases there may well be internal sampling decisions to make. Who might be the key informants and why? Will women have a different perspective to men, or will people carrying out certain roles have a different 'take' on the world to others? The difference here with survey research is immediately apparent because the setting itself becomes the case under study, therefore one is sampling within the case (Hammersley and Atkinson, 1995: 45–6).

The organizing principle for sampling in interpretive research is often theoretical sampling where the researcher is testing her theory through selecting cases that can confirm or falsify it. However, as Jennifer Mason describes, this does not necessarily mean that the settings, groups, people, etc. are somehow representative of other similar settings, groups or people, but rather 'because they provide *access* in an interpretive sense to something that you are interested in, rather than actually being what you are interested in' (Mason 1996: 96). Although you may have sampled particular people, it may be their experiences or the interactions between them that are interesting, but to get at those experiences or interactions you needed to sample those particular people. An illustration of this is how researchers choose focus groups. Gomez et al.'s (1999) research (see Chapter 3) on the attitudes of young people toward Youth Foyers began with the theoretical proposition that the ways various groups of young people would use a Foyer would differ. For example, young women would have different priorities and experiences to young men, the unemployed to the employed, those in younger groups (16–18 years) to older groups (19–25 years). The compositions of the focus groups were chosen accordingly and allowed the testing of this proposition.[6]

The researcher is, then, theorizing about how particular kinds of people might think or behave, but it does not have to be people; it could be economies, particular times (such as meal breaks in a factory), documents or contexts. What each has in common is that they are chosen on the basis that the researcher theorizes that they will yield the best information, or can be the best test of a theory.

One of the difficulties in talking about sampling in interpretive research is that is it easy to create the impression that there are a set of relatively fixed procedures that mirror those used in survey research. This is not the case. The great strength (and difficulty) of interpretive research is that it is procedurally less prescriptive and more reflexive at every stage. Good interpretive research requires the researcher to constantly reflect upon what he or she has found and the relationship to those (or that) being researched. Decisions about who to interview, what to ask, or what to observe must be capable of revision as the research progresses. There is, then, a much more direct feedback mechanism between findings and methods. It follows from this that the selection or sampling process is both more flexible and more integrated into the research.

To return to my earlier example of researching Welsh language communities: although initial sampling selections may theorize the known differences between communities, as the research progresses either sampling within the case (here the particular language community) may take on greater importance, or it may be realized that the community characteristics originally theorized might be less important than those subsequently discovered. The more exploratory the research and the less propositional the theorizing, the more flexible subsequent sampling will be.

Conclusion

Sampling and selecting take their character from the type of research undertaken. In survey research we aim to explain identified differences hypothesized within a population. The aim of sampling is to produce a miniature version of the population that accurately replicates the key attributes in which we are interested. The best way of doing this is through the probability sample, in which every member of the population has an equal chance of being selected into the sample. This way of sampling permits us to measure statistically the differences that might exist between sample and population – to be able to express our statistical 'confidence' in the sample. Accurate sampling of a large population is often achieved by stratifying it, or identifying naturally occurring and representative clusters. Survey research (especially market research) often uses quota sampling as a substitute for probability sampling, but the accuracy of a quota sample is dependent upon both the accuracy of the data about the population on which the quotas are based and (in interviewing) how accurate the selection of respondents is.

Sampling in surveys is close to the common-sense intuition about choosing people, or things at random and although can be statistically quite complex, the fundamental idea is easier to grasp. In interpretive research although one is selecting and arguably 'sampling', the reasoning is wholly different and possibly even contradictory. On one hand the researcher (usually) wants to make some kind of *moderatum* generalization and therefore whoever or whatever has been selected must be seen, at least in the weak sense, of being representative of a wider population or 'universe', yet on the other hand most interpretivists would deny (for good reason) that generalization from sample to population is a goal at all. Unlike survey research, in interpretivist research there is no logically necessary link between sampling and latter generalizations. Instead selection is made on the basis of *a priori* characteristics that can provide access to data that will illuminate prior questions, or test a theoretical proposition. A further difficulty in making such selections is that though these identify what might be key variables in arriving at any understanding or test of propositions, in interpretive research most of the variables remain hidden until the research has begun, thus requiring the interpretive researcher (unlike the survey researcher) to be flexible about sampling throughout fieldwork.

Questions for reflection and discussion

1 The University of Poppleton Students' Union want to conduct a survey on student attitudes toward the services offered by the Union. Two teams of interviewers are sent to interview every fourth student leaving either the library or Students Union bar. What are the strengths and weaknesses of this sampling strategy?
2 Is quota sampling as good as probability sampling?
3 What would have been a better sampling strategy for *The Sunday Times* (see Box 4.3)?

Try this

A publisher wishes to launch a new fashion magazine aimed at men between 18 and 30. The publisher needs to know to which groups he should promote the magazine. What might be a cost-effective, but rigorous sampling strategy?

Suggested further reading

Some of the literature on sampling can get very technical indeed. Most books on survey method (especially the above cited, by David de Vaus) will discuss sampling, but the most accessible book I have come across is Arlene Fink's *How to Sample in Surveys* (1995).

Notes

1 For example, physicists 'generalize' from instances (say, the cooling of an electric element) to laws (say, thermodynamics). Other natural scientists generalize from probabilistically obtained samples to the larger units they represent (populations). When this can't be done, weaker generalizations might be possible from other kinds of samples or selections. The generalizations possible are always linked to samples or selections.

2 Some 95 per cent of all US households have a telephone. In the UK this is around 99 per cent for professional classes and 90 per cent for unskilled manual workers.

3 In cluster samples, sampling error increases with each stage, but fortunately this can be compensated for by increasing sample size.

4 Think of it like this. A 95 per cent accuracy is probably OK for an election, but you and I probably want a little more accurate probability attached to the safety of the brakes on our cars. In engineering it would have to be a lot better than 99.9 per cent!

5 Saying they will vote Labour doesn't necessarily mean they will do so.

6 The result was both heterogeneity and in some aspects homogeneity in both aspirations and experiences. Although the groups were selected on characteristics, only one characteristic was held constant at any one time. Thus, for example, the 'women only' group would have had a range of different ages and the unemployed group would have had men and women.

Survey Research

In this chapter:

Design issues

- Descriptive and explanatory surveys
- Cause and association
- Experimental designs

Methods of data collection

- Interview schedules: advantages and disadvantages
- Telephone interviews and CAPI
- Self-completion surveys: advantages and disadvantages
- Internet research

Quality in quantity

- Validity
- Reliability
- Non-response
- Data analysis: some preliminary thoughts

People have very different ideas about surveys. On one hand, there are plenty of people, very often in non-social science professions, who seem to think that designing and conducting a survey is easy. On the other hand, university social science students faced with this task for the first time often think they have picked the wrong degree. As with so many of these things, the answer is somewhere in the middle. Surveys come in different varieties. Relatively simple descriptive surveys can be undertaken after just a minimal amount of training, but there is an awful lot of difference between the design, execution and analysis of a one-page self-completion questionnaire and a complex interview schedule of the kind used in large-scale government or academic surveys. Nevertheless the reasoning and the principles underlying good, quality survey research, whatever the level of sophistication or complexity, are similar and once the key principles are understood, it is fairly easy to move from simple to complex surveys.

This chapter is about design and quality issues in surveys. Some of the issues in survey design are interwoven with overall strategies of research design, but I will discuss these in Chapter 9. In the next chapter I will deal with the specific issue of measurement and questionnaire design and in Chapter 7 I will describe some of the key principles of data analysis. In these chapters I shall pitch my discussion to the less difficult level of survey research, but there will be occasional nods in the direction of the more sophisticated possibilities the social survey opens up.

Descriptive and explanatory surveys

Descriptive surveys

A great many surveys simply collect data in order to describe something: the readership of a newspaper, people's tastes in chocolate bars, views on taxation, capital punishment, etc. These are the simplest of all surveys, though they may collect data on a vast number of variables and the design of the survey and its questions might be quite sophisticated. Moreover, they allow descriptions between populations, or over time. The General Household Survey, for example, collects a range of data on British lifestyles and attitudes at regular intervals. Comparisons between similar surveys in other countries, or over time are possible and the GHS, along with other national surveys and censuses, may later be used to produce more complex secondary explanatory analyses (see for example Dale, et al., 2000). Nevertheless in themselves they go no further than to simply describe.

Explanatory surveys

Often, however, surveys set out to *explain* things in the context of a theory (see Chapter 2) rather than *describe* them. This presents a challenge for the survey researcher, for unlike experiments in the natural sciences, surveys cannot show that A caused B, though they can show that the association between A and B is so strong that a causal link is very likely. However, a strong association does not mean one thing caused another. The most famous illustration of this was the case of the storks and babies in Oldenburg, Germany in the 1930s. It was noticed that an increase in the human birth rate coincided with the presence of large numbers of storks (Glass, 1984). The storks, of course, had nothing to do with the birth rate – as charming as that proposition may have seemed – but instead both the raised birth rate and the increased number of storks were attributed to good harvests. Why this is I'll leave to your imagination.

The maxim is that association is not causation.[1] So what to do about it? Well, this really depends on what it is you are trying to explain. If you just wanted to know how many girls and how many boys studied mathematics beyond age 16 in a city or country, a well-constructed sample of schools and then students should tell you quite accurately, but trying to explain *why* more boys than girls continue mathematical study is more difficult because you are shifting from mere description to explanation. Explanations are answers to 'why' questions and are usually thought of as explaining a cause or causes. This particular question was addressed by Stephen Lamb (1997) using a sample of Australian high school students from Years 10, 11 and 12. His finding was that boys develop more positive views of mathematics than girls. Girls believed that mathematics was not relevant to their career choice, yet among middle-class girls there was a greater likelihood that they would continue studying mathematics beyond year 10. Though Lamb found associations between certain attitudes to mathematics and mathematical study, or career aspirations and mathematical study, it is hard to prove these attitudes and aspirations are the whole cause of fewer girls than boys continuing to study maths. It is quite possible that the attitudes and aspirations of the girls who drop mathematics are 'caused' by a further variable, which has not been identified, but is not present in the case of those girls who continue mathematics beyond year 10. In Lamb's study there is a suggestion that the variable may be class, but one's social class is a socio-economic position and implicitly is a standing proxy for a socialization process.

For the most part the debate about cause and association is one indulged in by philosophers and statisticians, and usually survey researchers have to be content with the best possible association between two or more variables. Nevertheless in designing the research and later in analysing it, we want to be able to infer the best explanation (Lipton, 1991) and if at all possible avoid storks and babies scenarios. In other words, when we want to show that X is an explanation of Y, this will usually involve us in eliminating, or attempting to eliminate A, B, C, etc. An inference to the best explanation requires us to show that all other candidates for explanation are less likely. It cannot conclusively prove X caused Y, but it can tell us whether this is the most probable explanation.

Experiments

Strictly speaking, experimental designs are separate from survey designs, but the use of survey method is often embedded in an experiment, especially in evaluation research (see Chapter 9). Descriptive and explanatory surveys depend only on observations, that is we 'observe' respondents' characteristics and views through our questions, whereas an experiment is the deliberate manipulation of some aspects of the environment by the scientist. In the early years of North American sociology, experimental designs, with or without the incorporation of surveys (Oakley, 2000: Chapter 8), were a much used strategy. In the social sciences, as opposed to psychology and medicine, they were never so widely used in Europe, but have begun to gain popularity in evaluation and in socio-medical research (Clarke, 1999: 42–54; Oakley, 2000: 314–20). Unlike in psychology, the social sciences are rarely able to use 'true experiments' (Campbell and Stanley, 1966) because these require that the groups used in the research are identical in key respects and cannot be 'contaminated' by external influences. A 'true' experiment will usually be conducted in a closed setting of a laboratory with participants randomly assigned to experimental and control groups. In the experimental group a 'treatment' will be applied, but not in the control group. Quite often the members of the each group are not aware of whether they are members of the experimental or control group. At the end of the treatment the results of each group will be compared.

However, because these conditions can rarely be met outside of the laboratory and researchers still want to use experimental designs, quasi-experimental designs are frequently used and these usually depend on the use of surveys. The reasoning in them is similar to true experiments in so far that experimental and control groups are identified and one undergoes a 'treatment', in such cases usually an intervention in the form of a social pro-gramme, and the other does not (Clarke, 1999: 47). When separate experi-mental and control groups cannot be devised, then it is sometimes possible to compare a group over time, before an intervention and afterwards. Quasi-experiments are not conducted in closed laboratories, but in the social world itself (the hospital, school, village, etc.).

There are a number of criticisms of experimental method, which although they may not rule out the design completely, should be taken into considera-tion by the researcher. I will briefly summarize them. First, humans are conscious, self-reflecting beings and when they are aware they are being experimented on may well change their behaviour accordingly. This was dis-covered in the early years of experimental sociology in North America and is termed the Hawthorne Effect[2] (Madge, 1963: 169–209). Therefore whether changes in behaviour are due to the experiment or the participants' aware-ness of participation is often hard to establish. Second, experiments conducted in the field have often not produced clear-cut findings for a variety of environ-mental and methodological reasons (Oakley, 2000: Chapter 10). Third, experi-ments do not take due account of context and mechanism (see Chapter 2). Experiments concentrate on the outcome – the hypothesis is proven or not proven, but does not show why the intervention has succeeded (or perhaps more importantly failed). As Pawson and Tilley point out, in discussing the findings of their evaluation of prison education programmes for inmates, for the programmes to work the participants themselves must co-operate and choose to make them work (1997: 103–14). Even in the relatively closed environment of a prison, programmes operate in context and local and non-local mecha-nisms exist. The biggest problem in experiments is that the researcher cannot be sure that experimental and control groups are the same, in the key respects, at the outset. Finally, the 'treatment' in a quasi-experiment may involve a posi-tive intervention in providing facilities or resources for the experimental group, but not the control group. The allocation of such resources then has ethical implications. If the allocation has beneficial results for the experimental group, then those in the control group have been placed at a disadvantage; and vice versa if the results are detrimental to the experimental group (see Oakley, 2000: Chapter 11 for a discussion of the ethics of experiments). I will discuss ethical issues more fully in Chapter 8.

Experiments are the strongest form of explanatory research, for instead of relying on the passive observation of attributes and attitudes, they depend on active intervention. This intervention can be problematic for the reasons described. One possible solution to this problem is to conduct experiments on the same group over time, before and after an intervention – what are sometimes called 'single case experiments' (Robson, 2002: 146–7). Evidence for effect might be established through an analysis of appropriate official statistics over time, or through surveys conducted before, then after, an intervention. The repetition of experiments (with dual or single groups) in which possible intervening variables are controlled in the survey, may be the closest the researcher can get to truly explanatory research in open systems.

Longitudinal studies

There are a variety of longitudinal designs, but all depend on taking measures of a group[3] at least twice, over time (see Ruspini, 2000). The time period may be months or years. Their great advantage is that change or continuity in individual characteristics or views can be studied over time. The commonest designs are panel studies in which a group of people are followed over time, cohort studies in which people with a common characteristic (birth date, graduation date, etc.) are studied at various future points, for example the British National Child Development Study which was based on all of the people born in one week in 1958. Many studies, using one or another longitudinal design, are very large scale, for example the Longitudinal Study, based on linked data from the ten yearly census in England and Wales, has one million 'members' (Hattersley and Creeser, 1995). Most survey longitudinal designs require resources beyond the reach of most researchers, partly because the study must take place over a long enough period to be able to show change or continuity and, second, they require large samples because of attrition, where participants are lost to the study.

More informally it is possible to build in a longitudinal element (though using repeated measures on the same variables) in smaller scale research. In a PhD study of migration intentions in young people, Philipa Aldous used a relatively simple self-completion questionnaire on 1500 year 10 secondary school pupils and then followed up a sub-sample of these, on two occasions, using an interview schedule (see next section) when they were in years 11 and 12. Whilst this study did not have large-scale resources and methodological sophistication, the design did at least have the merit of following the same people over three years and using repeated measures on key variables (Aldous, 2001).

Methods of data collection

Having decided upon a survey design, what it is to achieve, how ambitious, complex or simple it is, consideration needs to be given to how the data are to be collected and this requires the researcher to weigh up a number of factors with regard to resources, the nature of the population under study and the topic area. Different methods of data collection each offer both opportunities and constraints. The principal methodological difference is between interview schedules, in which an interviewer asks the questions of a respondent, and self-completion questionnaires which the respondent completes on their own.

Interview schedules

Interview schedules generally have very much more scope than self-completion questionnaires. Generally they can be longer, more sophisticated and more flexible, will achieve better response rates and will be treated more seriously by respondents than self-completion questionnaires. It is easier to put a questionnaire aside (in our household on top of the fridge) with the intention of completing it sometime than to tell an interviewer standing on your doorstep to go away. Especially in many well-planned surveys the interviewer has either made contact by phone earlier and arranged an interview time, or the respondent has been alerted by letter or general publicity (see Chapter 4 on reducing non-response). Once the respondent has agreed to the interview, they usually take it seriously and because people like talking about themselves, they will very often enjoy the experience. A device often used in surveys is an Interview Assessment in which the interviewer completes a short questionnaire about the quality of the interview. This is especially useful when interviewing groups with learning difficulties (who may require assistance from a third party), the elderly or those who may be under the influence of drugs or alcohol. Furthermore the possibilities for scaling and filtering of questions (I will discuss this in the next chapter) allow both a check on consistency of reply and some selection of respondents into different categories.

Interview schedules require interviewers, and interviewing, even with a standardized questionnaire, is a skilled task. A large part of the budget of market research companies is spent on interviewer training. Indeed, becoming a market research interviewer is one of the best ways to learn about surveys from the bottom up. It is certainly a good way to distinguish a good from a bad interview schedule and good from bad sampling strategies. Poor interviewing can cause refusal and non-response, item non-response (see below) or introduce bias into the survey. The interviewer should not 'interpret' the question to the respondent, should not offer overt encouragement through showing approval or disapproval and indeed should attempt to ask questions of each respondent in the same way. Skilled interviewers are, however, able to use prompts, or probe for information that does not emerge from standardized questions. But more of that in the next chapter.

A final important advantage of interview schedules is that they can be of varying lengths, in some cases up to one and a half hours. However, one should not lightly embark on such lengthy interviews lightly. Not only do they run the risk of respondent boredom (and ensuing problems of validity and bias), they also need to be analysed!

The length of the interview is related to location. A long interview is more acceptable in the respondent's home than on a busy street corner. Indeed location, or more properly, the spatio-temporal dimension, is crucial for success in most cases. Completing a transport survey on the quality of a bus service at a bus stop is terrific until your respondent's bus arrives. Interviews on sensitive or confidential topics should not be conducted in earshot of another person, or in a location where the respondent feels uneasy. Interview location should maximize the credibility of the interview, increase the 'onto-logical security' of the respondent and should minimize likely interference from external influences on the interview (Frey and Oishi, 1995: 31).

Interviews do have disadvantages, mostly that they require a lot of resources. Conducting a few hundred interviews can take weeks. Contact times with respondents, especially in their own homes, are often longer than the interview itself, because the interviewer will usually spend a little time on introductory 'small talk', explain the purpose of the survey and after-wards make an exit that does not appear too hurried. This is both ethically appropriate and puts respondents at ease. Furthermore, interviewers must travel to where the interviews are to be conducted and in rural areas inter-viewers frequently spend more time travelling than interviewing. Contacting sample members can be a frustrating and time-consuming busi-ness. These days less people are at home in the daytime and home inter-views must be conducted in the evenings or weekends. Finally, and most importantly, good interviews can command good rates of pay and this can be a major part of research costs.

Telephone interviewing

This is also discussed under telephone survey sampling in Chapter 4. Telephone surveys will have a poorer response rate than those conducted through face-to-face interview and it is widely held (though disputed by Frey and Oishi, 1995: 37) that they must be shorter. Certainly visual aids cannot be used as in the face-to-face interview and generally speaking the interview schedule must be less complex. An exception to this is Computer Assisted Telephone Interviewing (CATI) where respondent answers are entered directly into the computer and according to the responses, the soft-ware can 'choose' an appropriate next question.

Many of the advantages of telephone interviewing are obvious: the inter-view does not have to travel anywhere and it is quicker. Additionally the anonymity of the interviewer–respondent contact can actually benefit surveys where sensitive questions are asked.

An innovation in recent years is Computer Assisted Personal Interviewing (CAPI). As with CATI the researcher enters data directly into the computer using software such as *SNAP* or *PinPoint*. The difference is that in CAPI the researcher does this in face-to-face interviews. From small beginnings in the 1980s this method has flourished, especially in market research. I was among the first interviewers to use this approach on a study of business travellers' preferences in train design. The level of customization of the questionnaire engaged respondent interest, though back in the 1980s the power pack that accompanied the 'laptop' was about the size of a tractor battery. Things have changed and interactive nature of this method has been even more enhanced by much more powerful hardware and sophisticated software. Analysis of the data is easier (because it has already been entered) and one layer of potential error (data entry from questionnaire) is removed. Its biggest disadvantage is that of cost, though a sign of the times is that the British Office of National Statistics (ONS) now uses CAPI on many of its large-scale surveys.

Self-completion surveys

Everyone seems to be getting in on self-completion surveys. The commonest form these take are customer satisfaction surveys (that is if we ignore the spurious ones from charities and marketing companies). Self-completion questionnaires seem to be the intellectual bargain basement of social research. They are often badly designed and poorly worded. I recently received a questionnaire from a leading financial institution that began with unwarranted familiarity: 'Dear Malcolm, I am writing to you personally to ask for your views ....' The first question then asked me to say whether I was male or female!

Fortunately most self-completion surveys are better designed. In terms of advantages and disadvantages they are almost a mirror image of interview-based surveys. A bulk mail-out of postal questionnaires, even with a (necessary) reply-paid envelope will be considerably cheaper than carrying out the equivalent number of interviews. There is a greater anonymity on sensitive topics and they are ideal for very short questionnaires that do not warrant employing an interviewer. Because they are less complex they are easier to analyse and there is no risk of interviewer or environmental bias.

The downside is that their necessary simplicity can constrain the design of the questionnaire and the type of question asked (but more of this in the next chapter). Respondent misunderstanding of a question cannot be detected and indeed a general level of competence and literacy in the respondent is a prerequisite. This does not mean that people who do not understand the question, or misunderstand the question do not complete the questionnaire, but rather that they may get someone else to complete it for them. Self-completion questionnaires have their very own kind of bias. However, the worst problem is poor response rate and difficulty in detecting systematic non-response (see below), especially in postal questionnaires. However, despite all these disadvantages, the self-completion survey is very often the only economically viable one for most organizations and money spent on improving response rate through follow-up mail-outs and incentives, such as prize draws, is often less than on training and employing interviewers.

Internet research

It seems very likely that in the next few years web or email-based question-naires will become more widely used (Ò Dochartaigh, 2001). Internet research, because of its speed, relative cheapness (no interviewers needed), the absence of interviewer bias and data entry errors has become very popular in market research. In this field, as with CAPI, the market research industry has been the first to widely use such techniques and to consider technical and sampling problems (Comley, 2001). The technical problems of questionnaire design are not the major problem (see Chapter 6), but as in the earlier days of telephone interviewing, it is the difficulties of sampling that set limits on such research.

Email questionnaires can be sent to user communities in the form of a census, though in my own university typical response rates are low and this creates particular difficulties in a census (see Chapter 4). The principal aim of the researchers who wish to use the Internet is to be able to use some form of probability sampling, through, for example, Random Digit Dialling (RDD). A commonly used technique is a survey which samples every second or nth page, but such studies sample heavy users disproportionately (the more or the longer you are logged on, the more likely you are to be sampled). More obviously Internet techniques can only be used to survey a fairly narrow socio-economic group (those who can afford Internet access), which partly explains the interest of market research – these are the consumers with spending power!

Quality in quantity

One of the best known natural laws is that of Murphy – what can go wrong will go wrong. However, the researcher can save himself or herself a lot of heartache and disasters by considering a number of (what I've termed) 'quality issues' during the design of the survey. Some of these issues I'll deal with more specifically in the next two chapters, but for the moment let us suppose you have identified your research question and you have some research hypotheses you wish to test (Chapter 2); you have identified your population and sampling strategy (Chapter 4) and you have decided what kind of survey you will conduct and how you will gather your data. Now consider the following points.

Validity

The validity of a survey – whether it is measuring what it is supposed to measure – is an important issue that has both philosophical and technical dimensions and is closely bound up with the matter of operationalization discussed in Chapter 2. *Construct validity* refers to the extent to which variables accurately measure the constructs of interest. If it is claimed that a survey is measuring social class, it should measure social class – not a related variable such as income. Construct validity is an issue at both a theoretical and a technical level and is well illustrated by research on ethnicity using the UK Census. Ethnicity and 'race' have been vexed concepts in social science (Carter, 2000) and often seen (wrongly) as interchangeable. Although the Census has begun to recognize that there are a multiplicity of ethnic groups in the UK and it is possible to self-derive by selecting an 'other' category and writing in one's ethnic group, the main Census categories are derived from older concepts of race and ethnicity mainly using colour as a proxy for ethnic distinctiveness. In 2001 these were:

> White (*British; Irish; any other White background*)[4]
> Mixed (*White and Black Caribbean; White and Black African; White and Asian; any other Mixed background*)
> Asian or Asian British (*Indian; Pakistani; Bangladeshi; any Other Asian background*)
> Black or Black British (*Caribbean; African; any other Black background*)
> Chinese or other ethnic group (*Chinese; any other*)

The ethnic status of the groups varies from the huge and disparate collection of ethnic groups which makes up 'white', to the narrower category of Bangladeshi. Persons from Africa or the Caribbean are categorized by their colour. Inevitably the validity of each of these categories is different and consequently the validity of any measurement based on them will vary. Comparisons between Bangladeshi and Pakistani people will be more 'valid' than those using the 'white' category which tends to function here as some kind of measure of the absence of ethnicity. Nevertheless there is plenty of research which treats these categories as unproblematically valid representations of ethnicity. Research conducted on, say, deprivation of one kind or another that uses only these categories can only find associations between deprivation and the ethnic groups as defined. Define the categories differently and the whole landscape of deprivation and ethnicity changes. As Steven Vertovek (1994: 262) observes of Leicester (where 28.5 per cent of the population are members of ethnic minorities), while Pakistanis and Bangladeshis are nationally the worst off groups, in Leicester it is Gujaratis. People of Gujarati descent may originate from Bangladesh, India or East Africa. The category Gujarati does not appear on the Census and unless they 'self-derive,' Gujaratis must select one of the standard categories and their ethnic distinctiveness is lost. The use of standard Census categories of ethnicity would therefore not give the most accurate picture of poverty and ethnicity in Leicester.

At a theoretical level standard Census categories do not have construct validity for they fail to adequately capture a concept of ethnicity recognizable to many ethnic groups, or as I have shown in the above example concepts which are of interest. At a technical level they partially succeed because they do measure what counts as ethnicity in the Census, except that they measure some categories better than others.

A response one might make to this charge of poor construct validity in measuring ethnicity, is how else can it be done? How far would we have to subdivide ethnic categories in order for their representation to be valid to all constituencies of interest? Even if this were viable, establishing a person's ethnic group or class could take up much of the questionnaire. Though self-identification using the 'other' category can alert the researchers to the presence of other groups, this is not an accurate measure of their numbers. Mr Charalambous may tick 'white' whilst his brother living in the same street might tick 'other' and write in 'Greek'.

Arguably one will never achieve perfect construct validity, but prior research to develop the categories can improve it (see Ahmad, 1999, for a discussion of this). Interpretivist research in a locality can help clarify what people understand by a concept we wish to measure, or (in respect of the above example) what is the likely ethnic composition of an area. As Mark Litwin (1995: 43) observes: 'Construct validity is the most valuable yet most difficult way of assessing a survey instrument [and] ... is often determined only after years of experience with a survey instrument.'

Other forms of validity in surveys are more straightforwardly technical issues. *Criterion validity* is a measure of how well one survey performs against another in measuring the same thing. This can be broken down into concurrent validity, where one compares a survey instrument against an established method, or predictive validity, in which the ability of different surveys to predict events, etc. are compared. In concurrent validity this may become an issue because the new survey instrument is supposed to be an improvement on the old, or it is not possible to use the established method because it is too expensive or difficult to apply in the circumstances. For example, standard measures of social class cannot be applied when measuring the social class of the parents of youth respondents. These measures are based on occupational categories and young people often do not know their parents' occupation, or they misdescribe it. Instead other measures such as number and age of cars in the household, household ownership of certain consumer goods are sometimes substituted.

In predictive validity different methods of political polling (such as street interviews, telephone interviews, omnibus surveys,[5] etc.) can be compared for accuracy of prediction.

Content validity is often a way in which construct validity can be improved. It refers to the appropriateness of an item for measuring a concept. Though usually treated as a technical issue, it is nevertheless subjective and relies on asking various relevant people to assess a measure. A good example is the measure of homelessness. As with ethnicity, its definition has never been straightforward and in any particular survey its operationalization may be best achieved by asking various people to assess the validity of the measure for them. In surveys I undertook in two UK cities this was done through asking members of various statutory and voluntary agencies and homeless people themselves to asses the definitions used. Litwin (1995: 36) uses the example of the development of a scale to collect data on marital interaction as a dimension of health-related quality of life. The scale was to be used on cancer patients undergoing chemotherapy and was first tested on three oncologists, three psychologists, two social workers, one oncology nurse practitioner, four cancer patients and two spouses of cancer patients. Each of the reviewers were asked to rate each item on a scale and the whole scale for appropriateness and relevance to the issue of marital interaction and to further list any items they thought to be missing.

Reliability

Reliability is the measure of how consistent something is. I once had a car with a very unreliable fuel gauge. Sometimes when I filled the tank up it would register only two-thirds full, and on one occasion I ran out of fuel altogether although the gauge told me that the tank was still one-quarter full. When a survey is conducted, it is important that you obtain the same result on repeated occasions and that any differences in response between people, or over time, if asked of the same person, are the result of different circumstances and not something to do with the survey, or questions, scales, etc. within it.

Reliability is somewhat easier to check than validity and indeed most national censuses and large-scale government surveys will check back for consistency of response (Dale and Marsh, 1993: 129–54). This can be done by asking a person at time *t1* a series of questions about themselves, and repeating this at time *t2* (see de Vaus, 1996: 54), or by comparing the respondent's answers on some objective measure. The UK Census asks a question about the number of rooms a household has for its own use. Although guidance is provided on what counts as a 'room', the responses given are subject to high levels of misclassification. The reliability of the measure is established by an interviewer returning to a sample of households and asking a series of detailed questions about the accommodation, the answers to which are checked against the original Census return for the household (Dale and Marsh, 1993: 143–8).

How does unreliability arise? In the previous example it arose from respondents differently classifying a room. The fault therefore lies with the question, though in fairness this is a very difficult question to phrase and the form it takes is probably about as good as it can get.[6] Unreliability frequently does arise from respondents understanding the question differently or not being in a position to answer the question (I will discuss this further in the next chapter), but it can also arise from interviewer effects, such as the age, sex, dress or ethnic background of the interviewer. Finally, respondent answers are subject to interpretation at the coding stage and two different coders may classify a response differently (de Vaus, 1996: 54).

A survey can be reliable without being valid. Consistency of response may be obtained, but that consistency may be due to consistent misinterpretation by the respondent or the particular question or scale not measuring what it is supposed to be measuring. A watch that is consistently five minutes fast is reliable, but not a valid measure of time. However, a measure that is unreliable can never be valid because accurate findings cannot be obtained from measures giving inconsistent results.

Reliability can be improved in a number of ways. Through the training of interviewers and matching them to the appropriate populations, through consistency checks of data entry, but mostly through the thorough testing of the questionnaire and items within it. This I will discuss further in the next chapter.

Non-response

A perennial problem in surveys is that of non-response. The sampling frame, the selection and administration of the study may all be superb, but some people just refuse to answer. Often, frustratingly, the people who refuse are the very ones the researcher wants to include in the analyses. A survey of non-voters suffers from the same conceptual problem as the non-voting in the first place, i.e. those who won't vote are also likely to be those who don't respond to surveys. As I noted in Chapter 4, particular groups are known to be poor at responding (people aged 18–30; men; the elderly; or those who live in inner cities). It is important to stress that the non-response in particular groups is often a function of their partial exclusion from civic society in the first place.

Surveys carried out 'cold', either through interviews or postal questionnaires, attract the fewest responses. In Western countries social researchers have to first of all to convince potential respondents they are not selling insurance or encyclopaedias, or some other dubious service. This is especially the case when many direct sales representatives begin their pitch by saying 'I'm conducting a short survey, …' or (in my case) the post regularly contains a 'survey' from a charity, which on closer inspection turns out to be a plea for a donation. Research conducted on how much the British public trusted market research showed that 58 per cent felt market research interviewers were trying to sell them something and 63 per cent thought that their details would be passed on (Savage, 2000) – and these were the people who agreed to be interviewed at all! Survey researchers have to get past these obstacles and the more that can be done before the survey (usually), the better the response rate.

There are measures available to deal with non-response:

- First, we can 'over-sample'. In practice there is often a huge difference between selected and achieved sample – especially in self-completion questionnaires. Response rates in these are usually well under 50 per cent. Therefore if one wishes to achieve a sample of 1000, it is quite common in postal surveys to mail out 2000 or more questionnaires. The 'over-sampling' may be in particular strata, or across the board. If, for example, we can anticipate a 40 per cent response rate across a whole sample, but a 20 per cent response rate within a sub-group, then the sample for that sub-group should be increased accordingly. If in the event the sub-group confounds us by responding closer to the average for all of the sub-groups (say, age bands), then one can 'weight' the sample from the sub-group down to that of the whole sample.

- Conversely, a poor response rate in a sub-group can be compensated for by weighting upwards, in order to make one respondent count for one and a half or two, etc. (see Moser and Kalton, 1971: 182–6 for a discussion of this).
- Non-response can be at the level of the individual, or the item. That is, although a questionnaire may be completed, some questions may be unanswered for various reasons. In these cases it is sometimes legitimate to use imputation, that is from the information we have in the rest of the questionnaire we can legitimately impute missing values. We cannot usually impute opinions, but characteristics are possible. For example, in innumerations of homeless people in two UK cities my colleague Brian Cheal and I used four identifiers for each person counted (Williams and Cheal, 2001). These were date of birth, initials, sex and length of time in the city. These data were then entered into SPSS (see Chapter 7). The aim of the research was to estimate the total number of homeless people from a calculation based on the number of times particular individuals were innumerated. In many cases, one of the identifiers were missing for a particular person, but if three of the identifiers had been observed before, then the fourth could be imputed. As it had been counted before it was possible to 'impute' the missing value. Moreover, individuals were often innumerated with the same people (partners, children, etc.) on more than one occasion. Thus if data were missing for AB, but AB had been enu-merated with DB and JB and this had occurred before, then it could be assumed that the AB was the same person on each occasion. Imputation is not rocket science, but in large surveys and especially national censuses (Mills and Teague, 1991), it can play a crucial role in filling in the gaps.
- Obviously one wishes to design surveys which produce responses to each and every question and there are techniques for helping researchers get closer to this goal (more of this in Chapter 6), however, a primary task is to get a response at all. There are many well-tried strategies for this in both face-to-face interviews and postal questionnaires. For example, in the first case fruitless visits can be minimized by arranging interviews by phone or letter first, or making sure the interviewer calls at an appropri-ate time. In a community where most adults are working, daytime response on weekdays will be poor. Indeed, most British market research companies insist that interviewers make four calls at an address, one of which must be in the evening or weekends (Kinnear and Taylor, 1996).
- When a survey is to be conducted in a geographic community, such as a town, district or county, a lot can be done through publicity in the local press, TV or radio, such as an interview with the person who commis-sioned the survey, or is leading it, saying why it is important for people to respond. Variations on this approach can be used for postal or interview-based surveys.

- Interviewer training and appearance are important. How an interviewer looks and approaches the interview can make a difference to response, as can questionnaire design in respect of item non-response.
- Market research companies pioneered the use of 'inducements' to respondents to participate. Often this takes the form of a prize draw in which all respondents are entered. Inducements are not always ethically appropriate, but can increase response rate considerably in postal/self-completion surveys, up to 71 per cent from around 35 per cent in national studies (Thompson, 1996).

Data analysis

I won't say too much about data analysis here, because this is the topic of Chapter 7. However, when designing a survey it is important to consider what you are going to do with the data once you have it. Two kinds of design error can occur (and they are not mutually exclusive): first, it is possible to gather far more data than you either have the competence or resources to deal with. Generally speaking, you should not collect more data than you will use and when you consider what data you need to gather to test your hypothesis(es), you need to think about how it will be analysed. It is therefore necessary to be clear about analysis issues before even gathering the data. If the survey is explanatory, will this require complex scales (see Chapter 6), will it require univariate, bivariate or multivariate analyses (see Chapter 7)? Do you have access to a spreadsheet application such as Excel, or if your analyses are complex, SPSS? Finally do you have the resources (especially time) to enter the data, analyse it and report on it before your deadline (there's always a deadline)?

The second kind of design error is closely related to issues of validity and operationalization. Will (or indeed, can) your survey collect data that will operationalize your hypotheses? Consider the problem of wanting to say something about the social class of girls who continue maths and those that don't. We could ask the parents, but that presents problems of access (will Jane complete a questionnaire honestly or at all if she knows you are going to interview her parents?) and resources (it means another survey). We have to ask the girls and this is hard because adolescents can be a bit vague about what their parents' occupation is and this is a important component in allocating a social class to respondents. This means that other questions about lifestyle (possibly about consumer goods, holidays, housing, cars, etc.) might be asked. To just ask 'What is your mother's (and father's) occupation?' will not allow you to say much about class.

The example I give is a particularly difficult problem, but often this kind of error simply occurs because the researcher does not anticipate he or she will need data on particular topics. To continue with the same hypothetical example: if no data were collected on whether the girl had siblings, their age or their sex, it would be impossible to say whether this had any effect, yet it is quite possible that the presence/age/sex of siblings might not have been considered important at the design stage.

Conclusion

The various aspects of survey research do not fit into neat boxes, but are often an interplay between philosophical, technical and resource issues. This becomes apparent at the design stage when the researcher will realize the importance of the clarity of the research question and the ensuing research hypotheses. It is true that some surveys are straightforward and descriptive (though not all descriptive surveys are straightforward), but the more ambitious the research question, the more complex the design. This, it will be seen in the next chapter, extends to the questionnaire itself, but also to the analysis of the data.

Questions for reflection and discussion

1 Consider some circumstances (that is research questions, respondents or locations, etc.) in which interview schedules would be better than self completion questionnaires.
2 Thinking back to Chapter 2, how is operationalization related to issues of validity and reliability?
3 Would telephone interviewing (using RDD) to mobile numbers be a good idea?

Try this

Your local hospital wishes to conduct a patient satisfaction survey. Bearing in mind sampling issues from Chapter 4, draw up a list of advantages and disadvantages for using a postal survey, interview schedule or telephone interviews. Remember you will need to identify what a 'patient' is and when, in relation to their contact with the hospital, they should be surveyed.

Suggested further reading

Possibly the most authoritative book on the social survey is the classic Moser and Kalton book *Survey Methods in Social Investigation* (1971).[7] However, this is a bit of a tome and something lighter will suffice for most people. Alan Aldridge and Ken Levine's *Surveying the Social World* (2001) is very accessible and useful additional reading for all of the chapters on survey method in the present volume. A good short 'how to do' type book is Susan Thomas's *Designing Surveys that Work* (1999). Arlene Fink has written several short books on various aspects of the survey in the Sage 'The Survey Kit' series. *The Survey Handbook* (1995) is a useful practical overview. In the same series, Mark Litwin's *How to Measure Survey Reliability and Validity* (1995) is good on these topics.

Notes

1 By causation I mean that causes are temporally ordered events in which A preceded B and B could not have come about without A. While there can be no causation without association – association shows causation might be present – it can rarely be conclusively proved in a survey that A caused B. (See Papineau, 1978: Chapter 3 for a full discussion. Some, Moser and Kalton (1971: 213) for example, hold that causation can be shown by logical inference between variables and provide examples, but even they concede that 'The real life situation is immensely more complicated than the above, because … a large number of potentially disturbing variables ought rightly to be considered'. Some survey researchers will claim that complex correlations can demonstrate causation, but this is a rather controversial issue amongst statisticians and philosophers of social science.

2 Named after a study begun in 1924 (where the effect was first noted) and conducted in the Hawthorne Plant of the Western Electric Company plant in Illinois.

3 Strictly speaking, data can be collected for an item (usually an individual) or a variable, but the latter is less common.

4 'Any other' categories are self-selecting and will not form part of most Census analyses of ethnicity.

5 Omnibus surveys are conducted by leading market research companies on a regular basis. Several different clients pay to insert questions about the market for their goods and services and often among these batteries of questions one or more on voting intentions may be inserted.

6 In 2001 the question asked 'How many rooms do you have for use only by your household?' Specifications of what did and did not count as a room were then given.

7 There are later reprintings with supplementary bibliography.

6

Questionnaire Design

In this chapter:

- Context
- Content
- Appearance
- Asking about attitudes, beliefs and behaviour
- How to begin
- Types of question and question wording
- Questionnaire layout and contingency questions
- Piloting and testing

This chapter introduces some of the principles and techniques of questionnaire design. The design of the questionnaire itself should not be approached independently, but seen as integral to the successful design of the survey, and this includes anticipating how one might analyse the responses obtained. Good questionnaire design is about maximizing the validity and reliability of the survey. I recall proudly showing my first questionnaire to my research methods lecturer and asking him if it would tell me what I wanted to know. Ever diplomatic, he replied, 'Well, it'll tell you something ….' The survey asked a lot of questions, but few really measured what they supposed to measure and others, because they were ambiguous, would not have produced a consistent response. The layout was good, though.

In this chapter I will begin by considering fairly briefly what I consider to be the three key dimensions of questions: context, content, appearance. This will set the scene for a more detailed focus on specific design features and strategies, beginning with the tricky question of how to begin!

Context

How and from whom the data are to be collected will determine the kind of questionnaire that needs to be designed. First, as I noted in the previous chapter, self-completion questionnaires are generally simpler than interview schedules. The layout of the questionnaire and the questions asked will take a different form. While, for example, it is OK to ask, 'What is your sex?[1] on a self-completion questionnaire, to ask this in an interview may produce unintended consequences. Self-completion questionnaires cannot contain complex instructions and interview schedules should not usually have long lists of things to be read out by the interviewer.

Second, who are the respondents? Will they be able to understand the question, or indeed the context of a survey at all? To participate in a survey requires a lot of tacit cultural knowledge that we in Western cultures take for granted. The researcher needs to be sensitive to other factors such as age or disability, or when a self-completion questionnaire (or any questionnaire for that matter) would be inappropriate. Even among those quite capable of participating in a survey it is important to be sure that they have sufficient knowledge to be able to answer the questions. There's not much point asking someone in the American mid-West about US policy in the Middle East if they think you are referring to Pennsylvania, or, for that matter, most French people about the merits of veganism!

Content

Questionnaires consist not only of questions. They will contain instructions to the respondent, or interviewer, they may contain 'filters' to take some respondents on different routes to others and they will often contain things that are to be read out by the interviewer, or respondent. The format may be very 'closed' providing a limited number of responses to be chosen, or the respondent may be encouraged to respond in their own words in 'open' questions.

Most questionnaires will contain different kinds of questions. First, factual questions about *attributes*, such as:

What was your age last birthday?

They may be about *attitudes*, such as:

Do you think that convicted murderers should be executed?

They may be about *beliefs*:

Do you believe in the existence of an afterlife?

Or they may be about *behaviour*:

How many times did you visit the clinic in the last month?

Beliefs and attitudes are not always clearly separated. For example, it is possible to use the language of beliefs to describe political attitudes, say, a 'belief in socialism' and attitude scales often measure how strongly someone believes something to be the case. In other words, we use this language interchangeably about questions of knowledge and opinion. In either case we can hold opinions or our certainty in knowing particular things with different intensities (Oppenheim, 1992: 176). Political opinion will often be stronger than an opinion about the merits of one rock band over another and depending on levels of certainty, questions of knowledge can shade into attributes, for example, a question such as:

How many police officers do you believe are on patrol in Poppleton on most Saturday nights?

Some people (police officers, for example) are likely to know this, while members of the public would have different levels of knowledge.

Many questionnaires ask questions about beliefs and attitudes through statements with which the respondent is asked to express agreement/disagreement (I will return to this below).

Finally, when considering the content of questionnaire the researcher is rarely a pioneer. Others have usually been there before and for many topics there are well-tested questions that can be used in a variety of contexts. Not only does the researcher benefit from the development work of others, but the standardization of certain questions permits comparison between studies. In the past few years a number of question 'banks' have been established, often containing well-tested questions from large government surveys. A good example is the UK Centre for Applied Social Surveys (CASS) question bank at http://qb.soc.surrey.ac.uk/. This contains a huge range of questions on crime, demography, households, social class, etc.

Most surveys will also contain 'face sheet information', sometimes called 'classifying' or 'personal' data (Oppenheim, 1992: 109). This is background information on the attributes of respondents that allow comparison both across the survey and between surveys on the variables operationalized from the research question. Face sheet variables usually include sex, age, ethnicity and social class. In Western societies these are key defining variables and often can explain important differences in attitudes and attributes. Views vary on where face sheet information should be placed. To start off with a battery of such questions may seem irrelevant or intrusive to the respondent and it is usually better to place them at the end of the questionnaire. However, when using quota sampling, in face-to-face interviewing, the researcher needs to ask at least some of these questions to establish whether the respondent is suitable for the sample ('in scope'), see Chapter 4.

Appearance

Though content is of primary importance, what a questionnaire looks like will often make important differences to its completion. In designing the layout and the 'look' of the questionnaire it is important to bear in mind three simple objectives: (1) to get it completed (and completely completed!); (2) to get it completed accurately; and (3) to permit accurate analysis. Self-completion questionnaires have to be both attractive and simple to complete. Interview schedules can be less aesthetically pleasing, but must be clearly laid out and contain unambiguous interviewer instructions and routing.

In both there are some generic guidelines:

- Do not try to get too many questions on a page.
- Do not use a 'busy' design with lots of arrows and boxes.
- Use the largest typeface that is practical.
- Use a typeface that is easy to read. Arial is often a good choice.
- In interview schedules use **bold** for questions and CAPITALS FOR INSTRUCTIONS. Different colour fonts can be useful here.
- Coloured paper can make self-completion questionnaires more attractive and easier to read for some people. However, avoid dark colours and remember yellows, oranges and red are 'warm' colours and blues and greens 'cool'.

If you are conducting a self-completion survey and, if resources allow, it is worth discussing design with a graphic designer. If you are designing an interview schedule, try to discuss layout with an experienced interviewer. Though design issues are very important in the finished product, initially it is better to begin with context and content.

How to begin

It is important to assume that when work begins on designing the questionnaire the researcher is clear about what it is he or she wishes to find out and what the context is (i.e. who is to be questioned and how – self-completion questionnaire or interview schedule?). Start by writing questions down, initially in the way they arise from the hypothesis (see Chapter 2) without worrying too much about wording. For example if your hypothesis was that 'university students cannot afford nutritious diets', then there are a whole series of questions about what they eat, when they eat it, how much of it they eat; what their income is, how much is spent on food, and which kinds of food; and how much is spent on other things such as rent, clothes, entertainment. Then there are questions about who they are and what they are like (face sheet information), which in this case might include questions about their course, where they originate from and where they live in term time.

Having done this, try grouping the 'rough' questions into cognate sections and ask at this point whether these questions, assuming they are properly operationalized into indicators and measures, will truly test the hypothesis. The actual process of operationalization is one that often scares the beginner, but approached in an incremental way, starting 'rough' and gradually refining makes the process relatively straightforward.

How the questionnaire begins will make a difference as to whether the respondent stays the course and completes the questionnaire or even whether they will respond at all. Before you can ask any questions it is necessary to have a short introduction that will either be read out (in an interview) to the respondent, or that the respondent will read. It sets the scene, it should reassure and should stimulate interest and co-operation. For example:

> Good morning, my name is ... As you may have heard on local radio, the University of Poppleton is conducting research on the future of children's education in the city. I wonder if I could take just a few minutes to ask you *your* views about children's education? Your answers are strictly confidential and will only be used for statistical purposes.

Types of question and question wording

We now need to start turning the rough questions into questionnaire questions and to do this we need to get into the mind set of our respondents. In phrasing our questions we want to achieve 'stimulus equivalence' (Oppenheim, 1992: 121), between the question and the response and between respondents. That is, when we ask respondent A a question she understands what we understand by it, likewise respondents B, C, D ... etc. However, with few exceptions there is no necessary or direct correspondence between asking and finding out. In everyday conversations we have the opportunity to clarify meaning and correct misunderstanding through subsidiary questions or statements. In questionnaires we cannot establish this kind of folk validity, because the need for reliability requires us to ask the same question of each respondent. Elucidation or clarification is not permissible. Moreover, just because someone answered your question does not mean they understood it in the same way as someone else or that their answer meant the same thing.

Types of question

We saw above that questions can be roughly divided into those that ask about facts, behaviour, attitudes and beliefs. A good starting strategy is to see which of the 'rough' questions fall into each of these categories and then consider the best ways of asking them.

CATEGORICAL QUESTIONS: The commonest and simplest of questions are categorical. They may be yes or no answers, or just categories of which the respondent must choose only one. These correspond to the nominal or categorical level of measurement described in Chapter 2. For example:

Which means of transport did you use to complete the longest part of your journey today?

Plane ☐

Train ☐

Bus ☐

Car ☐

Motorcycle ☐

Bicycle ☐

Other (please describe) ☐

Note: This question is self-completion. If it were in an interview schedule, it would require an instruction for the interviewer to read out the categories.

They may be categorical questions, but the respondent may choose more than one category, for example:

Which of the following items do you have in your kitchen? (TICK ALL THAT APPLY)

Washing machine ☐

Tumble dryer ☐

Dishwasher ☐

Microwave oven ☐

Freezer, or fridge-freezer ☐

Electric food processor ☐

Although each of these examples are factual questions, the same format can be used for behaviour attitudes or beliefs. In the previous example we could have asked 'Which of the following countries would you consider taking a main holiday in?' and providing a list.

ORDERED CATEGORIES: Quite often we wish to ask the respondent to place things in some kind of order, perhaps of preference. The responses are categories but they are ordered categories, though we do not quantify the difference between categories. These correspond to ordinal level measurement. We may ask, as in the example below, for the respondent to estimate the likelihood of their being promoted in the next five years. We cannot assume that, in their answer to this question, respondents who answered 'very high' are saying that they think they are five times more likely to get promotion than someone who answered 'very low', but nevertheless we must suppose that the respondent is providing a personal estimate of the probability of promotion and that there is a ranking.

How do you rate your chances of promotion in the next five years? Would you say that they were ...

Very high	☐
High	☐
Moderate	☐
Low	☐
Very low	☐
Not sure	☐

However, because variables with true numeric values (interval or ratio measurement) present the researcher with wider analysis possibilities, it is quite common to try to measure things that have a natural ranking (or one that can be improvised) with measurable differences between the values. Some things, such as income, height, distance, etc. fall naturally into this type, but other things, especially to do with attitudes or beliefs do not. They need a little bit of help. For example the previous question could have been asked like this:

> **I'd like to ask you about your chances of promotion. On a scale of one to ten, where ten is very likely to be promoted in the next five years and one is very unlikely, where would you place your own chances of promotion?**

Here the language of measurement is very much more explicit and allows us to treat the response as if it had the same mathematical properties as, say, miles, or height.

However, a word of caution here. When we measure the distance in miles between A and B, unless we were mistaken, each of us would come up independently with the same answer. If we ask Jane and Joe to assess their chances of promotion, Jane may be a pessimist and Joe an optimist in relation to their 'real' chances, but they both answer 6. In this example, we are measuring people's subjective views about their chances of promotion, but this kind of format is also widely used to ask 'factual' questions, about income, age, distance travelled to work, etc. and depend only on the accuracy of the answers given.

ATTITUDE SCALES: Space in questionnaires is usually at a premium yet attitude questions, in particular, can take up a lot of space. Quite often, then, researchers will use a matrix to ask a number of attitudinal questions at the same time. One advantage of this is that in analysis respondents can be allocated an overall 'score' for adherence to a particular attitude. This kind of scale, known as a Likert scale, will usually consist of a number of statements the respondent is asked to agree or disagree to.

I'd like to read out some things people have said about universities. Would you please say whether you strongly agree, agree, disagree or strongly disagree with each?

	Strongly Agree	Agree	Disagree	Strongly Disagree
University education leads to a good job	☐	☐	☐	☐
University education is not for me	☐	☐	☐	☐
I would send my children to university	☐	☐	☐	☐
We need more university education in Poppleton	☐	☐	☐	☐
It's good for youngsters to go away to university	☐	☐	☐	☐
I don't know much about universities	☐	☐	☐	☐
You don't need to go to university to get on in life	☐	☐	☐	☐

The example is a fairly simple one, but notice that the statements can be either positive or negative and that these are mixed together. A disadvantage of this is that in self-completion questionnaires with a large number of positive and negative statements, a respondent may accidentally treat a positive as a negative and vice versa. However, the advantages outweigh the disadvantages, not just in terms of space saved, but as a validity check. How is this done? Well, in a large number of items a positive and negative version of the same measure may be interspersed. If, for example, a respondent strongly agreed with each of the following, then we would have cause to worry about the validity of the measure.

The US government should aim to build a constructive dialogue with North Korea

The US government should sever all economic and diplomatic contact with North Korea

Such contradiction is actually quite common and may be the result of layout, wording or, in the case above, a problem with the level of knowledge of the respondent (see Oppenheim, 1992: 147).

SEMANTIC DIFFERENTIALS: Here respondents are asked to situate their attitudes on a scale ranging between opposite positions, for example:

How would you describe your holiday courier?

Courteous	1 2 3 4 5 6 7 8 9	Rude
Efficient	1 2 3 4 5 6 7 8 9	Incompetent
Friendly	1 2 3 4 5 6 7 8 9	Aloof
Knowledgeable	1 2 3 4 5 6 7 8 9	Inexperienced

Such scales assume an opposition between adjectives, but these are not always easy to derive. Strictly speaking, 'aloof' is not the opposite of 'friendly' nor 'inexperienced' that of 'knowledgeable'. Much will depend on context and questions can be pre-tested and developed by asking a number of people to suggest what they believe to be the best antonym to a word in given circumstances (see section on piloting below).

OPEN AND CLOSED QUESTIONS: All of the foregoing are 'closed' questions, that is, if the respondent is to answer he or she must select a predesignated reply. An open question (usually called open-ended) asks respondents to answer in their own words. For example:

What kinds of things do you do on your rest days?

Some respondents are not always forthcoming in volunteering responses to open questions, so in interviews it is quite common to use 'prompts' or 'probes'. The respondent may give a list of things in reply, such as 'shopping/playing with the kids/reading/visiting my parents'. When the respondent stops, the interviewer might then prompt with 'And what else?'. Eventually the respondent will say something like 'Nothing else I can think of.' Suppose, however, the respondent had answered in a rather taciturn way, 'Uh, just chilling out', then the interviewer may probe by asking 'What sort of things do you do when you chill out?' Prompts and probes in open questions can be used to great effect to get information from respondents that closed questions cannot.

In market research in particular, a favourite strategy is to ask an open question, say, about what brands of washing-up liquid the respondent has heard of and then follow this with a structured prompt, listing various brands and asking if he or she has heard of them. By using an open-ended question initially there is a test of respondent knowledge and memory, so if, say, the majority of respondents had named 'Sudso', without prompt, this would be useful data. Despite the attraction of flexibility and the potential to better tap into respondent subjectivity, open questions can be expensive on resources, i.e. they take more time (and may therefore cost more) to code and analyse and in small-scale studies operating on a short time scale or small budget, their use is best restricted. Aldridge and Levine (2001: 103) advise that open-ended questions should be used sparingly and a questionnaire should not begin with one. It is better first to draw the respondent into the study and establish rapport before more difficult open-ended questions are introduced.

Question wording

Question wording is something of an art: it depends on context and even whether something 'feels right'. A form of words that would be considered unworkable in one context may work in another. What follows is not set in stone but should be seen as a guide to getting the questions right. One of the best ways to get a feel for what is right is to consider what can go wrong.

AMBIGUITY: This can occur in a number of ways. A common error is to ask two or more things in the same question, what are called 'double-barrelled questions', for example:

Are you a parent and do you live in Poppleton? Yes/No

Is the respondent answering yes to being a parent, living in Poppleton, or both?

Negatives are another source of ambiguity, for example:

Rail services should not be re-nationalized. Agree/Disagree

The frame of reference, to do with time or amount of something might also be ambiguous.

Do you go to the cinema regularly? Yes/No

or:

How much do you earn?

But perhaps the commonest source of ambiguity is the use of a word or a phrase which might be understood in a number of ways, e.g.

Do you think drugs should be legalized?

Box 6.1 provides some possible unambiguous alternatives.

Box 6.1   Ways of asking

The left-hand column has the ambiguous questions from above and the right-hand column some possible (though not exhaustive) alternatives.

Are you a parent and do you live in Poppleton? Yes/No	**Are you a parent?** Yes/No **Do you currently live in Poppleton?** Yes/No
Rail services should not be re-nationalized	**Rail services should be re-nationalized. Agree/Disagree**
Do you go to the cinema regularly?	**Do you go to the cinema ...** Once a week or more Two or three times a month Once a month Every few months Less than once a year
How much do you earn?	**What is your weekly take-home wage, that is after deductions such as tax and National Insurance?**
Do you think drugs should be legalized? Yes/No	**Do you think marijuana should be legalized?** Yes/No

Note: by removing the 'negative' on rail services the question takes on a different complexion which may bias respondents towards agreeing, therefore a statement like this would probably be part of a battery of statements in a Likert scale. The cinema question is about periodical behaviour and a good general rule is to avoid vague periodic terms such as 'regularly', 'often', 'sometimes', 'occasionally' and provide unambiguous categories. The 'weekly wage' question may be accompanied by 'bands' of wages (e.g. under £100, £100 to £200) with which respondents would be prompted. The marijuana question might need colloquial terms such as 'dope', 'ganga', etc.

NECESSARY KNOWLEDGE: Surveys are often about quite specialist topics, but the difficulty is that though new legislation, local planning decisions, etc. may impact on people's lives, as we have seen, they may not have the necessary knowledge to answer a direct question. For example, the answer to the question:

Do you agree with the Council's long-term planning strategy for housing?

will depend on whether the person knows what that strategy is. If instead a series of questions were asked about whether x amount of houses and type of houses should be built in specific places, then it is quite likely the respondent will have a view. On the other hand, if you needed a view on the strategy as a whole, you could first ask whether the respondent was aware of it.

DIRECT OR INDIRECT QUESTIONS: We cannot always ask what we want to ask in a direct way, because the topic is difficult or sensitive. The following is an amusing example of the latter from de Vaus (1996) (originally in Barton, 1958) which nevertheless shows a number of useful ways of getting at difficult questions. So rather than asking:

Have you murdered your wife?

there are several indirect approaches:

a   The casual approach: 'Do you happen to have murdered your wife?'
b   The numbered card approach: 'Will you please read off the number of this card which corresponds with what became of your wife?'
c   The everybody approach: 'As you know, many people have been killing their wives these days. Do you happen to have killed yours?'
d   The other people approach: 'Do you know any people who have murdered their wives?' Pause for reply and then ask 'How about yourself?'

(de Vaus, 1996: 85)

SHOW CARDS: In face-to-face interviews 'show cards', or other visual materials can be useful (see Box 6.2). These can be used as a visual prompt to help the respondents remember the response options and can have an additional advantage of allowing the respondents to review the options open to them. They are also used to ask people about age, income, ethnicity, or to present attitude statements the respondent might feel embarrassed to have read out.

Box 6.2   A show card

The following was read out:

Please look at this card and tell me which of these holiday destinations you have visited in the last five years:

Showcard

Portugal

Spain

Italy

Germany

France

Austria

United States

Australia

New Zealand

South Africa

Canada

(Usually there would be an interviewer instruction such as PROMPT FOR
OTHERS on the questionnaire.)

MEANINGS: You know what you mean – well, hopefully – but does the respondent? Words and phrases can have different meanings for different groups. This may be to do with class or culture. In Britain, for example, working-class people traditionally called a midday meal 'dinner', whereas middle-class people took this meal in the evening when working-class people had 'tea'. This particular problem can be avoided by using alternatives such as midday meal and main evening meal (Aldridge and Levine, 2001: 99). However, meaning is not just about cultural or class difference, but may be about misinterpretation (thus this problem shades into 'necessary knowledge' or 'ambiguity'). The respondent may either not respond at all, or respond on the basis of an erroneous assumption about what was being asked.

LEADING QUESTIONS: Leading questions often use loaded words or phrases, for example:

**Did you realize that many painful animal experiments
have no relation at all to human survival or curing disease?**

To those new to survey design the injunction that you do not use leading questions seems to contradict the idea of using attitude statements. However, leading questions differ from attitude statements in that the latter should be constructed to match positive and negative views of a matter.

Leading questions are commonly used on 'fake' questionnaires first to get 'respondents' to agree to a moral consensus on an issue, then to make some sort of commitment, usually financial. Here is a recent example mailed to my home from a British charity whose real purpose was to elicit a donation from me:

With present resources, Macmillan cannot possibly reach all those who need our help. Do you believe that everyone deserves equal and ready access to the best information, treatment and care for cancer?

Agree strongly ☐   Agree ☐   Disagree ☐

Macmillan Cancer Relief relies on the support of the public to keep going. Knowing this, would you be prepared to support our vital work with a small, regular donation of just £2 a month?

Yes ☐ No ☐

Good researchers (as opposed to campaigners in the above examples) try to avoid leading questions, but it is possible to create opinions where none previously existed by asking questions. This can have important ethical implications, for example, to ask people about their fear of crime in a relatively crime free area can instil a fear of crime.

CONFORMING WITH THE NORM: Finally, researchers are faced with the problem of 'social desirability' bias. People quite often want to convince the researcher they do what would be normally expected of people 'like them'. They either want to conform to a social norm, or sometimes, just the opposite, they want to appear deviant:

> Some people will claim that they read more than they do, bathe more often than is strictly true and fill more pipes from an ounce of tobacco than would seem likely. They claim that they buy new tyres for their car when in fact they buy retreads; they deny reading certain Sunday newspapers of dubious repute; the clothes that they buy are expensive; they would seem to make donations to charity with great frequency and to visit museums almost every week! (Oppenheim, 1992: 138–9)

As Oppenheim goes on to say, this is a problem without an obvious solution. Making people aware that there are no right or wrong answers, but that it is important that answers are as accurate as possible can help, as can the use of 'positive' and 'negative' attitude statements, open questions and probing.[2]

Questionnaire layout and contingency questions

As I noted above, the appearance of the questionnaire is important. Questions may be well designed and operationalized, but if the layout in self-completion questionnaires is unattractive, response rate will suffer. A fussy, cluttered or over-complicated layout in an interview schedule can lead to error. De Vaus gives eight useful tips on question order:

1 Commence with questions the respondent will enjoy answering.

   a These should be easily answered questions.
   b Factual questions should be used initially.
   c Do not start with demographic [face sheet] questions such as age, marital status, etc.
   d Ensure that the initial questions are obviously relevant to the stated purpose of the survey.

2 Go from easy to more difficult questions.
3 Go from concrete to abstract questions.
4 Open-ended questions should be kept to a minimum and where possible placed towards the end of the questionnaire.
5 Group questions into sections. This helps structure the questionnaire and provides a flow.
6 Make use of filter questions to ensure that questions are relevant to respondents.
7 When using a series of positive and negative items to form a scale, mix up the positive and negative items to help avoid an acquiescent response set.
8 Where possible try to introduce a variety of question formats so that the questionnaire remains interesting.

(de Vaus, 1996: 94–5)

Whether one is designing a self-completion questionnaire or an interview schedule, it will be necessary to break the questionnaire up into sections (unless it's very short). These will correspond with the topic areas initially identified and will need some kind of introduction. This might be a short sentence, such as 'I'd like to ask you a little about your education after leaving full-time schooling' or it may be longer and even consist of a short vignette. Section introductions, or headings (in a self-completion questionnaire) serve not just to contextualize each section, but to help the interviewer or respondent navigate the questionnaire.

In most questionnaires not all questions will apply to everyone and some groups might need a section containing questions just for them. Imagine a questionnaire about perfumes and cosmetics. You would not want to ask most men which brand of eye shadow they normally used, or ask most women which brand of aftershave they preferred to use! The way groups are separated out is by means of contingency questions. Depending on how one answers such a question will determine how one is filtered through the questionnaire. In long questionnaires there will be a number of contingency questions and a logical, but possibly complex means of filtering respondents through. An example is provided in Box 6.3.

Box 6.3   An example of a contingency question

Have you moved to Poppleton within the last five years, that is since January 1997?

Yes ──────────────────────────────┐
                                     │
                                     │
                                     │
                                     │
No [GO TO QUESTION 2]   ▼

(a)   Which year did you move to Poppleton? _____

(b)   What was the name of the town you lived in, or the name of the nearest town, prior to your moving to Poppleton? _____

(c)   What was the main reason for moving to Poppleton?

      job or education

      better environment

      to be near friends or family

      retirement

      unhappy with where you lived before

Piloting and testing

It is possible for the overall design of the survey (formulation of research question, hypotheses and selection of sample) to be exemplary, but to be spoiled by poor questionnaire design. Mistakes in data analysis can be exasperating, but recoverable. Mistakes in what you ask or how you ask it can only be recovered by repeating the survey. Organizations, such as government research agencies, university research centres and larger market research companies, spend a lot of time in testing and developing the questions they use and in some cases small 'trial data sets' are created and analysed to try to anticipate later problems with analysis. The UK and US Censuses, for example, begin to pre-test questions several years before the census itself.

Almost everything to do with a survey can be piloted, including sampling, but as with so many other aspects of research, what is piloted and the amount of piloting will depend on resources of time and money. However, all new questions and the final questionnaire should be piloted on members of the target population. In many surveys a 'pilot' consists of administering the completed questionnaire to a few people. This is not wrong and is certainly better than nothing, but rigorous piloting goes much further.

One of the best ways to increase the validity of the questions is to get the population to whom they will be administered to help design them! A good way to do this is through depth interviews or focus groups where the topic of the research is discussed in depth and respondent understandings of concepts or meanings can be explored. The interviewer can ask questions such as, 'If I asked you X, what would you understand by it?' The most important thing about this stage is that it gives the researcher a chance to check if he or she is covering all that might be important about a topic in the population of interest.

The next stage might be to actually test a battery of questions on different sub-groups in the population. The respondents may or may not be aware that this is piloting, though I think that both for ethical reasons and because you can ask for their views on what was asked, the former is better. What are we doing when we test questions? Converse and Presser (1986: 55) list four aims:

1   Variation. Which questions will have the most variability in the population and which are the sub-groups showing variation? Of course the variation may not be statistically significant (see Chapter 7), but it might suggest the development of further contingency questions to explore issues in sub-groups.
2   Meaning. What the researcher means and what he or she *thinks* respondents might mean may differ. 'Family planning' might mean birth control to investigators and most people, but for some it means saving for a holiday (Converse and Presser, 1986: 55).
3   Task difficulty. Quite often people may understand what you mean, but find answering the question hard. To ask people how many kilos of coffee they consumed last year, is readily understood, but not readily answered. Market research questionnaires frequently ask people if they have heard of a range of products. If the respondent then confirms he or she has heard of particular products, a battery of questions follow about whether then would use them, recommend them, or if x is better than y. The questions are really unanswerable unless the respondent has a greater familiarity than simply having heard of the product.
4   Respondent interest and attention. Interviewers often report that people enjoy answering questions about themselves; after all, for 15 or 30 minutes or so the respondent is the centre of attention, but if the questions are tedious or do not arouse respondent interest, then they will become bored or fatigued. The result is non-response or poor validity because the respondent will say pretty much anything to get the interview finished. Holding respondent interest in self-completion questionnaires is vital and the task that pilot volunteers completed it is not enough, you need to know what they thought of it. Would they have completed it had they have received it in the post?

Piloting the questionnaire itself can test a number of things, but it is not always easy to tell whether difficulties encountered were the result of the juxtaposition of certain questions, the routing through the questionnaire, the layout/typeface, or whether it was just too long. In other words, the pre-testing of questions may have been successful and rigorous, but the questionnaire still does not work. Government research agencies and larger market research companies will send out experienced interviewers with pilot questionnaires and then debrief them at length, or for self-completion questionnaires employ a panel who will similarly comment on their experience. This can be replicated on a smaller scale and, indeed, I always ask my students to start by administering the questionnaire to their best friend and asking for honest feedback.

One of the trickiest things to get right is the routing through the questionnaire. Contingency questions will lead the interviewer (or respondent) to 'skip' forward to different questions with the risk that some people will miss questions, or answer questions not relevant to them. Converse and Presser suggest the following:

> The best way of proof reading the skip patterns is to turn the task over to several individuals, each of whom follows the route for a certain 'scenario,' such as these:
>
> (A) The respondent was born in Mexico in 1947 and came to the U.S. in 1966. This is her first marriage; her husband had two children by a previous marriage, who are now living with R and her husband. She first voted in the 1976 national election …
>
> (B) The respondent, age 56, has worked at an automobile assembly plant for 11 years as manager of the shipping department. He is married, without children. He and his wife have recently bought into an investment partnership that is buying real estate in Florida, and they hope to retire there when he is 62 …
>
> (Converse and Presser, 1986: 62)

Questionnaires in smaller (and low budget!) studies can be 'batch piloted'. Five questionnaires are piloted and 'errors' or problems corrected. A further five amended questionnaires are piloted and newly emerging errors are corrected. This procedure continues until there are no errors. Usually after about 15 questionnaires the most glaring problems are solved.

Conclusion

Questionnaire design is at the very heart of 'scientific' social science, for as I have noted, the data we analyse and the subsequent statistical output are only as good as the research design and the 'instrument' – in this case, the questionnaire. Yet as with other aspects of research, knowing the rules does not make you a good researcher (or designer of questionnaires). Only practice can do that and I continue to be surprised to find out how often standardized techniques fail to work in circumstances where one would have anticipated success and, conversely, where the 'rules' say something should not work but it does. Nevertheless such instances remain a minority of cases.

Oppenheim puts it rather well:

> Some people still design questions as if the process of interviewing or filling out a questionnaire were rather like unloading a ship, with every item of cargo labelled according to its contents and marked with a specific destination, so that it can be lifted out of the hold and set down as and when required. In reality questioning people is more like trying to catch a particularly elusive fish, by casting different kinds of bait, at different depths, without knowing what is going on at the surface. (1992: 120–1)

In the foregoing I have tried to show what the key ingredients of a good questionnaire are, but much of this is not set in stone and there is much more that could be said about questionnaire design. Sometimes the rules can and must be broken, but it is as well to know them first. Two last pieces of advice: if it works, use it, but be sure it works first. And whatever goes into your questionnaire has got to be analysed, so only ask those things that you are capable of, or have the resources to analyse.

Questions for reflection and discussion

1 Why do we need 'face sheet' information?
2 What might be a problem with asking someone the question 'How old are you?'
3 Omnibus surveys (see Chapter 5) often locate questions concerning voting intentions between questions on many different topics (as diverse as personal insurance, travel, consumer goods, etc.). Could this make a difference to how people might answer? Why?

Try this

What question, or battery of questions, would you use in an interview schedule to find out how religious the population of your town or city are?

Suggested further reading

Apart from the general books listed in the last chapter, two specialist books might be helpful. The first is another 'classic', A.N. Oppenheim's *Questionnaire*

Design, Interviewing and Attitude Measurement (1992). Jean Converse and Stanley Presser's little book *Survey Questions: Handcrafting the Standardized Questionnaire* (1986) is admirably condensed and straightforward.

Notes

1 Political correctness and a misunderstanding of the meaning of the term have led to the substitution of 'gender' for biological sex. My advice is stick with sex. A good test of 'face sheet' questions like these, is would your grandmother understand? Your grandmother knows about sex, but possibly not gender. Actually sex can be avoided by asking: Are you: Male ☐ Female ☐?

2 For example … who buys pork pies? Market researchers have long found difficulties in establishing who buys this British delicacy. Unfashionable for some time and generally regarded as high in cholesterol, they nevertheless remain a best seller. The trouble is, people are not prepared to admit to buying them!

7

Analysing Survey Data

In this chapter:

- Cases, variables and the data matrix
- Missing data
- Univariate analysis
- Probability
- Central tendency and dispersion
- Bivariate analysis
- Elaboration
- Statistical significance
- Hypothesis testing
- Correlation
- Multivariate analysis
- Regression
- Modelling and its limitations

Data analysis is the least scary part of research. After all, most of the difficult tasks such as designing and executing the research are done and if you are to start analysing then it implies there is something to analyse! It is also less scary now than it used to be. The software interface between the researcher and the data is very much more user friendly than even a decade ago and the amount of statistical or mathematical knowledge needed is minimal.

In this chapter I will assume a number of things. First of all I will assume that at least some thought has been given to analysis at the design stage, of both the research itself and the questionnaire. As I suggested at the end of the previous chapter some thought needs to be given to what is needed for analysis purposes and what can be meaningfully analysed. For example, measuring age in age bands precludes analysis with any smaller units of age, whereas if the age of each respondent is known, then they can be grouped later in different ways. Complex scales may save space and are potentially powerful, but may be quite challenging to analyse.

Second, I will assume that a separate data analysis text will be bought or borrowed. Most data analysis uses either SPSS (Statistical Products and Service Solutions – formerly Statistical Package for the Social Sciences) or

Minitab statistical packages (mostly the former). There are a number of excellent and accessible introductions. These will show you how to undertake such operations. My aim here is to describe the reasoning behind various techniques of analysis. At various points I will refer to two of these and where you can find instructions in SPSS to carry out the operations. The books are *Understanding Social Statistics*, by Jane Fielding and Nigel Gilbert (2000) and *A Guide to Computing Statistics with SPSS for Windows* by Dennis Howitt and Duncan Cramer (2001). Both describe access to SPSS; the latter is a little easier and more direct for this purpose, while the former uses large-scale survey data to introduce statistics in the social sciences. A third book I will occasionally refer to, not explicitly concerned with SPSS techniques, but nevertheless good at answering tricky questions and explaining things clearly is *Your Statistical Consultant* by Rae Newton and Kjell Rudestam (1999).

Third, I am assuming that most readers wish to know quite basic things about data analysis and if they want to know more, then they will go to other books afterwards or instead of this one. Again I'll make a few suggestions.

Fourth, I will avoid equations. Equations can be useful shorthand, but I suspect that their use in introductory methods texts is more an indication of machismo. When Stephen Hawking was writing his best-selling *Brief History of Time* he was told that for every equation he would lose a 1000 readers and the book appeared with one equation: $E = MC^2$. Like Hawking I want to sell books – so I have followed his example. In this chapter I have also adopted a convention – annoying to some – of highlighting *key words* just in case you wish to look them up in a more specialised book.

Data analysis – an overview

First of all, let us be clear: data analysis here is shorthand for numeric data analysis. One can conduct quite different kinds of analyses on interpretive data, but here we are interested in numbers. When you administered your questionnaire you obtained data from a number of individuals[1] and these are called *cases*. The data themselves consist of attributes, behaviours, attitudes and beliefs (see Chapters 2 and 6). These become our *variables*. The aim of data analysis is to discover the relationship between cases and variables and variables and variables. Now imagine for a moment you are interested in one case, let's call him Garfield. You have asked Garfield a number of questions about his age, his occupation, his attitude towards welfare, his politics, etc. Further suppose that you want to compare the characteristics of Garfield with someone else called Denzil. How might you do it? One way would be to write down a heading with Garfield's name and another with Denzil's and underneath list the characteristics which will then show the differences between them. Like this:

	Sex	Age	Politics	Occupation	Welfare
Garfield	Male	51	Republican	Banker	Individualist
Denzil	Male	49	Democrat	Teacher	Collectivist

Data files, where your survey findings are recorded, are organized in such a way, except that numbers are used to stand in for the verbal description. We may have a list of occupation categories which start at one and go to 80. 'Garfield' or 'Denzil' would be represented by a case number and their ages would just be recorded in the same way. It would end up looking like this:

	SEX	AGE	POLITICS	OCCUPAT	WELFARE
0001	1	51	1	1	1
0002	1	49	2	8	2

Note how longer variable names are shortened.

The data entered in each cell will correspond to the value recorded on the questionnaire. For example:

Which political party do you support?

Republican	1
Democratic	2
Green	3
Other (write in)	4
None	5

The above is not meant to be instructions on data entry, these are covered thoroughly, along with how to access SPSS in Chapter 1 of the Howitt and Cramer, but merely to clear up the mystery of how data get from paper to the computer.[2] When the variables and cases are all entered we have a *data matrix*.

Once the data are entered there are three main things the researcher is likely to be interested in. First, finding out what the values are for each variable (e.g. how many of the sample support the Republicans, etc.); how these variables might be associated with each other, for example, is support for the Green party associated with younger people? Third, how confident are we that our sample results accurately represent the population? Most data analysis is interested in all of these things, but the level at which the last two take place will vary enormously. Although you would never know it from reading most data analysis texts, most social and market research consists of the presentation of simple *frequencies*, that is the frequency in which particular values occur on each variable (say, the number of people in the sample supporting each political party); of *cross-tabulations* of two variables to show what the relationship is between them and finally the presentation of simple statistical tests to demonstrate the probability of such a finding occurring by accident.

Some research does go further, using more complex analyses – often examining the relationship between several variables – what is termed *multivariate analysis*, or how strongly variables are related (more of this below). In the rest of this chapter we will look first at some of the basics, what one might expect to come across in simple analyses and finally there will be just a taster of multivariate analysis.

Although data analysis need not be complex, it is nevertheless the case that our aim is to produce reliable statistical data but this can be hampered by incomplete data (see Box 7.1). Statistics can be summed up as the collection and interpretation of numeric data. It relies on mathematical principles, mostly to do with probability (you will recall there was some discussion of this in the chapter on sampling, Chapter 4), so while I will be mostly concerned with describing levels of analysis here (*univariate*, *bivariate* and *multivariate*) I will nevertheless discuss a few of the more important and basic statistical procedures that allow us to know what can be inferred from the data.

Box 7.1 Some of our data are missing!

What do we do when we find we have missing values for some variables? What we do about it depends on why it is missing and what is missing.

The refusal of people to participate at all can be problematic for the sampling strategy. This was discussed in Chapter 2, but even when people do participate, there can still be missing values for a number of reasons (this is not an exhaustive list):

- poor questionnaire design;
- interviewer error;
- curtailed interview;
- respondent doesn't answer a question (refuses, doesn't understand, etc.).

The first thing to do is to see if there is a pattern in the missing data. Is it to do with a particular question for one of the reasons above? Could an interviewer throw some light on why there is a pattern?

Next, see what difference it makes. Try comparing a sub-sample where the data are not missing with one where they are. For this you might use a *t* test.[3] If the two groups are similar in all respects but the missing values, then there is no big problem and you just have to decide what to do about the missing values. If the groups are very different then this

---

implies bigger decisions, at the very least, making a virtue out of necessity and comparing the two groups.

Having made the more strategic decisions about how serious/interesting the problem is there are three main things you can do:

- *Drop the case altogether.* This is probably best if the missing data are across several variables in few respondents.
- *Drop the variable.* Providing the sub-samples above are similar, then a lot of missing values on one variable indicate you should drop the variable.
- *Imputation.* Occasionally it is possible to logically or probabilistically 'impute' a value. A simple example: we can logically impute a person's sex as female, if later we discover she is, or was, pregnant! Usually it's harder than this and strategies such as randomly choosing a value from remaining cases, or entering the mean value of the variable are used.

There is an excellent discussion of the topic of missing data in Newton and Rudestam (1999: 156–68). How to deal with missing values in SPSS can be found in Fielding and Gilbert (2000: 62–3) and Howitt and Cramer (2001: 132-6).

Univariate analysis

The *univariate* distribution is at the basis of all statistics and is the most commonly presented. It simply shows the scores for the values within a variable and is what you will get if you ask SPSS to run frequencies for you (Howitt and Cramer, 2001: 24–6). For example, Table 7.1 shows the top ten destinations of holidaymakers interviewed at a major airport in the UK. The distribution of the frequencies for each destination is given alongside the percentages. Usually if one were presenting these data, only percentages would be given along with the total number in the sample (*n*), thus allowing the reader to work back to the frequency for each category. While a univariate analysis like this only tells you the total number in the sample visiting each country (and nothing about the people themselves), it is nevertheless useful for such basic analysis alone, but also for comparative purposes. We could, for example, compare the findings from different airports, or at different months of the year.

'Running frequencies' is the first step in the analysis of data, but also in checking its quality. For example, it is no surprise that the favourite holiday destination in the sample is Spain. Had the frequency distribution shown this to be Morocco, with Spain least popular, then this would suggest a

Table 7.1 Destination frequencies

	Number	Percentage
Spain	185	21.8
Greece	140	16.5
United States	102	12.0
Cyprus	91	10.7
Portugal	80	9.4
Turkey	65	7.6
Malta	64	7.5
Italy	52	6.2
Tunisia	40	4.7
Morocco	31	3.6
Total	850	100

problem somewhere in the research process (sampling, interviewer bias, data entry, etc.).

The categories in Table 7.1 were ordered according to the most popular destination, but they could have been ordered differently, because the variable is a nominal one (see Chapter 2).

What is probability?

Probability lies at the heart of statistics. It can be a fascinating and complex subject, but on a day-to-day basis we use probability all the time. When you toss a coin to decide who buys the last drink you are invoking the laws of probability. The coin has a one in two chance of coming up heads or tails. Likewise, a dice has a one in six chance of coming up with a six. Assuming the dice or penny is not 'loaded', eventually there will be a regular distribution of heads/tails or sixes, threes, etc. This principle seems to underlie most things in nature and it is this assumption that is the basis of statistics. We assume for example that populations are 'normally distributed' and when they are not, then this becomes interesting for the statistician or the scientist. We would expect, for example, that leukaemia would be evenly distributed geographically across a country. When it is 'clustered' into particular places, then we investigate. Statistics, based on the laws of probability, help us to find the uneven distribution in the first place and can help us to understand why this is the case.

The same laws of probability underlie our claims to generalization. The probability of something existing or arising in our sample should be the same as in the population – one dice bought from Woolworths has the same odds of coming up on six as any other of Woolworths' dice. Our variable analyses tell us whether the sample has certain characteristics and probability allows us to generalize. The same laws of probability underlie the statistical tests we use to see if our generalizations are legitimate!

Measures of central tendency and dispersion

The level of measurement permits us to describe univariate distributions in different ways because they have particular mathematical properties. Most importantly we often wish to summarize findings by talking about 'averages'. Averages are the most important measure of *central tendency*, that is statistical summaries of data designed to find the single number best representing several numbers. When most people think of averages they are actually thinking of arithmetic averages, for example, the average number of sunny days per year in a given location. Actually there are three kinds of average, but not all can be used at every level of measurement. The arithmetic average, usually called the arithmetic *mean*, is the most versatile statistically, but first a word about the others.

Only the *mode* could be used to describe the holiday destination data above, because it is a nominal variable. A good way to remember the mode is to think of how we employ the word 'mode' to describe something that is most popular. In Table 7.1 Spain presumably was the most 'popular' destination (and therefore the mode) because more people were going there. But it need not imply popularity. Had business travellers been questioned, Germany might have come out as the mode, but it may not have been the number one aesthetic choice!

The other ways of measuring 'averages' are the *median* and the (aforementioned) mean. Neither can be used on nominal data, the first because it measures the 'halfway' point on a set of scores and, second, in order to obtain the median in an even set of scores it is necessary to obtain the average of the two middle scores. You can't have a half-way country or an average of two half-way countries! The median can only be used when something is ranked according to sizes and can only be used on ordinal data or above.

The mode and the median are less used than the mean, though they can be very useful when a set of scores on an interval or ratio scale are widely *skewed* to extremes. For example, mean earnings in a location may be £25,000, but this figure may have come about because a minority earned a great deal more than this. Most people, however, earned a lot less with very few actually earning £25,000 (or thereabouts) and the median may be a great deal less than the latter figure, but a truer picture of 'average' earnings.

The normal distribution

Statisticians like perfection and elegance and the most perfect representation of this is the normal distribution or curve. The first thing to say about it is that it is not 'normal', especially in the social world, but represents a theoretical distribution in which most scores cluster around the mean with correspondingly less in a gradual curve in either direction from the mean. This is illustrated in Figure 7.1.

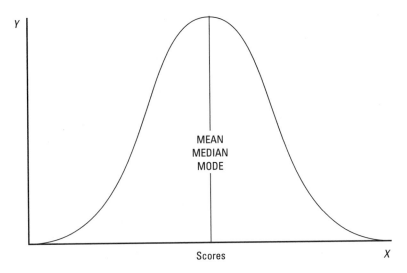

Figure 7.1   *A Normal Curve or distribution*

The thing to note about the normal distribution is that that the mean, median and mode all fall at the same point. Although 'real' normal distributions are rarely found, some distributions (for example, age) come quite close and often researchers will talk of a normal distribution when it is merely nearly normal! Perhaps the most important role of the normal distribution is it is the basis for a number of statistical tests which tell us just how much a distribution differs from a normal one. The normal curve becomes a kind of yardstick for other distributions.

Because the mean, median and mode are just averages they cannot tell us much about how scores are dispersed over a distribution. It is often important to say something about the *dispersion*. The simplest way of doing this is to specify the *range*, so, for example, we may know that that mean earnings are £25,000, but if we also specified the highest earnings recorded (say £980,000) and the lowest (£3,000), we could immediately see that there was a huge difference between the highest and lowest earners. To obtain the range we simply subtract the lowest score from the highest.

However, the distribution may not give a true picture of earnings, because only a very few earned £3,000 and perhaps only one person earned £980,000. An alternative measure of dispersion is the *standard deviation*. This shows the spread of scores in a distribution by summarizing an average distance of all scores from the mean. Therefore the more widely scores are distributed, the greater the standard deviation (represented as SD or *s*). To grasp the importance of standard deviations we need to go back to the normal distribution.

It can be seen from Figure 7.2 that on a normal distribution 68 per cent of all scores will fall within plus or minus one standard deviation of the mean and around 95 per cent within plus or minus two standard deviations and

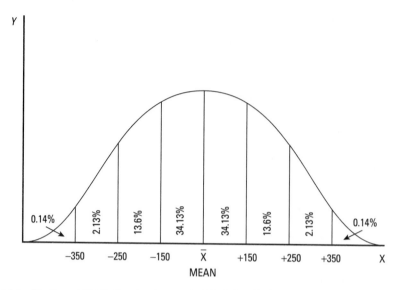

Figure 7.2   *The Normal Distribution showing standard deviations (SD)*

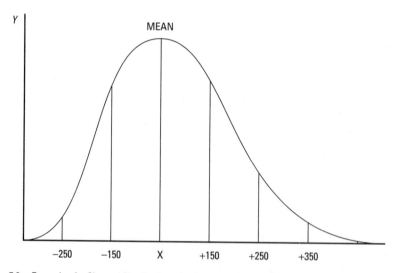

Figure 7.3   *Example of a Skewed Distribution with Standard Deviations (SD)*

99.7 per cent within plus or minus three standard deviations. Consequently, on a distribution that is not 'normal' (the kind we mostly deal with in social research), considerably fewer scores will fall within one standard deviation of the mean, as is illustrated in Figure 7.3. We would expect a lower standard

Table 7.2 Economic and migration data for South West Britain[4]

	Unemployment	% employed in manufacturing	% migrating in	% migrating out
Avon	9.1	15.1	11.9	12.4
Cornwall	12.8	11.0	11.1	23.2
Devon	9.8	15.9	10.6	18.8
Dorset	9.4	15.5	11.1	21.8
Gloucestershire	7.1	20.2	11.3	16.4
Somerset	7.9	19.6	12.5	19.0
Wiltshire	7.4	20.8	14.9	19.1

deviation if, say, student marks clustered around a mean than if they were dispersed with quite a lot of students scoring very low or very high marks. For a further discussion of the normal distribution and how to work out measures of central tendency using SPSS, see Howitt and Cramer (2001: Chapters 3 and 5) and Fielding and Gilbert (2000: 114–18).

There are limits to what can be done with a univariate analysis. It is a necessary step in analysis to help make sense of the data. As a strategy in research its most useful role is a comparative one, for example, a number of comparative scores across several variables can tell a powerful story. In Table 7.2 univariate data has been compiled to create a comparative statistical picture of the counties of the South West region of Britain. Very simple data present clear differences between the counties. Cornwall, for example, has the lowest percentage of people employed in manufacturing, but the highest unemployment. Gloucestershire is almost the opposite. While these data are unsurprising, the absence or presence of manufacturing jobs made little difference to in migration levels, though out-migration levels varied (Williams and Champion, 1998).

Bivariate analysis

In Table 7.2 data from different sources are simply placed alongside each other to illustrate difference. There is no attempt to show any statistical relationship between the variables; however, in bivariate analysis that is exactly what we wish to do.

In bivariate analysis we want to show what the relationship is between variables. This is really quite an everyday concept. There is a relationship between eating too much and feeling ill or between doing very little work and getting bad grades. In everyday life and in the physical world we speak of these as causal relations where B comes about because A happened. Statistics cannot show causal relationships, merely *associations*, but these associations can be stronger or weaker (see the storks and babies story in

Chapter 5). Indeed, however obvious and common sense the association between variables is, we can talk only of association. Nevertheless bivariate relationships are an important stage in explanation and as we will see, can be used to infer relationships beyond the two variables specified.

Contingency tables

The commonest form of bivariate analysis is the contingency table and it is very easy to produce in SPSS using the Crosstabs command.[5] For details of procedures see Howitt and Cramer (2001: 61–4) and Fielding and Gilbert (2000: Chapter 9). The most difficult decision is knowing which variables to *cross-tabulate*. It will be recalled from Chapter 2 that while we cannot really talk of causes, it is a helpful strategy to specify which variable might be affected by others. Therefore in deciding which variables should be cross-tabulated we start by specifying the dependent variables. Initial exploratory data analysis will often specify a series of research hypotheses, often quite informal,[6] about which independent variables might be affecting which dependent ones (which variable is *contingent* upon the other). Tables 7.3, 7.4 and 7.5 illustrate this. The research question attempted to explain low election turnout, first, by reference to age, second, by reference to sex and third, by reference to distance from the polling station. If the research hypothesized that the younger a person is, the less likely they are to vote, then this would have been confirmed for the younger groups. The 18–25 year olds were less likely to vote than the older groups, though the hypothesis would need refining because the 61+ group were less likely to vote than the 41–60 and the 26–40 groups.

In Table 7.4 the hypothesis was that women were more likely to vote than men and this was confirmed, although the third hypothesis that the further an elector is from the polling station, the less likely they are to vote was not confirmed. Only 3 percentage points separated the groups. These analyses would not be the end of the matter, because other independent variables would be explored and interactions between independent variables and then between them and the dependent variable might be explored through elaboration or multivariate analysis, but I'll come to these things presently. Note here that I am talking about *research hypotheses*; there is another kind: *statistical hypotheses*, which I will discuss later.

Usually the dependent variable is the row variable and the independent variable forms the columns. This is not a rule set in stone and sometimes it makes sense to use a different format. In these tables notice the column frequencies are not given alongside the percentages, but it is possible to 'work back' to these from knowing *n*.

In Tables 7.3, 7.4 and 7.5 whether one votes or not cannot determine one's sex, though being female means a person was more likely to vote. Obviously biology does not cause voting behaviour in any sense, but instead it comes to stand in for social behaviour associated with biological sex. So we do have

Table 7.3 Voting by age group

(%)	18–25	26–40	41–60	61+
Voted	22	41	42	38
Did not vote	78	59	58	62
n =	259	484	472	401

Table 7.4 Voting by sex

%	Males	Females
Voted	37	41
Did not vote	63	59
n =	709	907

Table 7.5 Voting by distance from polling station

(%)	under 1 mile	1 to 2 miles	2 to 5 miles
Voted	41	38	42
Did not vote	59	62	58
n =	868	505	243

some idea of a cause–effect relationship and this will mostly be the case in the relationship between dependent and independent variables, but more often than we would like it is messier and we do not know the direction of the cause–effect, and moreover we cannot specify which variables are dependent or independent. For example, in Table 7.6 two variables, 'satisfaction with current housing' and 'intention to move within five years' were variables measured in a survey of housing needs and aspirations. Here we cannot say whether levels of satisfaction drive an intention to move, or whether one's intention to move affects satisfaction. One must either get into some complex social psychology around meaning and intention, or at the very least conduct analyses with other variables – something we will come to below.

Elaboration

Elaboration is the process of cross-tabulating two variables while 'controlling' for a third (often referred to as the 'control variable', see also Chapter 2). In Table 7.6 the rather unclear result could be elaborated by running several cross-tabulations where a third variable is 'controlled' for, for example, whether or not respondents lived in rented housing, their sex, their age

Table 7.6   Satisfaction with housing and intention to move

	Definitely move (%)	May move (%)	Unlikely to move (%)	Definitely won't move (%)	n
Very satisfied	9	22	44	25	293
Satisfied	12	23	39	26	400
Unsatisfied	18	29	49	4	205
Very unsatisfied	7	35	51	7	119

Table 7.7a   Satisfaction with housing and intention to move: respondents under 55 years of age

	Definitely move (%)	May move (%)	Unlikely to move (%)	Definitely won't move (%)	n
Very satisfied	16	24	27	33	112
Satisfied	18	27	29	26	479
Unsatisfied	24	30	32	14	102
Very unsatisfied	23	40	30	7	72

Table 7.7b   Satisfaction with housing and intention to move: respondents 55 years of age or older

	Definitely move (%)	May move (%)	Unlikely to move (%)	Definitely won't move (%)	n
Very satisfied	2	12	54	32	53
Satisfied	7	14	49	30	96
Unsatisfied	14	24	35	27	69
Very unsatisfied	10	17	61	12	32

group, etc. This is what the table looks like if we control for age (Table 7.7a and b, above). Table 7.7a shows respondents under 55 years of age and Table 7.7b those of 55 years of age or over.

Controlling for age produced a slightly clearer story indicating that those in the older age group who were dissatisfied with their housing were less likely to expect to move in the next five years. This is not a surprising result: older people are often less able or willing to undergo the trauma of moving home than younger people. Indeed, other analyses indicated that 'satisfaction' is less associated with intention to move than income, being an owner occupier or being a member of a non-manual class.

Recoding and computing new variables

A further technique that helps the researcher to get the most out of simple univariate and bivariate analyses is that of *recoding* or deriving new variables from one's data. The commonest example of recoding is that of age. As I noted above, there is a greater flexibility if data are collected on individuals' ages rather than age bands. However, it would be fairly uncommon to present a cross-tabulation of age showing every year from zero to 99. More often the researcher will recode according to the hypothesis being tested in the elaboration. For example in Tables 7.7a and b above two age bands were derived because it was hypothesized that older people would be less likely to intend moving, regardless of housing satisfaction.

Recoding can also be useful when one is faced with small numbers in a data set. Cross-tabulations with small numbers, where the variables have several categories, can end up not being 'statistically significant', especially when using nominal variables and the chi-square test of significance (see below). For a discussion of how to recode, see Howitt and Cramer (2001: 137–42). For example, a social class variable of six categories could be reduced to manual/non-manual. Second, we may wish to recode one variable into two in order to conduct a series of separate analyses; for example, we may have initially measured children's subject choice with six categories: mathematics, chemistry, biology, English, history and art. Subsequently we may wish to conduct separate analyses of those children taking arts subjects, to those taking science. Thus the first three categories could be recoded as science and the second three as art.

Deriving (or 'computing') new variables is a slightly more complex operation – see Howitt and Cramer (2001: 143–6) – but can increase the power of analysis considerably. Suppose that in a data set we had information on the following:

Age
Marital status
Relationship to other household members
Household size
Dependent children

From these a new variable can be derived called 'household structure', which has 12 categories and looks as shown in Box 7.2.[7]

By using this newly computed variable we could produce much more sophisticated contingency tables (and elaborations) than by using its constituent variables alone. Not all computed new variables are as complex as this, though the task of computing any new variable requires some clear logical thinking, so that every case in your data set will 'fit' one or other category.

Generally, the techniques described are quite simple but useful, the real skill lies in knowing what to control for and how to create new variables through recoding or derivation, but most of all in being able to contextualize the results. As I noted in Chapter 2, data do not speak for themselves, they always have a context. In the study of voting above, for example, controlling for sex and then repeating the age analysis might bring us a little closer to the

---

Box 7.2 Household structure

Elderly person (65+) living alone
Elderly married/cohabiting couple
One person in household, younger than 65
2 or more non-married/cohabiting adults in household and no elderly
Non-elderly couple, no children in household
Married/cohabiting couple with dependent children only
Married couple with dependent children and non-dependent others or children
Married couple, no dependent children, with non-dependent children or others, no elderly people in household
Lone parent with dependent children only
Lone parent with dependent child(ren) with non-dependent child or others
Two or more families, most with dependent children, no elderly people
Complex households with at least one elderly person

---

groups less likely to vote – the youngest males in this case. To make sense of this we need to know the cultural context of young males in this particular society. Now it may well be that that other studies have shown that they are more likely to be unemployed, to belong to 'deviant' groups, etc., in other words, they are 'excluded' from civic society. Voting is likely to be irrelevant and unimportant to them. But to demonstrate whether this latter was true or not, we would have to do some further research and ask them.

Statistical significance

At the beginning of this chapter I said that an important thing we wish to establish in data analysis is how well our sample replicates the population. Now you may well believe that in drawing the original sample, if that sample was a large enough number to represent the population, that the work was done (see Chapter 4). Yet error may have crept into your sample as a result of non-response or bias, so that your sample no longer resembles the population. You may therefore want to compare your sample with another (known reliable) sample of the population to see how they match.

Second, you will want to know whether your sample was representative, whether the characteristics of that sample could have arisen by chance or not. For example, if you found that 4 per cent intended voting for an extreme right-wing party, then how 'significant' is this – how much can you trust such a finding to reflect the voting intentions of the population?

Non-statisticians (and even some statisticians) misunderstand what is meant when we say a finding is significant. To say something is statistically significant says nothing about its substantive significance. As Hays (1993: 68) points out, 'Statistical significance is a statement about the likelihood of the observed result, nothing else. It does not guarantee that something important, or even meaningful, has been found.' If our results showed that 4 per cent of the sample intended voting for an extreme right party and a statistical test showed this to be significant, then this may or may not be a substantively interesting finding. In Israel it would not be substantively interesting, where extreme right parties regularly poll in excess of 4 per cent, but in Canada or Australia it would constitute a finding of political importance.

Newton and Rudestam (1999: 68) suggest that we can think of statistical significance in two ways. First, as our ability (I prefer entitlement) to generalize from the sample to the population and, second, as the probability of making an error. In Chapter 4 you will recall I discussed the issue of confidence intervals and 'error'. To recap, if we said that we had a confidence interval of 3 per cent, at a confidence level of 95 per cent, we would be saying that in 95 out of 100 cases the prediction is accurate plus or minus 3 per cent. A pollster who predicts Labour will win 47 per cent on this basis cannot be accused of getting it wrong if they get 45 per cent!

There is no 'right' or 'wrong' answer here, just an expression of the level of confidence we can have in our results. However, (and certainly in political polling) it is unusual to see confidence interval expressed of more than 5 per cent, which means there is a + or − 5 per cent possibility that the result could have occurred by chance.

Hypothesis testing

The context in which we test for error is known as *hypothesis testing*. A statistical hypothesis has the same relation to a research hypothesis as statistical significance has to substantive significance. It may be that the statistical hypothesis being tested will be a crucial test of the research hypothesis, but they are not necessarily logically the same.[8]

Research hypotheses are posed positively – that X effects Y, but a statistical hypothesis is initially posed negatively – hence it is called the *null hypothesis* (its opposite is usually called the *alternative hypothesis*). If something is found to be statistically significant, then the researcher *rejects* the null hypothesis and *accepts* the alternative one.

A research hypothesis might be that among year 11 (UK) pupils there will be a greater level of enthusiasm for science subjects among boys than among girls. Suppose that we can measure enthusiasm in a way that allows us to obtain a mean and we wish to compare the mean of boys with girls, then the null hypothesis would state that the mean for boys on the enthusiasm measure is equal to or less than the mean for girls (in the population from which the sample was drawn). The alternative hypothesis would state that the mean for boys will be greater than the mean for girls.

Assuming we then found that the mean for boys was in fact greater, then we would reject the null hypothesis and accept the alternative one. The finding thus supports the original research hypothesis. As Newton and Rudestam point out (1999: 64), to reject the null hypothesis (and support the research hypothesis) is a risk that we could actually be wrong, but the likelihood of being wrong is expressed as the level of significance of the test. Box 7.3 discusses expressions for the wrong decision in hypothesis testing.

Box 7.3 Type I and Type II errors

You may have read of Type I and Type II errors. These are the expressions for the wrong decision in hypothesis testing. Type I errors are when the researcher rejects the null hypothesis when in fact the findings really confirmed it. Type II errors are when the researcher accepts the null hypothesis, but really should have rejected it. Because of the topsy turvy way statisticians describe these things, falsely rejecting the null hypothesis amounts to saying you were right when you were wrong and is considered a more serious sin than its opposite which might be seen as false modesty – thinking you were wrong when you were right!

Actually it is probably a little unfair to use the language of personal responsibility here. Type I and Type II errors occur as a result a misjudging the significance level or wrongly accepting/rejecting a significance level.

	Null hypothesis (H_0) is:	
The decision	False	True
Reject H_0	Correct decision	Type I error
Accept H_0	Type II error	Correct decision

The null and alternative hypothesis described above are what is known as a *one-tailed test*, because the research hypothesis specifies a directional effect, that boys will express more enthusiasm than girls. It measures only whether one of the distributions differs in a specified direction from the other. Sometimes, however, it is not possible, or we do not wish, to specify a directional relationship in the original research hypothesis, in which case we use a *two-tailed test*. This examines whether the mean of one distribution differs significantly from the mean of the other, but the direction of the difference is not specified. In the above example the null hypothesis would be that there was no difference between the means for boys and girls. Why, then, do we not always use two-tailed tests that do not commit us to hypothesizing a direction? First, theory (and hypothesis) testing underpins the logic of science and a clearer statistical articulation of the research hypothesis is afforded by a directional statement. Second, it is usually easier to show a difference between sets of scores if a directional hypothesis is chosen, because the power of the test is greater. Nevertheless a great deal of exploratory data analysis will be better served using two-tailed tests.

Hypothesis testing is central to bivariate analysis. When researchers run cross-tabulations in SPSS they will usually specify they wish to produce one or more statistical tests. This in itself is not complex and is part of the Crosstabs procedure (for a detailed discussion of hypothesis testing and SPSS procedures see Fielding and Gilbert, 2000: Chapter 11). However, knowing which tests to use and interpreting the results are a little harder.

Test of significance

Tests of significance can be divided into *parametric* tests and *non-parametric* tests. Parametric tests are so called because they make certain assumptions about the parameters describing the population from which the sample is taken. Generally speaking (though this is controversial among statisticians – see Newton and Rudestam 1999: 180–7), they are used when the variable(s) are sampled from a population with a normal, or near normal distribution and are at (at least) interval level. One of the most important is Analysis of Variance (*ANOVA*) which tests for the differences among the mean scores of two or more groups on one or more variables. A common test (or family of tests) encountered in introductory statistics texts are *t tests*. On one sample a *t* test can be used to find out if the mean of a sample is similar to the population and with two samples to see if the mean of the samples is different.

Unfortunately, even if we relax the assumptions about parametric tests, as some recommend, and include ordinal level data, this does not help us with a great deal of the kind of data we encounter in the social world which can only be measured at a nominal level. They consequently require us to use non-parametric tests. Fortunately there are several available (those commonly used include the *MannWhitney U test*, the *Wilcoxon* test and the *Kolmorgorov-Smirnov* test). Only some of these can be used on nominal level data (in this case Kolmorgorov-Smirnov), but the test most commonly used and reported is *chi-square* (written as χ^2). I'll say a little more about this test, because it helps us to grasp the logic of significance testing and many of the general principles can be generalized to other tests (see Table 7.8).

Chi-square is designed to test whether the difference between *observed frequencies* and *expected frequencies* is statistically significant. Recall that a researcher specifies a null hypothesis which states there is no relationship between the two variables (in Table 7.8 between income and university attendance). The expected frequencies are those which would exist if there were no relationship between them. The SPSS output in Table 7.8 shows these (Expected Count). Generally speaking, the bigger the chi-square value, the more confident we can be that there is a significant relationship. However, we need to consider two additional things. First of all, that the

Table 7.8 Annual Income* Attended University Crosstabulation

| | | | Attended University | | |
			yes	no	Total
Annual	under £5,000	Count	1	20	21
Income		Expected count	3.5	17.5	21.0
	£5,000–£10,000	Count	0	29	29
		Expected Count	4.8	24.2	29.0
	£10,000–£20,000	Count	12	95	107
		Expected Count	17.7	89.3	107.0
	£20,000–£30,000	Count	24	101	125
		Expected Count	20.7	104.3	125.0
	£30,000–£40,000	Count	8	36	44
		Expected Count	7.3	36.7	44.0
	£40,000–£50,000	Count	6	6	12
		Expected Count	2.0	10.0	12.0
	More than £50,000	Count	7	6	13
		Expected Count	2.1	10.9	13.0
Total		Count	58	293	351
		Expected Count	58.0	293.0	351.0

Chi-Square Tests

	Value	df	Asymp. Sig. (2-sided)
Pearson Chi-Square	33.647[a]	6	.000
Likelihood Ratio	32.946	6	.000
Linear-by-Linear Association	26.339	1	.000
N of Valid Cases	351		

a. 4 cells (28.6%) have expected count less than 5. The minimum expected count is 1.98.

significance level is acceptable (0.05 or less). Second, the size of the table. The more cells in the table, the greater the chi-square statistic (this is because its value is calculated by taking the square of the difference between the expected and observed frequencies for each cell and then adding up all the differences). In order to know whether the chi-square statistic is significant, we also need to know the number of degrees of freedom in the table. The underlying reasoning of the above description need not concern us – for an explanation see Fielding and Gilbert (2000: 264). What is more important is how to interpret the statistic.

Interpreting the statistic

In chi-square there is no single simple magic number to be read off, the test output needs to be interpreted. We are interested in looking at four things:

- The chi-square value (given as Pearson's chi-square). In Table 7.8 this is 33.647 (the bigger this is, the more likely a statistical relationship).
- The degrees of freedom (given under df). The more categories the variable is broken into, the higher the degrees of freedom. In Table 7.8 it is 6.
- The significance level (this is given in the column Asymp. Sig). This must be 0.05 or less. Notice that in the example in Table 7.8 this is given at 0.000, which means SPSS ran out of space to print the zeros and it is significant at 0.0001!)
- The expected cell count (shown underneath Table 7.8). In the example, four cells (28.6 per cent) have an expected count of less than 5. A commonly accepted criteria is that if more than 25 per cent of cells have an expected frequency of less than 5, then the overall chi-square value is less likely to be valid.

This last output is often taken nowadays taken as a rule of thumb as to whether the other output shows 'significance'. With a little experience you will only need the above information to make a decision about the chi-square test, but if you are unsure about significance you can check it by looking up the previous three outputs in a chi-square distribution table (such as the one given on page 309 in Fielding and Gilbert, 2000). Just look down the left-hand column for the appropriate degree of freedom, look across until you find the reported chi-square statistic, then look up the column to the top to find the significance level.

Though in the example given in Table 7.8 the significance level was 0.0001, there were 351 cases, but 232 of these were in two salary bands, thus there were many cells across the table with very few cases in them – hence 28.6 per cent of cells had an expected count of less than 5 and this was unacceptable. In this example significance was obtained by recoding the salary bands to produce fewer categories, however, the loss of categories produced a table that was substantively much less interesting. Unfortunately statistical significance is a problem for small-scale research and decisions have to be made about whether to present, or how much weight to place on findings that are not significant. Strictly speaking, these should be rejected, but there are some strategies of presentation or analysis that can help under these circumstances. I return to the presentation of numeric data in Chapter 10. One problem that can be overcome (and one not just restricted to small-scale research) is that of 2 × 2 tables where cell counts are sometimes too small to use chi-square. A useful similar alternative called *Fisher's Exact Test* can be used instead. For details of how to use this see Howitt and Cramer (2001: 121–2). A more advanced book of statistical strategies for small-scale research is that edited by Rick Hoyle (1999).

Correlation

Not all bivariate analysis consists of contingency tables with reported significance, as in the previous example. An alternative approach is to use *correlation* to measure the strength of relationships between variables. In this

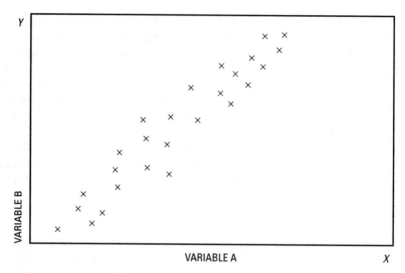

Figure 7.4   *A Positive Correlation*

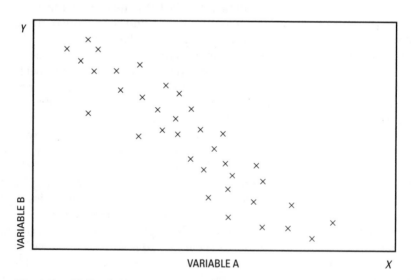

Figure 7.5   *A Negative Correlation*

approach the commonest statistic you will see used and discussed is that of Pearson's correlation coefficient (usually expressed as Pearson's r) which measures the relationship between continuous variables. However, social data can often only be measured at the discrete level (see Chapter 2) and Pearson's r would not be appropriate. Fortunately there are several statistics,

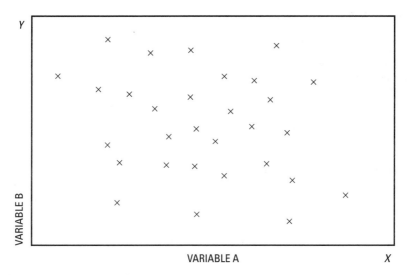

Figure 7.6 *A Zero or Non-Correlation*

which I briefly describe below, that allow us to use correlation with ordinal and even nominal level variables.[9]

The principle of correlation is simple. It measures the extent to which two things are related. If it was the case that the higher Poppleton Univesity students scored in their finals, the more they earned ten years later, then there would be a perfect positive correlation between achievement and earnings – represented as 1. If we then found that the more these alumni earned, the less they gave to charity, then there would be a perfect negative correlation between higher earnings and charity giving, represented as –1. A very strong positive or negative correlation in the data social scientists analyse is not that common and quite often our analyses will produce quite weak correlations, or no correlation at all.

How do we use and present correlation? First, when reporting on research one may say that there was a positive or negative correlation between two variables and just give the figure. This may be produced alongside a contingency table. However, a more powerful visual story can be told by presenting a 'scatterplot'. This also helps us to visualize what is going on when we run a correlation between variables. In Figures 7.4, 7.5, and 7.6 respectively we can see a positive relationship, a negative relationship, and no relationship.

I have simplified correlation here, because I think it is more important to get a grasp of essentials without getting bogged down in statistical detail. As an operation, like so many things in SPSS, correlation is simple and requires the researcher merely to tick a box . There are, however, a couple of other important things to say. First, variables may be correlated, but for similar reasons discussed in hypothesis testing above, the correlation may not be statistically significant. When conducting correlation you need to test for significance, choosing a

Table 7.9 Measures of association (correlation)

Correlation	Symbol	When to use
Pearson's r*	r	On interval or ratio scales. Best known use of correlation.
Spearman's rho*	ρ	Can be used on pairs of ordinal variables, but particularly useful when one variable is ordinal and the other is interval/ratio. Data need not be normally distributed.
Kendall's tau*	τ	Ordinal variables. Use when you wish to compare how similar the orderings are of two variables. Note there are actually three measures: a, b, and c that depend on different assumptions (see Argyrous, 2000: 181).
Phi or Cramer's V	V	These are similar measures. Use on dichotomous variables (male/female; manual/non manual, etc). Cramer's V can be used on nominal variables but can give only strength of association, not the direction (positive/negative).
Gamma	γ	Ordinal variables. Useful for comparing pairs of variables (say, intention to vote with social class) to see whether cases have the same rank on each.

Note: *These are default options when using bi-variate correlation in SPSS. You just choose one of them.

one- or two-tailed test (see sections on hypothesis testing and significance tests above). Again, this operation in SPSS just requires a box to be ticked. Second, there are several different kinds of correlation that depend on the kind of data used – in particular the level of measurement and care should be taken to select the right one in order to avoid a statistical *faux pas* (see Fielding and Gilbert, 2000: 209–18 for a full description of different measures and the procedure in SPSS). These are quite often produced as outputs alongside contingency tables and can be obtained by just ticking the appropriate box in SPSS. Table 7.7 summarizes the characteristics of five of the commonest measures used.

Statistical significance can tell us nothing about substantive significance, but a correlation (provided it is also statistically significant) can tell us how strongly something is associated. It should not be seen as an alternative to significance testing – it is doing a different job and is more of an alternative to or way of summarizing a contingency table.

Multivariate analysis

Sometimes we want to manipulate more than two variables at a time in order to find out whether another variable is affecting the first two. As I have shown, we can do this through elaboration, by 'controlling' for a third variable. Sometimes it is appropriate to produce tables where three variables are cross-tabulated. Quite often such tables are very 'busy' and hard to grasp and an alternative approach is needed. This is a similar kind of problem for which correlation was used to make sense of bivariate data. Multivariate analysis is often based on techniques with a similar kind of logic to correlation.

In this section I'm not going to discuss multivariate analysis in any great depth, because it can be a very complex area and daunting for the researcher just beginning quantitative analysis. Nevertheless multivariate techniques can be very powerful tools indeed and if one does quantitative research for any length of time eventually a research problem will present itself that calls for multivariate techniques. My aim in this section is to give some 'feel' for the logic of multivariate analysis and provide a step to more advanced texts.

Regression

While causal claims are hard to sustain in the social world, the principle of regression analysis is that it can 'determine how far the known data are consistent with a particular causal proposition' (Rose and Sullivan, 1996: 147). It brings us as close as we can get to causal claims in that it can tell us both the nature and strength of an association.

Although regression is the basis of multivariate analysis it can be conducted (as with correlation) with two variables. Indeed, there is little difference between simple regression and correlation.[10] Initially it's a good idea just to think in terms of two variables, though the point of multivariate analysis is to work with three or more variables. The important thing about regression is that it is *linear*. 'Linear' means straight and in regression implies that a straight line can be drawn on a graph to represent the relationship between two variables. It would be as if all the dots on the scatterplot in Figure 7.4 coalesced into a straight line. Regression analysis might then be seen as describing the degree to which data conform to the linear, or 'regress' from it.

Suppose that a dependent variable is graduate income and the independent variable, years after graduation. A perfectly fitting line would 'predict' income to rise from £10,000 at graduation to £30,000 ten years after graduation, because if you know the number of years after graduation you can predict income.[11] Now we know that in the real world graduate income does not rise in such a neat way. Some graduates will earn considerably more after ten years, some less and a few less than £5000. A scatterplot of real graduate income would be very much more dispersed, but nevertheless it would be possible to draw a line on the X–Y axis that showed both the direction (upward–positive) and the strength (the concentration of dots closer to the line).

Now imagine that we knew only the data for graduate income which ranged from £8000 at graduation to £45,000 after ten years and we were asked to 'predict' the income of an individual, all we could do would be to state the mean, which (as I noted above) may not be a very good measure at all if income is dispersed. The addition of a further variable (in this case, years after graduation) helps us to reduce the 'error' we would make in our prediction of a mean income. This is the principle on which regression (and most types of correlation) works and is known as *Proportional Reduction of Error* (PRE).

The addition of the second variable certainly reduces some of the 'error', but the addition of a third or fourth variable may well reduce it even further. Of course it may not, and that in itself becomes interesting.

Multiple regression and models

The principle of prediction and reduction of error remains in *multiple regression*. The $X–Y$ axis, whether the line is 'negative' or 'positive' and the amount of scatter still concern us, but we can no longer visualize a two-dimensional graph (visualizing three dimensions requires us to think of a plane and any more than that induces headache). Indeed, it is worth stepping back and thinking in a more methodological way about what we are doing.

The introduction of a third (or further) variable can be seen as an attempt to 'model' reality. Models are pretty similar to theories (see Chapter 2) in that we propose that the world is like X and then we investigate to see if it really is like X. Models based on regression analysis are a statistical model of reality. A model can never be as complex as the reality it models (otherwise it would be a replication not a model) so it is also a simplifying 'heuristic' or explanatory device. What is gained in explanatory elegance is lost in real-life likeness (I will return to this issue below). The most basic model is a two-variable analysis where we seek to establish the extent to which the independent variable 'affects' the dependent one. Indeed, the independent variable is sometimes called the *predictor* variable. As we saw earlier in the storks and babies example, a dependent and independent variable may well be associated, but this is a spurious relationship. The introduction of further variables should help to explain the relationship between the original two and should as a model is a better approximation of reality. However, rarely will three variables produce a model that is a full explanation and usually several more variables are introduced into the model.

Like most operations SPSS will perform multiple regression for you quite easily, but interpreting the output is harder. If you glance back to Figure 7.7 you will see that Pearson's Correlation coefficient was represented by the symbol r. The level of r shows the level of correlation between two variables. Similarly R stands for a multiple correlation between variables, however, usually the number we are most interested in is R^2 (which of course is R squared) and is called the multiple correlation coefficient. This tells you how much of the variability of the dependent variable is explained by the independent variable. The higher the figure, the more is explained and the better the 'fit' of the model.

Approaches to modelling

In practice researchers use a range of different kinds of model. Which kind of model will be used is determined by the kind of data they have, particularly the level of measurement and the nature of the questions they wish to ask. Examples are path analysis, log linear analysis, logistic regression and principal component analysis. Space does not permit me to discuss these, though once you have grasped the reasoning behind multiple regression it is relatively easy to understand why one would use these approaches and what they can reveal. Multiple regression can be summarized into three 'meta' procedures (Newton and Rudestam, 1999: 252–5).

First, the simplest procedure follows the reasoning described above, the *standard multiple regression* technique. Here all the variables are entered simultaneously in order to evaluate the statistical significance of R^2. No variables are eliminated and the researcher can assess the multiple correlation between the dependent variable and the independent variables and the impact of each individual variable when he or she 'controls' for the others.

Second, the researcher may wish to treat the independent variables as predictors and to see which set of them are best at predicting the dependent variable. The goal here is to maximize R^2 with the least number of predictor variables[12] (the jargon is 'to produce the most parsimonious model'). This procedure is called *stepwise regression* and variables are entered one by one starting with the one that has the highest correlation with the dependent variable and then following with the one that contributes the largest increase in R^2 after the first one.

A variant on this is *backwards stepwise regression* where the independent variables are entered together and the variables which contribute least to the total R^2 are removed first.

Third, and in a much more literal sense of a 'model', the researcher will use a statistical model to test a theoretical model. The choice of which variables are used and how they are entered is not on the basis of their relative contribution to the model, but on the basis of a substantive theoretical reasoning as to their importance. This approach, called *hierarchical regression*, is the closest to classical scientific method (see Chapter 2), but unfortunately, because of statistical assumptions required, it is not always practically possible.

Doing regression analysis is easy, as is the overall reasoning behind it. However, the difficulty lies in interpreting what you have got. For a discussion of how to use both using stepwise and hierarchical methods consult Chapters 28 and 29 in Howitt and Cramer.

Modelling and complexity

Multivariate analysis using linear regression has a number of limitations, some of which are better compensated for than others. The first of these is that the models assume that data are ratio or interval (though sometimes ordinal level data are used). In social research quite a lot of data are at a nominal level and require either different models, or need to be converted into a form suitable for linear analysis. Mostly the latter approach is used and *dummy* variables are created whereby a variable (say, sex) is given a score of 1 and 0. When a variable has more than two values, a series of dummy variables indicating 1 for presence and 0 for absence are used. This method can be somewhat cumbersome and does not permit such a treatment of the dependent variable, so other methods such as logistic regression and log linear analysis are used (see Tacq, 1997: 51).

Factor analysis (actually this presents a whole family of techniques) is used when the association between the variables cannot be expressed as a causal statement (see above) and is suitable when the researcher cannot specify a dependent variable. Factor analysis works on a slightly different principle to standard regression in so far as one starts with a number of variables which are reduced to a smaller number of variables (or factors). It depends on finding patterns in the variation among several variables by looking for inter-correlations (or factors), see Howitt and Cramer (2001: 209–18).

A second problem, both more abstract and contemporary, is the problem of linearity itself. This book, as the reader will have discerned, is methodologically sympathetic to a moderate realism, which depends on the principle that social phenomena have a real existence beyond what any individual may think or wish of them. In recent years several methodologists have argued that the nature of social reality is that it is complex. Now this is not the same as complicated. A jumbo jet is complicated, but a mayonnaise is complex (Cilliers, 1998: 3), that is it has *emergent* properties that are greater than the constituent parts and, in addition this emergence cannot be deterministically known. The General Linear Model (as the family of techniques I have described are known) is based on the assumption of mathematical linearity. A linear relationship, if plotted on a graph, forms a straight line, because the direction and change in one variable are constant in respect of changes in the other. Social relationships, even economic ones, are rarely like this and linear models cannot account for complexity and emergence because we can neither specify enough variables, nor the relationships between them.

There are two things we can do about this situation. First, we can – and this is the normative position I have described in the foregoing – treat the models purely as heuristics that might resemble the world in important ways, or we can attempt to build 'realist' models.

This second approach is one taken by Ray Pawson (1989, 2000; Pawson and Tilley, 1997) and Dave Byrne (2002). The former, as I described in Chapter 2, sees statistical outcomes as evidence of mechanisms, real processes that must be described with the appropriate social context. The latter uses exploratory techniques such as cluster analysis based on analysis of cases, rather than variables, to determine the ways in which individuals are similar enough fall into groups or clusters (see Byrne, 2002: Chapter 6 for a description of this technique). This approach is not so much a modelling of the world as an attempt to describe its general character and brings us closer to the assumptions and reasoning of interpretivism and the pluralistic approaches to research I describe in Chapter 9.

Byrne's approach is both innovative and radical and would require us to rethink much of the basis of our assumptions of statistics and may well be the shape of things to come. I am sympathetic to this approach and have argued for something similar myself (Williams, 1999b). However, further discussion is beyond the scope of this book and it must be assumed that the General Linear Model will continue to form the basis of statistical data analysis for some time yet, even if its results are seen only as a heuristic or are underwritten by a realist approach to context and process, or mechanism.

Conclusion: data analysis as exploration

For many methodologists what is known as '*ex post facto*' hypothesizing is considered to be a fallacious form of reasoning. To explore data looking for patterns and then hypothesizing what this may mean was seen as a form of inductive reasoning that had no means of disconfirmation – an anathema to the theory testing approach of science. Yet as I noted in Chapter 2, this plays down, even ignores, the role of theory building. Karl Popper believed that it did not really matter where one's theory came from (Popper, 1959: 108), but rather how it was tested. Yet where a theory comes from may well impinge upon its quality. If one theorizes on the basis that there is a relationship between X and Y and on testing we find no such relationship exists, what then?

Earl Babbie (1995: 396–7) discusses this question in relation to Samuel Stoufler's wartime research on the US army. Prior to Stoufler's research a number of contentions were influentially and widely held. Among these was the view that soldiers in units where there was little promotion would suffer low morale. Stoufler's research falsified this and the other contentions. He did not end the matter there, but from his data attempted to theorize why this was the case. He found that contentment about promotion was linked to expectation. If you saw promotions in your unit, but were not promoted then you were likely to be less happy than in a unit where people rarely got promoted.

Good data analysis is about exploration[13] and in my view exploration implies both theory testing and theory building. Researchers, once they have mastered the basics of data analysis, can have a great deal of fun simply trying new elaborations or models. Quite often something new or unexpected will emerge, which will lead to more formal testing. Good science is good detective work and a good detective is never constrained by dos and don'ts in thinking. The foregoing chapter has taken us from very simple principles of data analysis to a brief consideration of modelling. Much of this journey was intended to be illustrative, even (to use a currently trendy expression) 'sensitizing', but as I noted at the beginning of the chapter most data analysis is very much simpler. I end then with a piece of advice. To avoid drowning in a sea of SPSS output, do not get bogged down in over-complex data analysis or just do lots of cross-tabs for the hell of it. Explore by all means, but always keep in mind the research question and the *research* hypotheses you are testing – a disciplined creativity!

Try this

> Your research hypothesis is that adults who live alone are sick more often. You have collected data on the following variables: sex, age, household structure (see above), length of time in present household structure, occupation, social class, marital status, ethnic group, place of residence (town/county), type of housing (public/owner-occupied, house/apartment, etc.), days lost from work through sickness in past year, visits to doctor/hospital in past year, medical history (current/past illnesses).
>
> 1 Can you identify dependent and independent variables?
> 2 Suggest some analysis strategies using cross-tabulation.
> 3 Suggest some statistical hypotheses for your relationships.
> 4 Would you use any two-tailed hypotheses?
> 5 Unless you had a large sample the household structure variables would be likely to produce cross-tabulations that were not statistically significant. Given the research hypothesis, could any recoding be undertaken?

Suggested further reading

Most statistics books promise much in terms of accessibility, but just a few pages later they bombard the unwary reader with formulae. At some point I suppose one has to bite the bullet and learn this stuff, but it's more important to get going on data analysis first. Apart from the two data analysis books I refer to above, and the Newton and Rudestam book, there are a few other titles that take the reader gently into statistics. Alan Bryman and Duncan Cramer's *Quantitative Data Analysis with SPSS Release 10 for Windows: A Guide for Social Scientists* (2001) is well written and clear. Similar in scope to Fielding and Gilbert and could have stood in above and might have, except my partner was using her copy and I couldn't borrow it.

A good pop. science introduction to probability and prediction (which is what it's all about) is John Casti's *Searching for Certainty* (1991). Cathie Marsh's *Exploring Data: An Introduction to Data Analysis for Social Scientists* (1988) is now sadly out of print, but is a clear introduction to exploration approaches if you can get a copy. *How to Think about Statistics* by John Phillips (1999) is well-established and gentle introduction to the concepts, formulae and jargon. Among the more advanced books, Nigel Gilbert's *Analyzing Tabular Data: Loglinear and logistic models for social researchers* (1993) is easier than it looks, though avoid being tempted to use the GLIM package – you can do log linear and logistic regression (and all the other fancy stuff) in SPSS. Jacques Tacq's *Multivariate Analysis Techniques in Social Science Research: From Problems to Analysis* (1997) is very comprehensive, though not for beginners, and good on why as well as how.

Notes

1 They may not be individual persons. 'Units of analysis' can refer equally to countries, households, hospitals, etc. They should not be confused with sampling units. A sampling unit may be a household, but the corresponding unit of analysis (sometimes called unit of enquiry) may be the individual.

2 I am assuming here that most questionnaires are paper-based at present. Data entered using CAPI or CATI methods (see Chapter 5) is direct to the data file, though the organizing principles described are very similar.

3 t tests compare means, so data must be at interval or ratio level (see Chapter 2). Much of the data social researchers collect is at nominal level, so a chi-square χ^2 test might be used instead. See later in the chapter and Fielding and Gilbert (2000: 261).

4 In most tables it is good practice to show totals for rows or columns so that it is possible to work out the size of the percentage given. Nevertheless, sometimes, as in the case of Table 7.2, data are aggregated from a number of tables and the figure would not be helpful.

5 Contingency tables are commonly referred to as cross-tabulations (crosstabs for short), though a cross-tabulation can, strictly speaking, consist of more than two variables.

6 In other words hunches!

7 This version of household structure is computed from variables in the England and Wales Census Longitudinal study. For a discussion of its composition and examples of its use see Dale et al. (1996: 24).

8 Their equivalence is much more likely in experimental research than in survey research.

9 Usually nominal level variables are not used, or they must be treated in a special way that involves 'dummy variables'. See Fielding and Gilbert (2000: 281–5).

10 Correlation focuses on the degree to which data points are scattered around a line, whereas regression focuses on the slope of the line.

11 This $x \rightarrow y$ prediction is often expressed as $y = f(x)$. If it were a true causal process y would be a function of x.

12 The maths of some models calls for the *reduction* of a statistical criterion such as R^2.

13 A superb book, sadly out of print at the time of writing is Cathie Marsh's *Exploring Data* (1988).

The Ethics of Social Research

In this chapter:

- Ethical thinking
- Doing the right thing
- Harm
- Deception
- Privacy
- The principle of informed consent
- Can we act ethically?

In Chapter 1 I discussed the importance of objectivity as a grounding for commitment in social research. Objectivity is a social value in the same way that honesty or kindness is, but it also has the property of bringing us to reliable knowledge that can best serve the moral commitment that led us to do research in the first place.

The values that produce commitment drive our research and the value of objectivity helps us to better research, but it is not the only value existing in the research process itself. The difference between value freedom and the kind of objectivity I have argued for is that the former denies the existence of values, whereas the latter acknowledges their existence throughout the research process. When we do research it is not simply a matter of objectively pursuing truth in a social vacuum – the pursuit of truths in the social world is itself a social process with consequences for those it touches.

The whole process can be understood in a context of ethics. To behave ethically is to behave in a way that is considered socially appropriate, but more than that, it is a commitment to certain principles. Ethical principles underpin our moral commitment as citizens and underpin those things we do as social researchers. These principles may not be apparent, they are often implicit. When we make a donation to a charity or campaigning organization, or undertake voluntary work in the community, we do not usually explicitly ground our actions in particular ethical precepts, we just do what we think is right. However, in social research we need to be aware of what it is to act ethically.

In this chapter I want to introduce the idea of thinking ethically when we conduct research. First, I will briefly consider what is meant by 'ethics' and how ethical considerations permeate the research process. Second, I will discuss some particular ethical issues that arise in various stages of research or are associated with particular methods. I will provide some illustrations of what others have regarded as unethical behaviour in research and suggest that in certain areas a consensus of what is and is not ethical behaviour in research does exist. In other areas there is controversy and this is equally important, because every so often researchers must make ethical decisions that they must justify to themselves and others. These decisions are by no means clear-cut, but are a little more readily made if the reasoning for making them can be made explicit.

Ethical thinking

Every society has ethical principles, rules for how one should behave. These change over time and are different between societies. Ethical principles can themselves become precepts in laws or underpin laws. Laws of privacy or freedom of information are derived from ethical principles. In theist societies ethical precepts usually originate in religious doctrines, but in secular society where 'humans are the measure of all things' such certainties are absent, although there may be a quite high degree of consensus about certain things (Downie, 1971). There was, for example, a universal revulsion in the medical profession against the 'experiments' performed on concentration camp inmates by the Nazis and this led to the creation of the Nuremberg Codes, a code of ethics intended to regulate medical research (Homan, 1991: 10). This code has been widely influential since, not just in the medical profession but also in the social sciences.

Mostly it has been philosophers who have attempted to derive meta-ethical principles of ethics, or at least to understand and describe how humans arrive at ethical decisions. The study of ethics is complex, but for our purposes can be simplified into two important, but very general meta-ethical positions, those of utilitarianism and deontology. Each of these has subdivided since they were first formulated (or identified) as first principles and in practice people will often derive particular ethical precepts from both.

Deontological ethics are traceable to Kant (Korsgaard, 1996) and can be summarized as the view that some acts are morally obligatory. Early theist ethics were very prescriptive about what a person should or should not do, but both the sanction to do, or not to do, lay with God. In contrast the Kantian deontological ethic is grounded in a respect for persons and is often described as a rights-based ethic (O'Neil, 1993: 202–4). Kant's injunction was that people should always be treated as ends and never means and is captured in his injunction that one should only adopt and act on principles that everyone could adopt. A 'means to an end', if it violates that principle, by adversely affecting others, would be contrary to such an ethic. It is not outcomes that matter, but the intention to act morally.

Now translated into the language of social research, it means we should not conduct such research that will create harm or distress, even though the outcome might well be beneficial to a wider group. On the face of it, such an approach to ethical thinking sounds at least straightforward, if we apply the Kantian 'test' of how to act. But, as you can imagine, this is rarely the case.

I, like so many social scientists (as well as natural scientists) hold a deontological position toward doing certain kinds of research, that to do such research may either violate the rights of those researched or could lead to outcomes which do so. I, for example, will not conduct research that might benefit certain political regimes or do work involving the armed forces or the defence industry. However, though I take this position, I realize it is not morally straightforward. The example of military sociology illustrates this.

This has occupied a small yet influential place in the sociology of organizations for some time and is exemplified by the work of Samuel Stoufler (see Chapter 7). Stoufler's funding came from the US Department of Defense (Madge, 1963: 287) and of course was forthcoming because it was anticipated that the army would derive some benefit from the research. I do not know whether the army thought it got good value, but what we know now is that his study was a classic in the sociology of organizations. The insights of the research had benefits far beyond those that may have accrued to the army, for example, the way black soldiers were treated within the army helped sociologists to understand ethnic prejudice and discrimination in wider society. Much more recently work by Joan Chandler and Lyn Bryant and colleagues on the integration of women into the Royal Navy (Bryant et al., 1995) and Christopher Dandeker and David Mason (1999) on the issue of recruiting women and ethnic minorities into the British armed forces was likewise funded by those forces. Now here is the ethical dilemma. The bottom line for all armed forces, whatever the justification, is that they exist to use force and, if necessary, to kill. Yet, at the time Chandler and Bryant carried out their research for the British Navy this had been a position that had been fairly abstract, at least since the 1982 Falklands War. Moreover what was learnt by Bryant et al., about the views of the women and the male attitudes toward them has a currency that goes well beyond the Navy. The insights of each of these research projects are potentially beneficial for women and ethnic minorities wishing to enter any organization that has traditionally been dominated by men.

As a social scientist I can see this, yet as a citizen who has opposed nearly every military campaign the British armed forces have been involved in during my adult life, I feel compelled to hold on to my opposition. One could then be uncomfortable with the overall *raison d'être*, but nevertheless argue that the concrete benefits of the research outweighed adherence to an abstract anti-military principle.[1]

The reasoning I outline is a form of the second major strand in ethical thinking – utilitarianism. Utilitarianism itself divides into consequentialism, which can be defined as the morality of an action is judged by its consequences, and hedonism, the view that happiness must be maximized and unhappiness minimized.

Arguably most social research treads a line between hedonism and consequentialism, both in its political motivation and its execution. My own research on homelessness provides an illustration. My entry

---

Box 8.1 Ethics and health promotion research

Is health promotion, like goodness, something we can all favour? Not necessarily, for like goodness a lot depends on who it is good for and what will count as good. Since the World Health Organisation Ottawa Charter of 1986 five principles have underwritten much of Western public health policy: building healthy public policy, creating supportive environments, strengthening community action, developing personal skills and re-orientating health services. However, national and local politics within and outside of health services will provide different expression to these principles. They can lead to local and individual empowerment or they can shift the responsibility from government to provide the economic means for healthy communities to individual responsibility (Sidell et al., 1997:2). The link between adverse socio-economic conditions and poor health will not be broken by the rhetoric of 'healthy lifestyle choices', but it may succeed in shifting the blame on to the individual for his or her fate.

Much health promotion has been evidence based. Evaluation research (see Chapter 9) has been widely used to measure outcomes of particular promotions. Evaluations may measure tangible improvements in the health and well-being of a community, but they may equally measure ephemeral or tangential outcomes. For example, many British health authorities have been anxious to widen participation in breast screening programmes (and have used evaluation research as a means to assess how well such programmes have worked in terms of participation). But, as Alison Dines reports (1997: 118–19), individual participation may only improve one's odds for not getting cancer from 1:2400 to 1:2900; 14,000 women need to be screened to save one life; (in the UK) on average 142,000 women will be recalled with false positives and conversely many cancers will be missed. Against this, for the individual (the stress induced by a false positive diagnosis aside), the benefits obviously outweigh any disadvantages. Evaluation research of participation, whatever its outcome, can be used to promote participation and only research which demonstrates the extent to which such programmes reduce the numbers of cancers can provide a true picture of effectiveness. But if this is, say, a reduction of 1:500 for an individual, does this count as effective, or is effectiveness to be judged in resource terms?

To be a researcher in health promotion and indeed other policy fields is never an ethically neutral activity.

---

into studying homelessness – or more generally housing need research – arose out of a political involvement with the issue before I became a researcher. Much of this work (see Williams, 1999a; Williams and Cheal, 2001) has been concerned with counting how many homeless people are present in a location and is intended to provide data that can inform housing and homelessness policies and in this respect has perhaps been useful. Yet the method I and my colleagues use requires us to record the initials, date of birth and sex of those homeless people observed in particular locations over a certain time period. The recording of these data is often part of the routine monitoring activities of agencies and the homeless are mostly unaware they are being 'counted'. The ethical objection here is that their personhood is violated because things are being done with these data without their informed consent. In deciding whether to do such research one must balance the rights of the individuals and their potential 'unhappiness' with potential 'happiness' that might accrue from developing effective housing need policies.

The short pieces of autobiography above illustrate both how it is possible to be utilitarian about some things and deontological about others, but also how even reasonable liberal academics can mount equally plausible opposite cases. The message is that ethical decisions are often lonely ones and ultimately there is no clear algorithm on what it is to act ethically. Box 8.1 provides another example of an ethical problem.

In the next section I will examine those areas where there has been varying success in achieving consensus about the right thing to do. Sometimes such consensus finds its expression in Codes of Ethics, though quite often these are much more than advice on how to proceed within a consensus and are actually prescriptions on what to do and what not to do. These kinds of prescriptions are not only controversial, they can lead to dilemmas for individual researchers on how to act. I will turn to these now and the difficulties faced by individual researchers in the final section.

Doing the right thing

Many discussions of ethics in social research simply concern the rights and welfare of the participants themselves, while the value commitments which led to the research in the first place are ignored. Psychologists in particular have developed strict codes of ethics to protect participants in research, yet the research they conduct is often controversial. Conversely there are a number of celebrated cases where the opposite has occurred: laudable research aims have driven the research, but the research itself has been marked by ethically controversial treatment of participants. Amongst the most famous are Stanley Milgram's studies of behavioural obedience. In

Milgram's experiments participants were duped into believing they were inflicting increasingly severe electric shocks on other participants. The aim of the studies was to asses the obedience of the participants when asked to administer ever greater 'shocks' to commands from the experimenter. The person receiving the 'shocks' was in fact a confederate of the experimenter and was acting. However, the effects on the participants were traumatic as Milgram himself reported: 'I observed a mature and initially poised businessman enter the laboratory smiling and confident. Within 20 minutes he was reduced to a twitching, stuttering wreck, who was rapidly approaching a point of nervous collapse'. (Milgram, cited in Kimmel, 1996: 59). Milgram did not carry out his experiments through sadistic curiosity, or even in a moral void. His was a genuine quest for knowledge in the context of a post-war society both fascinated and repulsed by (what was seen as) the blind obedience to fascist and other totalitarian regimes.[2] Many argued that if we could understand the psychology of obedience, then we would begin to understand much about totalitarian regimes (e.g. Fromm, 1977; Adorno, 1982).

Though technically one could separate out the ethical decision-making on what to research, from how to research it, but it could be argued that to do so would itself serve to abrogate one's responsibilities to act ethically. In my view the two are equally important, though I accept that, especially in the first case, it is all but impossible to formulate specific advice or prescription on the right thing to do. However, I do believe it should be possible to make transparent the generic questions we should ask when making up our minds about what we should research. This is made both more imperative and more difficult by the current climate of research in most Western countries.

Increasingly there are calls for 'relevant' research aimed at specific economic or social goals (see the example of health promotion in Box 8.1). Much of the sub-discipline of evaluation research rests on the measurement of performance against targets, which in turn have a direct fiscal impact on the funding for those projects (Clarke, 1999). It is not that evaluation or 'relevant' research is bad in itself, it is just that it throws up a huge range of ethical decisions about the aims of the research or the projects which the research serves. Sometimes these are implicitly or explicitly mutually contradictory in their ideological underpinnings, requiring a 180 degree ethical turn by a researcher prepared to work on project A or B. What sort of researcher would that be? The assumption is often of the autonomous academic both free and equipped to make decisions about what he or she will work on, but the reality is, alongside the growth of 'pragmatic' or 'relevant' research, an increasing tendency for researchers to be employed on a jobbing basis, both inside and outside of academia and equally often to be social researchers *per se*, as opposed to sociologists, educationalists, political scientists, etc. (Williams, 2000c).

For many in this position, the choice of what to work on has to be considered against a need to work at all, but even this requires an ethical decision about balancing the interests and welfare of oneself and one's family with a wider and often more abstract interest. The ethical decision-makers are equally those who commission and devise the research. However, deciding whether to work on or commission a project in the first place does not end the ethical decision-making about the nature of the project itself. The following are some of the key generic questions researchers, or those commissioning research, must ask:

How do we decide on the nature/quality of evidence from other studies?

All research must begin from theoretical assumptions (see Chapter 2), but this is not just a methodological issue; it is potentially an ethical one that is closely bound up with that of objectivity. A researcher can think he or she is being objective, but previous data or theories might have been marred by political considerations or poor design/data collection. This becomes an ethical issue when one knows these things to be flawed and data/theories are selected according to their being conducive to what one wishes to find.

What effects will the research have on others?

No research act is socially neutral. The literature in psychology, anthropology and sociology is replete with examples of research that had well-intended aims having serious effects on participants, or others who happened to be in the vicinity.[3] Western researchers in the 'golden age' of anthropology were sometimes the first outsiders some societies had ever seen. The act of research itself fundamentally changed many such societies, both by the contact itself and the recycling of the anthropologists' views back to the societies they studied.

Even fairly mundane research in urbanized Western society can have unintended consequences on others. That research is being conducted at all can focus people's minds on things that might not have occurred to them. In order to increase response rates to surveys researchers often aim for maximum publicity, but the publicity itself brings the issue more squarely into the public domain. Research on fear of crime, for example, can potentially increase fear of crime, though of course to know the latter, further research would be needed!

Community studies, though less popular than they were, often evoke local divisions and passions. These studies examine life, usually in towns and villages, from a number of perspectives. This usually requires the researcher(s) to live in the community, but usually they are not 'of' that community (see, for example, Frankenburg, 1957; Vidich and Bensman, 1960; Payne, 1996). Consequently some members of the community may wish to 'co-opt' them to a particular viewpoint, whereas others either do not wish them to know certain things, or see their community portrayed in particular ways. One of the most celebrated examples of this was Galliher's study of 'Plainville' (Homan, 1991: 5). Although the town's real identity was not deliberately divulged, its identity became known with the consequence that residents complained that the account given stressed its negative and backward features to produce a more interesting account. Although ethical discussions usually cite community studies, this issue can be more widely generalized to organizational studies and social networks.

Should highly controversial findings be published?

Has the scientist the right, or indeed duty, to publish their findings? In an open society this is a difficult question to answer and methodologically can run counter to objectivity. If a researcher finds out X and X will make a difference to future research questions or methods, then surely the researcher needs to put X into the public domain?

This was the view advanced some years ago by the psychologist Hans Eysenck in his intervention in the 'nature–nurture' debate (cited in Morley, 1978: 8–12). In 1969 a fellow psychologist, Arthur Jensen, had published findings on the IQ differentials between black and white Americans. Though not discounting environmental factors, he maintained that on balance the lower IQ scores for the black participants were likely to be attributable to genetic factors. This debate has had social consequences ever since and there have been other researchers, such as Herrnstein and Murray (1994) whose findings have continued to provide ammunition for the political far Right. For them ethnic and gender inequality in society were 'a ratification of "genetic justice"' (Nelkin, 2000: 22). Jensen's findings were published just a few years after the assassination of Martin Luther King and the battle for civil rights was most certainly not yet won in the Southern States. Whether or not Jensen was right, it remained that such findings provided the intellectual justification for racism (see also Box 4.3 for how poor sampling can have consequences for race relations).

We don't really know whether he was right or not, even today. Certainly evolutionary psychologists and some sociobiologists support theories that all but discount environmental factors in favour of genetic ones, but despite the passion with which they are held, they remain unsubstantiated theories (O'Hear, 1997). Furthermore many of those who take the 'genetic' line accept that the difference in genetic make-up between black and white people is certainly not a major component of IQ.

So Jensen was either wrong, or certainly not wholly right, but published his findings with a conclusion that suggested the genetic explanation was right. Perhaps, then, just on the basis of methodological objectivity he should have reconsidered. But is this a case of being wise after the event? I don't think so, because even he admitted his findings were not conclusive and given their potentially disastrous consequences, he should have conducted further work and, as the Popperians would say, subject his hypotheses to the most rigorous tests available (see Chapter 1).

Knowing how 'right' we are is not easy to call and probably only postpones the decision to publish. How much certainty we can attach to findings is a scientific decision, but one with ethical consequences. As in so many areas of ethics, there is not a right or wrong answer, but a balance sheet of consequences to be drawn up.

Often, however, the decisions are made for us. Those who work for governments or even private companies may have restrictions on publishing findings without prior clearance as a condition of funding or employment. The decision then passes into the political arena with the researcher having to decide whether to work on the project at all. Decisions on the publication or suppression of findings are only partly scientific and the decision of the scientist is that of a citizen, albeit an informed one, perhaps carrying a special responsibility for the burden of consequences that may arise (see Williams, 2000a, for a discussion of the scientist as citizen).

> What will the findings be used for and what will others claim on the basis of the findings?

The last question implies a special moral role for scientists. Obviously we cannot always know what findings will be used for. Market research for tobacco companies will clearly benefit those companies and the researcher has to decide whether he or she is in favour of this or not. Yet even here it could be argued that the researcher has a responsibility to at least take into account the fact that this *is* a moral issue, whatever the final decision. However, quite a lot of the time it is quite hard to know how people will use findings, either in their 'raw' state or as the basis for a (perhaps selective) secondary analysis. Every researcher has stories of how politicians or the media have used their findings to advance a particular view, or just simply to create a sensation. My own example concerned a study some years ago, which used longitudinally linked British census data and showed that young people who left Cornwall did better, in socio-economic terms, ten years on than either those who either stayed in Cornwall, or moved in (Williams and Harrison, 1994). The week after publication the *Sunday Independent* displayed the banner headline 'Boffins say "get out of Cornwall"'. Quite apart from my bemusement at being characterized as a 'boffin', I was amazed that in the subsequent weeks local politicians co-opted our findings to support quite opposing views: that Cornish youngsters were too stupid to do well, that they were brighter and therefore leaving; that the outward migration was good for Cornwall, that outward migration was bad for Cornwall!

Martin Shipman succinctly sums up the unintended consequence of a community research project in a small town in New South Wales.

> [Wild] moves there and gets the local paper to publish a description of the work he will be doing for his doctorate. Three years later his PhD thesis is ready and he converts it into a book, carefully changing all names to ensure anonymity. Lawyers work with him to cut out libellous bits. When the book appeared, journalists were not that easily fooled. The headlines in the newspapers soon announced 'THE BOOK THAT SET A TOWN ON FIRE'. Wild writes an apology in the local newspaper. But soon he is taking part in a film of the book and looking back is pleased that he has exposed the pretensions of the 'bosses' and members of the Rotary Club. (Shipman, 1988: 148)

Most of us, however, don't get film offers.

These generic issues can rarely be considered in isolation; one will often imply or be a facet of the other and in none of these issues can there be simple prescriptions. So how then can we make ethical decisions?

Some 'core' issues?

Much of the literature of social research ethics has concentrated on the ways researchers may harm or violate the rights of participants. I want to move on to discuss these, but with two initial caveats. First, that often these can be generalized beyond participants to wider community. Indeed, as I have suggested above, publication and the misuse of findings are potentially damaging for many more people than the participants themselves. Second, despite the attempt to develop the principles concerned with harm or violation of rights into codes of ethics, they can still only help us to become sensitive to potentially harmful effects of our research.

The avoidance of harm

Physical harm is relatively easy to identify and experiments such as the Tuskegee syphilis study (see Kimmel 1996: 3–10)[4] were so obviously deleterious to the participants that a very strong 'hedonistic' argument about wider benefits would be needed to justify them. However, by definition, the 'harm' of psychological experiments is potentially psychological. It seems to me that it took that discipline a long time to recognize this and experiments such as those of Milgram (above) were routinely conducted until the 1970s. Nevertheless it was psychology that first considered harm as an issue in the experiment. Indeed, direct psychological harm is more likely in experiments, yet even self-completion questionnaires have the potential to cause great distress. In 1997 researchers at the Universities of Wolverhampton and Birmingham were forced to abandon a survey researching post-traumatic stress disorder. The self-completion questionnaire was sent to a sample of residents of Dunblane, where a number of children had been shot in the local school some months before.[5] The researchers withdrew the questionnaire and apologized. In this case the potential harm was obvious, but it is not always possible to foresee 'harm', nor is it always clear what constitutes 'harm' , or what is simply inconvenience. Were the residents of 'Plainsville', or those in Wild's study 'harmed' or merely inconvenienced? Nigel Fielding's study of the far Right British National Front (Fielding 1981, 1982) did much to expose the workings of a racist organization and many of those party members who co-operated with Fielding, could be said to have been 'harmed' by his research, but against this, one could claim that the party's racism had a potentially wider harmful effect.

The avoidance of deception

The use of this principle in codes of ethics has created enormous confusion as to whether, or under what circumstances, a researcher can deceive. As with the issue of 'harm', the awareness of the ethical implications of deception arose from psychological experimentation. The consensus among psychologists, at least, is that some form of deception is impossible to avoid in experiments and much of the literature has consequently emphasized remedies that might be applied in experimental research. Singleton et al. (1988), for example, suggest that researchers should do the following:

1   Debrief as soon as possible after the research.
2   Carry out the debriefing slowly and carefully, making sure subjects understood what was going on.
3   Express their own discomfort about using such techniques.
4   Point out that in a good experiment everyone is fooled.
5   Adopt the principle that 'a subject ought not to leave the laboratory with greater anxiety or lower self-esteem than he (*sic*) came in with'.

However, for the most part, these remedies are inapplicable in survey or ethnographic research. Most field research requires that the researcher's identity is concealed, or partly concealed, and the ethics of this have long been controversial (see especially Bulmer, 1982). Debriefing, or screening for harm, is rarely possible and the decision as to whether deception in ethnographic research is justified is one the researcher, or possibly his or her peers, must make.

While some researchers take a deontological view that covert methods should never be used, most do not rule them out altogether. The point at issue is not the deception itself – mild deception, or acting as Erving Goffman (1959) taught us, is part of everyday life – rather it is the harm which may accrue to those being deceived. As I suggested in respect of Fielding's study of the National Front, 'harm' is not always a straightforward concept. Usually, then, researchers will balance issues of harm with those of benefit either to a body of research literature or to particular groups in society.

Second, much depends on the nature of the covert research. Simple overt observations (or 'people watching') in social settings 'deceive' those observed, but the absence of interaction between observer and observed means that harm can only arise from the subsequent reporting and use of the findings (Kimmel, 1996: 134). When interaction is present, particularly when a researcher befriends those researched, perhaps to gain access, then harm is possible. However, arguably, unless such interactions involve specific risks of harm that arise only because the research is being conducted, then the risk of psychological harm is no greater than that likely to exist in any day-to-day interaction. The researcher might differentiate on the basis of known and unknown risks. Hypothetically, a researcher would know that he or she was placing a contact at risk if he or she asked the contact to act as a gatekeeper, when doing so might entail psychological or even physical harm.

Conversely, a conversation with someone during fieldwork could have the unintended effect of changing the latter's behaviour and thus placing them at risk. In the second case such a risk would likely be no more than the person might face in any non-research interaction.

Finally, and at a much higher level of risk is the strategy of 'entrapment'. This is when field 'experiments' 'are conducted to investigate moral character by providing opportunities for subjects to engage in dishonest behaviour or perform otherwise reprehensible acts' (Kimmel, 1996: 151). Usually such research sets up situations which will allow people to cheat, lie or steal in order to observe the circumstances in which people will do such things. Because most university research proposals are now scrutinized by ethics committees or panels, such research is rarely allowed to proceed. However, Allan Kimmel cites Webb et al. as justifying such deception when the honesty of people in positions of public trust are studied, such as taxi drivers, physicians, and automobile mechanics on the grounds that 'these individuals occupy roles that have some bearing on public welfare [and] the potential benefits to society may outweigh the risks involved' (Kimmel, 1996: 153).

The right to privacy

Although an important issue, this is a somewhat less difficult problem for social researchers and most of the time there are clear guidelines, or laws on what must be withheld or disclosed (the Data Protection Act in the UK, for example, or the Freedom of Information Act in the USA). Privacy is more likely to be violated by accident than design, particularly in surveys. Survey data are usually anonymized. This means that respondents are not anonymous, but their identity cannot be discerned from the output from analyses. Unfortunately small cell sizes have the potential to reveal a person's identity. For example, housing need surveys which select a particular neighbourhood for analysis may 'control' for housing type (terraced house, detached house, mobile home, for example) and then cross-tabulate tenure type with household structure inadvertently making visible the household of Homer and Marge Simpson!

Government surveys and censuses often go to great trouble to anonymize records (Dale and Marsh, 1993: 119–25), and sometimes insist on the inspection of any output prior to publication. However, it is likely to be smaller-scale surveys where this becomes an important issue.

Nearly all ethnographic researchers anonymize the individual members of the community and usually the community itself. However, one would not have to have been a super-sleuth to work out the identity of Lynd's 'Middletown' or Galliher's 'Plainville' (Lynd and Lynd, 1929; Galliher, 1964). Individual privacy can be a key issue of harm when deviant groups are studied. Dick Hobb's studies of the criminal and near criminal milieu of London (1988; 1995) necessitated complete anonymity for both 'criminals' and police. It was a difficult feat to achieve without a fictionalization that would undermine claims that such studies are research.

However, the most famous example of social research practice deception is shown in Box 8.2.

Box 8.2   The 'Tearoom Trade'

No discussion of social research ethics can ignore the work of Laud Humphreys (1970). The 'tearoom' in this case refers to men's lavatories where casual homosexual encounters take place. Humphreys, a sociologist, was a participant observer playing a passive role of 'watch queen' while observing the sexual behaviour and characteristics of the participants. What was controversial, however, was that he maintained records of car registration numbers which he then traced to homes of the participants using state police automobile records (ibid.: 38). One year later and as part of a health study he was working on, Humphreys contacted a sample of 50 of the original participants and conducted interviews with them.

The deception Humphreys practised, particularly his tracing the participants to their homes, has been widely criticized for the risk it posed for them and the invasion of their privacy (see, for example, Warwick, 1982). The risks were indeed real in that Humphreys himself notes in, various places, that known participation in homosexual activity in this period (the 1960s) could lead to moral and legal sanctions.

Humphreys' defence of the research was specific in terms of the care he claims to have taken to protect his informants' identity (to get the addresses from automobile records, for example, he posed as a market researcher) and it was general in respect of defending covert research. His argument was that benefits of the research outweighed the risks of the method, particularly that he was able to show that homosexual activity was not just restricted to a discrete minority, but was an activity indulged in by 'respectable' family men. In this respect he may well have been right. The book made an impact not just on social researchers, but as an important contribution to the understanding of the gay community.[6] At the end of the book he asks us to consider whether researchers should ever carry out covert research in sensitive areas. His argument is, as one would expect, in the affirmative, but it remains a legitimate area of ethical debate (see Bulmer, 1982).

The principle of informed consent

Informed consent implies that those being researched not only know that they are being researched, but also that they should be able to comprehend why. As with the avoidance of deception and the right to privacy, informed consent is more possible under some circumstances than others. In the experiment or social survey it is often feasible to explain the purpose of the research without revealing the detail of research strategy. However the issues are how much information one should give and how well respondents/participants can understand the information they are given. Strictly speaking, fully informed consent would place those researched in the same knowledge position, with respect to the research, as the researchers! Clearly this is not feasible, so the researcher must decide how much information to give, but as Roger Homan points out: 'What passes for information is very often no more than a softening up of respondents and a selection of those facts most likely to facilitate access' (1991: 76).

In my experience there is some truth in this and especially in market research where those commissioning the research have commercial interests of their own to protect. Nevertheless the public are less easily fooled than they were, especially when so many 'market researchers' are direct sales-people and not researchers at all (see Chapter 5). Consequently market and social researchers need to win public trust and this is often done by providing the maximum amount of information possible about a forthcoming study. Prior mailshots, newspaper adverts and radio commercials are used to tell potential respondents about the study in order to maximize response rates. Self-completion questionnaires might be sent with FAQ sheets (frequently asked questions) or other information that allows the respondent to respond (or not) after learning more about the study.

The UK Market Research Society insists its member organizations give out a standard information sheet providing information about the generic purpose of market research and providing a contact number where more information can be obtained. This practice, often with specific study information, is becoming widespread, but alongside this, introductory remarks in an interview schedule will often inform the participant of their right to withdraw at any point.

All of this is impossible in covert ethnographic research. By definition there can be no informed consent and the best the researcher can do is to attempt to re-enter the field and de-brief participants, possibly with the help of the original gatekeepers (see Chapter 3).

Although the ability to comprehend the purpose of a study will vary enormously between adults, there are some groups in society, such as children and those suffering from dementia or mental illness, who are seen as being unable to provide informed consent. Informed consent is then by proxy of parents, relatives, carers, etc. imposing a greater responsibility upon the researcher to inform those who give permission.

All of this assumes that the researcher knows the purpose of the data collection. Quite often, especially in large-scale government surveys, the purposes may be multiple, or may only emerge once the data are collected. Censuses are a case in point. Those countries which have a national census usually make it available (in anonymized form) to researchers and even private companies, who will use the data for analyses often not even contemplated at the time of the census. This raises a further issue – that of secondary analysis. While respondents might be informed of the purpose of primary data collection, they cannot be informed of any secondary analysis that might be contemplated in the future. Secondary analysis is more popular than ever and in the UK researchers are encouraged to make their data available for further analysis by placing it in the Essex Data Archive (http://www.data-archive.ac.uk). While the archive itself is subject to ethical procedures, those who participated in the original research almost certainly did not give their informed consent for a secondary analysis to be conducted, which may use the data for altogether different purposes to that of the original study.

Conclusion: Can we act ethically?

Ethics occupy a particularly important place in social research. As I suggested in Chapter 1, social research had its origins in and is still driven by both commitment and science. Our commitment to political and ideological values arises from our being agents in the social world, but as researchers we investigate that social world often to provide information that may help us pursue actions in respect of those commitments. My advocacy of objectivity in Chapter 1 might be said to stress the science, but one can go too far and a lack of commitment leads to a disjuncture between being a researcher and a social agent with beliefs.

Being ethical is about achieving a balance between being an objective researcher and being a morally bound citizen. The difficulty of this is that my moral boundaries are possibly not yours and consequently decisions on what to work on and for whom will vary, that is, assuming we have the choice. All research depends on resources and those who have the power to dispense those resources for research will have power over the research. Now that does not mean that government agencies and charities, etc. necessarily have disagreeable or repressive ideological agendas. The wider ethical implications of most research are more a question of emphasis, that funders favour this programme over that, or prioritize one area of public policy rather than another. Researchers have little power over this process, even if they are senior researchers seeking funds for their own projects and even less if they are researchers who must work on the projects of others in order to make a living.

However, this does not free researchers from responsibility in this area, for there is one position all researchers can agree upon and that is the need for an intellectual open society where one is free to publish the findings of objective research, even if these might be inconvenient to certain parties. As researchers, to be ethical at this level is to try to be honest about analysis, presentation and dissemination and to resist the blandishments or threats of others. It is also about being objective and reflexive about one's own position. Arthur Jensen can be said to have published in the face of opposition, but in this case it was to publish research that was ideologically convenient to him. A reflexive consideration of his position would have led him to admit partiality and an objective view of the research would have led him to stress the fallibility of his findings, that the conclusions were logically possible, but not irrefutable.

Being ethical at this level is about a balance between science and commitment. We as social agents will have commitments that will drive research, but the theories and hypotheses those commitments produce must be rigorously tested if we are to claim to be objective and, as I argued in Chapter 1, objectivity itself is the best servant of commitment, because it helps us to discover error in those views. Ethics at this broader level is closely related to objectivity.

Second, there is no sharp divide between the ethics of the underlying politics and ideology of the research and the ethical practice in method. Both are about the consequences for others of our actions as researchers. Milgram's experiments had consequences at the level of politics and ideology in that they told us much about authority and at the level of method, because of the harm inflicted upon the participants in his experiments. But to contemplate using these methods in the first place implies a consequentialist decision about means and outcomes.

Being ethical at the level of method is both easier and harder. It is easier for two main reasons. One there does exist an informal consensus about what one should and shouldn't do and it is a consensus that has emerged since the controversial studies of Milgram, Humphreys, etc. and places emphasis on avoidance of harm and the informed consent of participants. It is also easier because professional and university codes of ethical conduct will either proscribe or advise against research that offends these precepts. Yet being ethical is also harder, because in order to do certain kinds of research, or possibly do research at all requires a particular reading of such codes.

Clearly informed consent must be violated to do a great deal of field research, yet it is violated to an extent every time we administer a survey. Respondents cannot possibly be informed in such detail as to make them as knowledgeable agents as the researcher himself or herself, otherwise there would not be any point to doing social research, which must (like any other form of science) depend on privileged knowledge. No one would suggest that researchers should not conduct surveys because they violate the principle of informed consent, though many are uncomfortable about participant observation for this reason, but what can count as informed consent is not and cannot be specified as an algorithm. To a greater or lesser extent this is the case for most ethical precepts.

Being ethical is, then, not like being numerate where there are clear and measurable criteria. Being ethical is a much more personal and subjective quality and it is about the realization of oneself as a moral agent and being able to reflexively evaluate the consequences of one's own actions on the lives of others.

Questions for Reflection and Discussion

1 Can the ends ever justify the means in social research?
2 Is secondary analysis free of ethical issues?
3 Can field research ever be ethical?
4 Is the principle of informed consent helpful to researchers?

Suggested further reading

The literature on ethics pretty much divides into the broader, often philo-sophical, questions of ethics and science and the ethics of the methodological approaches themselves. The David Morley edited collection *The Sensitive Scientist* (1978) is long out of print, but very good if you can find it. One of the more sophisticated discussions of science and society can be found in Steve Fuller's *The Governance of Science* (2000). One of the few books on social science ethics that considers political and ideological issues is J. Barnes' *Who Should Know What?* (1979). There are fewer books than one would expect on the ethics of methods in social science, but Roger Homan's *The Ethics of Social Research* (1991) and Allan Kimmel's *Ethical Issues in Behavioral Research* (1996) are very clear and comprehensive. Several professional organizations such as the British Sociological Association (BSA), the American Psychological Association (APA) and the (UK) Market Research Society (MRS) produce codes of ethics. These can be accessed via the organisations' websites:

> BSA http://www.britsoc.org.uk
> APA http://www.apa.org/
> MRS http://www.mrs.org.uk

Notes

1 When you start working for the military how far do you go? In 1999 a veteran US anthropologist caused great controversy when he accused fellow anthropologists of spying for the US military in Central America. He didn't name names, but there are several docu-mented examples: Samuel K. Lothrop spied for the USA in the Caribbean in the First World War and in Peru during the Second World War: Christian Snouck Hurgronje used his knowl-edge of Indonesian Muslim culture to assist the Dutch colonial rulers with counter-insurgency (Bunting, 2002).

2 Few discussions of Milgram's experiments consider why he carried them out. One exception is that of Erich Fromm (1977).

3 There are numerous examples in the Kimmel and Homan books cited.

4 The Tuskegee syphilis study was conducted by the US Public Health Service and began in 1932 in Macon County Alabama. It investigated the long-term effects of untreated syphilis in a sample of 399 semi-literate black men. The subjects did not know they were part of a

study and were even duped into undergoing therapeutic and often painful 'treatment'. The subjects were not told they were suffering from syphilis and although the experiment continued into the 1960s, even by the mid-1940s the mortality rates for the untreated subjects was twice as high as for those who received treatment (Kimmel, 1996: 9–10).

5 Reported in the *Guardian* 15 January 1997.

6 Indeed, though last reprinted in 1974, in the summer of 2001 it was still on sale in gay bookshops in London.

9

Designing Research

In this chapter:

- Resources and research design
- Literature reviews and desk research
- Secondary analysis
- Exploratory research
- Theory testing and theory building
- Problem solving and action research
- Evaluation research
- Multi-method research and triangulation

At first glance it may seem perverse to present a chapter on strategies for designing research after chapters describing methods of doing it and making sense of it. Yet it is important to have some grasp of relative strengths and weaknesses of particular methods, as well as an understanding of theory and data before embarking upon a study design. In the discussion of quantitative analysis in Chapter 7 you will recall that I pointed out the importance of considering how one will analyse the data before designing the survey. This injunction is just as relevant to interpretivist approaches to research. Detailed tape recordings of conversations, for example, can only realize their full analysis potential if there are resources to fully transcribe them, but at the same time such transcription may not always be necessary.

This chapter describes some of the key issues and decisions to be made when designing research. In the first part of the chapter I will consider resource implications and some key elements of design. In the second part I will return to the issue of methodological pluralism, briefly discussed in Chapter 2, but this time in the context of multi-method research designs.

The process of designing research

In Chapter 2 I described the journey from abstract theory to method with the emphasis on testing and developing theory. Though theory (usually middle range) is implicit in all research, the testing and developing of theory are usually the central concern of academic research. The research question in a great deal of public and voluntary sector research is often tied quite closely to immediate and practical issues. These practical issues may not just be about using research to solve a problem (for example, attitudes towards housing development in a community), but about resources – how much money you have and how much time. This, in particular, is a key issue for individual research of the kind conducted by students, both undergraduate and graduate.

Resource issues

The research design adopted will depend on the nature of the research question, the type and amount of knowledge already available on the question and resources for conducting the research and the analysis. While the research design is question-led, it is resource-driven. The analogy might be that of an expensive audio system. Most music lovers know that there are technically near perfect systems that will deliver excellent sound, but they also know they can only afford to pay a certain amount of money for a system. It is OK to start by thinking about the research equivalent of a top of the range system, but at some point the resource implications must be considered and often there is a 'trading down' (though occasionally a trading up) (Hakim, 2000: 150–2).

Resources are not just money, they can be time, equipment, access, skills and expertise. These things are not always apparent when we read a research report or article. Even a Binatone has to be made to sound as if it were a Bang and Olufsen! We do not hear, for example, that 195 people were interviewed because that's all there was time for; that multivariate analysis was not used because the researcher hadn't got that far in the SPSS book, or that two focus groups were conducted, because there was no way they could run to a survey.

I'm not suggesting here that research is usually cheap and dirty. Some is, but a lot is good and makes excellent use of the resources available. Here are some examples of resource implications that need to be considered.

- Depth interviews cost more in time per person than focus groups. If the research is exploratory, then the latter may be adequate, but if exploratory research relies on information from a few key informants, then the group interaction of focus groups is an unnecessary indulgence.
- If it is intended (again in small-scale or exploratory research) to interview just a few people, then a survey is not the best way of doing it. Consider using semi-structured interviews.
- Participant observation can be expensive in time and money. When Dick Hobbs was conducting his fieldwork among East End petty criminals and police officers, he was funded to undertake PhD research (see Chapter 3), but this kind of fieldwork can take months, even years. Paul Siu's study of Chinese laundrymen took 20 years (Siu, 1987). Some observation exercises can be brief, but the question one should ask is whether

such a brief foray into the field is really going to tell you more than depth interviews with key informers?

- When the decision is made to conduct a survey, the inevitable question is, self-completion or interview schedule? Often there are good methodological reasons for using one or the other (see Chapters 5 and 6), but sometimes the methodological desirability of one over the other must be tempered by resource constraints. Interviews take longer, interviewers must be paid and often have to travel between interviews, respondents may have to be tracked down. All of this takes time and money. On the other hand a postal survey will take many weeks. Respondents need time to reply and further follow-up mail outs must be made. If the research is to be done quickly, then in terms of time, interviews will be quicker.

- Open-ended questions are expensive and some market research companies charge clients a premium for each. Generally speaking, the simpler a survey, the quicker and cheaper it is. If you are interested in in-depth opinions of a particular sub-set of the sample, then it is better perhaps to consider a simple survey and follow-up depth interviews. Don't make a survey do too much 'qualitative' work.[1] The opposite is also true. Going along to conduct depth interviews with lots of standard questions begs the question of why a survey isn't being used.

- When designing the survey consider that you (or someone else) have got to analyse it and even with new versions of SPSS, the data have to be entered and 'cleaned', variables defined, labelled, and so on. Once the tables start rolling out they have to be interpreted. Don't ask more than you can analyse, but also be careful to ask all you will need![2]

These do not exhaust resource questions by any means, but perhaps give a flavour of how to tackle them. Most importantly these things must be costed for money, time and material resources. For example, if one is using interview schedules try to work out how long each interview will take, consider travelling and contact time. How long will the, say, 300 interviews cost in person days and how much does an interviewer cost per day? Remember interviewers often need to make more than one call at an address before they are able to make contact with the respondent. How many interviewers can be afforded? In most studies labour costs of researchers, interviewers and clerical staff will account for two-thirds to three-quarters of total budget. If data are to be transcribed from depth interviews, focus groups, etc., then how long are the interviews and how long will it take to transcribe each? Is there access to (and skills to use) NUD*IST or Nvivo?

Just occasionally resources do not exist to do the research. By this I mean that in order to answer a research question a particular design is necessary. But the resources to carry out the research, using that design are unavailable. If a cheaper alternative is proposed, it may give the appearance of answering the question (particularly to lay persons), but it is bad research. During the course of writing this chapter I was contacted by a certain British county council who had not got time to conduct a survey on residents' views on council services, but proposed that instead I might like to organize two focus groups ... to gauge the views, attitudes and opinions of over 250,000 electors! If this were possible, then surveys would be pretty well redundant.

Literature reviews and desk research

However elaborate or simple the research design, the starting point must be finding out what has been done, what is known already about the subject and indeed what kind of methods have been used in similar studies before. Market researchers call this beginning with 'desk research' and academics refer to 'literature reviews' (Fink, 1998). The kind of 'desk research' or 'literature review' undertaken will itself depend on the research. A researcher in a local council whose brief it is to find out citizens' views on housing development would search for studies in other communities, especially looking at the ways in which the public were consulted. The search would not usually take her into the academic literature of community studies/urbanization/counter-urbanization, etc. However, an academic researcher who wanted to examine the social relations of property development in a community would examine a wider literature on the built environment, the political economy of local capital and the social relations of spatial communities. See Pratt, 1994, for an example of this.

As a rough rule, the more academic or theoretically ambitious the study, the deeper and wider the literature review. Academic research usually requires a thorough search of electronic databases such as the Web of Science http://wos.mimas.ac.uk or Scirus http://www.scirus.com/.[3] Though this is nowadays unavoidable, it does not exhaust the search possibilities; moreover, some experience and skill is often required to find the literature in a particular area. One cannot be too literal: entering the search terms 'housing and health' will produce some hits, but a bit of lateral thinking might be required, say, by thinking of what kind of health problems poor housing might create (e.g. respiratory illnesses) in order to search that literature. I have often found that once a few papers have been identified it is then possible to follow up other material through looking at their bibliographies. Eventually the same papers will start to make a number of appearances and one gets some sense that the key literature has been identified.

Literature reviews or desk research will often change the shape of the research, by changing the research question or suggesting a different methodological approach. Sometimes, like Scott of the Antarctic, you will find that someone else got there first. Some years ago, when working freelance for a market research company, I remember talking myself out of designing a survey of consumer preference for vacuum cleaners by discovering that there was plenty of research already available! It is at this point that secondary analysis may become a viable option.

Secondary analysis

Secondary analysis is the further analysis of numeric data or texts (the latter might be interview transcripts, etc.). In most medium-sized or large studies a great deal more data are collected than are analysed to answer the original research question and in some cases (national censuses, for example), there is no research question as such and the data are gathered as a multi-purpose resource. Often such data sets (the ONS Longitudinal Study or the Sample of Anonymised Records are (British) census data sets specifically intended for secondary analysis (see Dale and Marsh, 1993; Dale et al., 2000). Such large data sets contain scores of variables and usually data are collected from large national samples. Provided the original questionnaire (and you should look at this first!) contained questions that translate into variables that will answer your research question (or you can compute or recode new variables from these), then secondary analysis is an enormously powerful tool.

In the UK, the Essex Data Archive (http://www.data-archive.ac.uk) holds thousands of data sets, quantitative and qualitative, of various sizes and ages that are available to researchers to use. However, some caution is needed in using secondary data. Not only does the researcher inherit the data and its analysis potential, but also any difficulties of sampling, bias, poor question design, inaccurate data entry, etc. These are things that it is important to find out about before embarking upon the further analysis of a data set. While the original research might have directly asked question(s) of interest that will become dependent variables, the type and range of the independent variables will severely restrict analysis. If, for example, you wish to know about home ownership, the UK Census provides data on who owns their home, who has a mortgage on their home and who rents publicly or privately, but if you want to know how ownership might be related to earnings, then Census-derived datasets are no use to you because the Census contains no income data.

The whole research project may be based on secondary analysis and if it is and survey data are used, then much of what was said in Chapter 7 still applies, as does the link between theory and data and its later presentation. The main difference is that somebody else collected it (see Hakim, 1982; Dale et al., 1988). One last point: not all secondary data are equal. Data archives, such as that at Essex University, hold many data sets of varying sizes. Smaller data sets will be less useful, because of small sample sizes, geographic clustering, or a limited range of variables. They are also unlikely to be of such good quality as data sets derived from large national studies. The latter are better resourced and based on larger samples, (often) better trained inter-viewers and have been more thoroughly piloted.

Exploratory research

Strictly speaking, literature reviews and desk research are exploratory research and they can shade into secondary analysis. The latter may be used in an early exploratory phase of research, but exploratory research is usually employed when one wishes to begin work on a little researched area, or is developing methods for a later more formal study. Thus exploratory research is often the precursor to a larger project, or even a multi-faceted research programme that investigates several different, but related areas.

One may employ any kind of method for exploratory analysis (see Box 9.1), though elaborate surveys would be very unlikely. Mostly informal interpretive methods are used, interviews with key informants or possibly focus groups. The exception to this may be when one wishes to test specific techniques or methods, such as scaling devices (see Chapter 6) or less used interpretive methods such as video.

Box 9.1 Exploratory research: homelessness in Plymouth

In 1994 the University of Plymouth undertook a preliminary exploratory study of the subject that became a multi-method study to quantify and describe homelessness in the city (Williams and Cox, 1994; Williams et al., 1995). The study was later extended to the south coast resort of Torbay.

The exploratory research primarily aimed to discover what data were collected on homelessness in the city and the methods of collection employed. A secondary aim was to raise awareness of the research among the various agencies that would later be asked to assist in data collection.

The exploratory research took approximately seven weeks. Initially a researcher contacted a list of agencies[4] (supplied by the local council) and asked them (a) if they collected homelessness data; and (b) if they did, to provide their data for the previous 12 months. At the same time the researcher arranged a time to meet with representatives of the organization when she undertook informal depth interviews to explore the nature of the agency networks among the homeless in the city and to identify the key personnel who could participate in later data collection, or act as 'gatekeepers' to homeless groups.

Finally, a review of homelessness data from other similar-sized cities and urban homelessness research in the UK was undertaken.

Exploratory research can be about developing ideas, or just testing hunches, though the example in Box 9.1 is mostly a data inventory. Nevertheless the methods are often quite informal. It is probably unnecessary to transcribe interviews, for example, and the kind of theory – method link that I discussed in Chapter 2 will be less explicit or developed. Against this relaxing of theoretical and methodological conditions, it is also illegitimate to claim too much from exploratory research. Often it is not published and in a university if it is, it is often as a 'working paper' (see Chapter 10). Some exploratory research can actually finish at that stage, or it may suggest a completely different direction. However, as with a literature review, it is a crucial step if one is not to waste time later re-inventing the wheel, or repeating the mistakes of others.

Theory testing and theory building

This is the approach to research that underlies most academic research, though many humanistic researchers would see it as an overly scientific way of describing what they are doing. Nevertheless, even in field research – unless the study is very exploratory – there will be some ideas or a likely focus of interest that will drive the research. Such conjectures will be found to be wholly correct, partly correct, or incorrect. Usually, in quantitative research, direct tests of a hypothesis will demonstrate a statistical relationship, or lack of it, but there will rarely be a stark confirmation or disconfirmation. In interpretive research (and some quantitative research) specific directional hypotheses are not often used, but rather the researcher begins with some background knowledge of the setting and addresses a number of questions implied by a broader theoretical framework. For example, Angela Bolton and her colleagues have used photographic techniques to study young people's workplaces. In some ways the use of photography is exploratory, but under-lying an openness to the data are certain theoretical assumptions. The deci-sion to photograph how 'The bundles of towels accumulated in the back room of a hairdresser's contrast with the row of neat hairdryers and styling tables' (Bolton et al., 2001: 512) suggests a prioritization of those things the public does not see, but are possibly the most central part of the reality of the young people who work there. Indeed, one could theoretically locate it in Goffman's notion of 'front stage' and 'backstage' roles (Goffman, 1959). The research helps us to build theories of young people in the workplace through descriptions of the workplace.

Theory testing and theory building usually imply each other, though there may be a methodological emphasis on one rather than the other. Theory building and exploratory research also merge into each other, though with some approaches to theory building, such as grounded theory (see Chapter 3) the approach is far from informal. Nevertheless, a great deal of theory build-ing is done using interpretive methods, though theory testing can employ either. In the latter case decisions about which methods to use in the design will depend on whether theories concern conditions, behaviour or meanings and how its possible to study them.

Problem solving and action research

A great deal of bread-and-butter research involves problem solving and though it is certainly not atheoretical, it is often about gaining information about a problem or problems, in order to provide a resolution. The problem–research link is at its sharpest in action research. Here researchers work within a community and provide direct feedback to the community, or its leaders, activists or policy-makers. The aim of research is not primarily to build a stock of knowledge for its own sake, but to use knowledge for action, which in turn creates further experiential knowledge. Box 9.2 shows how this can be done even in the relatively domestic setting of a block of apartments.

Box 9.2   Action research

Goode and Bartunek (1990) describe research the former conducted in an apartment block where she lived. Problems of mail security had been a source of concern to residents for some while and blame for these problems had been directed at the caretakers. Goode initiated an action research programme by first of all talking to a group of residents, explaining what action research is and what could be done. This small group of collaborators then undertook the research, which, first, sent an information letter to residents, and then conducted initial interviews with residents and caretakers. Third, they set up an information session for any interested parties and, finally, interviewed all of the interested individuals. Data produced was analysed under headings such as organizational strengths, existing mail security problems and existing group structures and problems. Once these things had become transparent it was possible to set up task forces to address particular issues.

The researcher in this case was uniquely privileged in that as a long-term resident she had credibility with the neighbours, but as a researcher she had the skills necessary to initiate a specialist task. (Coghlan and Brannick, 2001: 57–8)

Action research is to more theoretically driven social research perhaps what technology is to science. Relatively well-tried techniques are brought directly to bear on problem solving, somewhat like conducting a geological survey in order to understand why mining activities are causing building subsidence.

Action research is not always appropriate for problem solving. Usually it is conducted at a relatively micro level and can tell us very little about (or help us address) problems in a wider context. It might be conducted in a rundown housing estate in order to improve the physical environment, but this alone could do nothing to resolve underlying social structure problems such as high levels of unemployment. There is also the question of whose side the researcher is on. Quite often action research is not initiated by communities,[5] but by outsiders who both perceive a problem and provide resources to research and solve it. As Matthew David (2002) observes, the interests of each group and how these interests are perceived may diverge and become a source of conflict.

For these and other reasons not all problem solving research is action research and the information–problem tackling chain may have a lot of links in it. Moreover the research itself may highlight different problems from those anticipated. Problem solving research is usually in the public or voluntary sector and is most often *ad hoc*, though like other forms of research may have an exploratory phase or use secondary analysis. Research I conducted for Guernsey States Education (Williams and Williams, 2002) was motivated by earlier research using Census data which showed that Guernsey-born citizens were less likely to occupy professional or managerial positions than migrants to the island. This prompted a more general concern about the skills base of the islanders and, as a result, a survey of qualifications and education, along with attitudes to these, among a cohort of adults educated in Guernsey, was undertaken. At the time of writing the research is being debated by policy-makers, but it does demonstrate the existence of a skills deficit and confirms the earlier research. Note that while this research is clearly about finding information about a problem, it contained elements of secondary analysis and testing. Research designs, like so many other things in research, are ideal types.

Evaluation research

This is certainly so in the case of the divide between 'problem solving' and 'evaluation research'. While the former need not be evaluative and may employ the logic of testing or exploration, evaluation research might be said to be about problem avoidance through increasing efficiency or satisfaction. Evaluation research can be described as research which evaluates the impact or effectiveness of social interventions. It is a design, or indeed some might argue a method, of research (Clarke, 1999) that is very important in the public sector. Evaluation research has become very big business indeed in the past ten years and is used widely in health, education and local government.

Its origins go back to the early days of scientific sociology in the United States and to the advocacy by Francis Chapin of the use of experimental methods in the evaluation of public policy (Oakley, 2000: 168). Indeed, evaluation research is well suited to the experiment, or quasi-experiment (see Chapter 5), because it allows the comparison between where an intervention has been made and where it has not. An old evaluation experiment, though in a subject area as relevant today as it was when conducted in 1967, is described by Ann Oakley (2000: 247–8). At this time in the USA physics teaching was becoming regarded as stale and a new curriculum was proposed in order to attract students back to the subject. In this evaluation experiment a group of teachers were randomly assigned to teach the new curriculum and another group (the control group) taught the old one. Though no difference between the groups in cognitive performance was found, the new curriculum was found to be more enjoyable for the students, but, as Oakley remarks, this may have had something to do with the enthusiasm of the teachers for the new curriculum.

Evaluation research has become controversial and this is mainly because of what it measures and for whom. The problem of not really knowing whether it was the intervention or something else that created the effect is a criticism of experiments in general and particularly those used in evaluation research (see Chapter 5). However, this is not a difficulty restricted to experiments but one that afflicts, to one extent or another, any inferred relationship between a dependent and independent variable. But not all evaluation research is about experiments. Much of that conducted nowadays measures effectiveness or satisfaction. Effectiveness can be satisfaction, particularly in the evaluation of services provided to a community. In the UK the 'Best Value' initiative places not just emphasis on financial effectiveness in local government (and increasingly the public sector generally), but how effective councils, health authorities or other quasi-governmental bodies are in delivering services (Martin, 2001).[6] Tracey Collett carried out an evaluation of the housing services of a British local authority (Collett, 1998). The methods she used were the standard ones of focus groups, depth interviews and questionnaires. Much of the focus was on client satisfaction with the services, but in housing services (as in many other areas) this is hard to measure. The allocation of scarce public housing, for example, will leave those who got the housing they wanted happy and those that didn't, unhappy. There is hardly any situation when this would not be the state of affairs and says nothing about the quality of housing services. Thus, Best Value in housing services has to be measured by other indicators, such as length of time a client had to wait to get an appointment, the efficiency of the council officer and effectiveness or clarity of arbitration procedures.

Many public programmes and indeed university curricula are designed on the basis of measurable outcomes. The difficulty is knowing what counts as 'effective' outcomes, with the consequent temptation to measure only those things easily measured or politically convenient. This if X is an outcome and X is achieved, then this counts as success. Good evaluation research, however, is not about counting ticks in boxes, but as Ray Pawson and Nick Tilley have argued (1997: 216) also about shaping the underlying processes and structures, about understanding the outcomes of initiatives and how they are produced. Furthermore, not all evaluation is 'summative', that is measuring outcomes, but may instead be 'formative', whereby feedback is provided to 'people who are trying to improve something' (Scriven, 1980: 6). This type of evaluation is often quite informal, normally using interpretive approaches and built into the day-to-day activities of the service or project being evaluated. In this respect it has parallels with action research in that it provides an interactive information–change process.

Multi-method research

It should be apparent from the foregoing that good research design should not eschew any form of method or combination of methods. The aim is to produce the best possible answer to the research question. This is the principle of methodological pluralism, but it also implies that one should be ready to use more than one method in research. In the second section of this chapter I want to look at how we can combine methods in a design and the possible advantages and pitfalls of this. Multi-method research can imply a number of approaches from the relatively informal use of more than one method to the much stronger ontological assumptions of the triangulation of methods whereby interpretive and quantitative methods are used to corroborate each other.

These two opposites help us to frame what is intended when more than one method is used in research. The commonest use of multi methods is (a) to use interpretive methods to provide the basis for a survey or (b) to use interpretive methods to broaden or deepen the findings of a survey (see Hammersley, 1996, for a discussion of typologies of multi-method research).

The use of focus groups, depth interviews and observations allows the researcher to produce surveys that are more likely to be grounded in the everyday experiences, expressions and meanings of those researched. A survey is much more likely to be successful if its construct validity is under-written by prior interpretive research. This is especially important when it is intended to use a survey with a group with particular cultural characteristics. For example, surveying teenagers (or even talking to them at all!) without a ready appreciation of their ever changing argot is hazardous. At the time of writing the judicious use of the words 'bad' , 'skanky' or 'cool' will do much to reduce non-response – though by the time you read this all may well have changed. One 16 year old of my acquaintance assures me that a survey question addressed to his (male) contemporaries about their musical tastes should ask 'what genre' they are in to. This is not a word I would normally use in questionnaires, but I'd be willing to give it a go in a pilot!

Though it is not always possible (for resource reasons) to begin with inter-pretive research, it invariably improves the validity of surveys (or even experiments). Indeed, one could turn the matter on its head. If we do not conduct interpretive research first, then from where do we get the concepts and language we use in surveys? Either from previous surveys, or informally from what we 'just know'. The former assumes a conceptual and linguistic validity in the earlier survey (and its transferability to the current one) and the latter assumes cultural proficiency in the population to be surveyed. These may be reasonable assumptions, but good science would test them!

Using interpretive research to follow quantitative research was once less common, as Alan Bryman (1988: 137) noted, yet this strategy does permit a detailed exploration of meaning and context and is increasingly used in large-scale studies. The Chicago Urban Poverty and Family Life Study (Wilson, 1997) used two surveys: a large-scale survey of inner city residents and a second survey with a sub-sample of the very poorest people. The researchers then conducted two very large ethnographic studies. The first comprised interviews with 99 respondents from two very contrasting neighbourhoods. Sometimes several interviews were conducted with the same respondent. Finally graduate students were employed to walk around the neighbourhoods observing and getting into conversation with the residents.

This study, though very much in the tradition of US urban sociology (Lindner, 1996), is perhaps unusual in the breadth and depth of data yielded, but even small-scale studies can usefully employ interpretive methods after survey work to amplify responses or resolve anomalies. Housing need studies, for example, will often use a community survey to establish the extent and nature of housing need, but this will be in respect of standardized categories. Depth interviews which explore housing histories and their relationship to factors such as household circumstances, health and illness or employment help researchers make sense of why different groups express housing need (van Zijl, 1993).

Increasingly researchers use a variety of methods to discover different aspects of the research question. However, in these forms of multi-method research, while there may be a weak transferability of findings from one stage to another, so that findings from later depth interviews will be in agreement with and expand upon the results of earlier attitude statements in a survey, there is usually no claim that the resulting sum is any greater than its parts.

However, the second and much more sophisticated version of multi-method research seeks to improve the validity of the research (and therefore its believability). It makes much stronger claims about the logical relationships between the methods. For many this *is* multi-method research and it is indistinguishable from triangulation. It is described by John Brewer and Albert Hunter as a means '*to attack a research problem with an arsenal of methods that have nonoverlapping weaknesses in addition to their complementary strengths*' (Brewer and Hunter, 1989: 17 [emphasis in original]).

The term triangulation originated in trigonometry where it is a method of calculating the distance to a point by observing it from two other points. The best-known advocate of triangulation in sociology is Norman Denzin (1978, 1989). He describes two main approaches of *inter*-method triangulation, including two or more methods, and *intra*-method triangulation which uses two or more techniques or variants of the same method.

The use of inter-method triangulation more obviously conforms to Brewer and Hunter's maxim above and would usually employ contrasting interpretive and quantitative methods to attempt to eliminate the weaknesses of each. Intra-method triangulation recognizes that even within a particular method, weaknesses can be exposed by using different variants. In Collett's 'Best Value' research, described above, a sample of focus group members were recruited to take part in depth interviews in order to control for the problems inherent in the group dynamics of focus groups (see Chapter 3). Similarly one could combine interview schedules with self-completion questionnaires, covering the same topics but possibly using different scaling techniques. Denzin's concept of data triangulation is elaborate and includes replications of studies in different settings, micro and macro level research.

The aim in both is to produce data which show agreement (or not) between methods. This can be achieved more rigorously nowadays with the use of sophisticated coding techniques developed by interpretive researchers for use in applications such as NUD*IST and indeed the analysis potential of triangulation has been further enhanced with the possibility of importing data from NUD*IST into SPSS and vice versa (see Richards and Richards, 1994, for an early example of using NUD*IST in combination with survey methods).

Denzin also recommends the use of more than one researcher in order to provide different perspectives on the research question. This can be very valuable, both at the fieldwork stage of interpretive research, but also in the analysis and interpretation of data. This issue does not arise in the administration of interview schedules because these are standardized.[7]

A third type of triangulation is theoretical triangulation. Actually this a grand name for an issue which has been around a long while in natural science (Hacking, 1983: 12–15) and quite a while in social science, but in both cases it is rare because it involves the interpretation, or analysis, of findings from quite different theoretical perspectives. This is perhaps more likely at the level of secondary analysis than primary which would almost certainly involve the posing of the research question in quite a different way depending on the theoretical perspective. In other words, the theoretical perspective will influence the type and way the data are gathered (see Box 9.3).

Box 9.3 Triangulation in transport research

Cunningham et al. (2000) discuss the use of methodological triangulation in transport research. In order to successfully market their services and to develop management strategies for them, transport providers need to understand how consumers evaluate the quality of their services. Yet customer evaluations of service quality are difficult to measure with just a single method. Instead data were collected from the general public as well as from transportation officials using surveys, focus groups and an analysis of 'critical incidents'. The results showed the areas of transportation activities with which respondents were currently satisfied or dissatisfied. The consistencies as well as the inconsistencies between the results of the surveys and focus groups from the two groups of respondents allowed a comparison of the relative importance of the services provided.

Brewer and Hunter's assertion that 'Multimethod research tests the validity of measurements, hypotheses, and theories by means of triangulated cross method comparison' (1989: 83) sounds like a recipe for rigour and indeed this can be so, but a number of writers have warned confirmation obtained in this way may be the result of a commonality of error in initial conditions (see, for example, Seale, 1999: 56–61 for a discussion of the objections). If, for example, the initial survey sampling was flawed, then any checking of measurements, hypotheses and theories in, say, depth interviews with a sub-sample will be invalidated by the initial sampling error. Conversely if there is a disagreement between findings obtained in method one and two, can it be established which was wrong?

In either inter- or intra-method research there is no guarantee that one is a check on the other, or one validates the other. Nevertheless a commitment to methodological pluralism and a degree of methodological modesty about the possibilities of one or other method, does have the potential for better research design. The *moderatum* generalizations derived from interpretive research (see Chapter 3) can produce testable hypotheses for a subsequent survey and the puzzles generated in the analysis of survey findings can often be resolved by micro-level research.

Conclusion

Every piece of research is unique, because by definition each tackles a different research question, or in the case of replication of research, the same question in a different place or time. This means that every design is a bespoke one and a generalized specification for research design, or designs, cannot really be produced. Yet every research design requires the researcher to tackle some of the same or similar questions about what research has been done before, what is the most efficient method or methods and how these can be balanced against available resources. In my view, when considering these things one should remember that as a researcher one is a scientist and although all scientists face resource questions, astronomers cannot study the heavens with binoculars, nor biologists micro-organisms with a magnifying glass. In all of our decisions about design, we should not lose sight of the importance of matching the method, or methods, to the question. The methodological pluralism I advocate in this book is not simply a liberal doctrine of breaking down methodological barriers, but also a recognition of the limits of methods. Good research design is about knowing the limits and possibilities of each methodological approach and selecting these in the most efficient and resource-effective way.

Box 9.4 shows the ten questions to ask when designing research.

Box 9.4   Ten questions to ask when designing research

1   Are you clear about what is the research question?
2   How big is the project – is it part of a broader research programme with wide research aims or is it single one-off piece of research?
3   Is it exploratory or does it have an exploratory phase?
4   What is the logic of the research: theory testing, building, problem solving, evaluating?
5   Is the emphasis on characteristics, behaviours, meanings or underlying mechanisms?

---

6 What is the 'unit of analysis' – individuals, households, events?
7 Which method or methods might best provide data?
8 What is the time scale for the completion of the research?
9 What is the budget and what resources will this provide (inter-viewers, support staff, computers, facilities/expertise available for analysis etc.)?
10 What is the relationship between the resources available (8, 9) and the design emerging from 1–7?

Try this

Greenburgh is a city of 250,000 people who live in 12 wards of approximately equal populations. In recent years the city centre, which lies in a valley, has become heavily polluted and congested with traffic. Parking is inadequate. The city council believes there are two possible solutions to the problem: (a) to develop an 'inner orbital road' with several Park and Ride schemes that would use buses to transport commuters into the city centre or (b) to develop a comprehensive urban transport system (mainly bus-based, but with an east–west light railway) and city centre vehicle restrictions. Solution 1 is slightly more expensive. It is anticipated that the first solution would be more attractive to those commuting from outside the city, but the second more attractive to the citizens of Greenburgh.

Your research company is to bid for the contract to measure public opinion on each of these solutions. The population is that of Greenburgh and the surrounding commuter belt. The population of the commuter belt is around 130,000. The city council is concerned that the research should be both accurate and as cost-effective as possible. Draw up the initial parameters of a research design. If you are working in a class, it might be more interesting to divide into two groups and produce rival 'bids'. If you have access to local research costings, try to build these in and produce outline costs.

Suggested further reading

Many books on research design are in fact methods books in disguise, though it is hard to discuss design without discussing methods. I have found the Catherine Hakim book mentioned above, *Research Design: Successful Designs for Social and Economics Research* (2000) addresses design issues very centrally. John Brewer and Albert Hunter's book, also mentioned above, *Multi-method Research: A Synthesis of Styles* (1989) is the 'classic' work on multi-method research, though, in my view, the authors conflate the concepts of multi-method and triangulation. Abbas Tashakkori and Charles Teddie have more recently produced a similar, but perhaps slightly more pragmatic book *Mixed Methodology: Combining Qualitative and Quantitative Approaches* (1998).

Notes

1 Although I have mostly used the term 'interpretive' throughout the book to describe interpretive/qualitative/ethnographic approaches, in survey research it is standard practice to use the term 'qualitative' in relation to open-ended questions.

2 Unless you anticipate returning to further analysis at a later date.

3 Arlene Fink (1998: 33) provides a list of some key US databases, though the availability and nature of web-based resources change rapidly, so any suggestions in books are likely to have a limited life.

4 'Agency' in this case was broadly defined as all those statutory and voluntary organizations that would have contact with the homeless. These ranged from council housing services and social services to housing charities, the police and the health service.

5 By communities here I do not just mean physical communities, but any community of interest, from the inhabitants of a housing estate to the employees of a large corporation.

6 This paper is an introduction to special issue of Policy and Politics partly given over to a discussion of Best Value.

7 However, while the instruments themselves are standardized, there may be effects from using different interviewers, or carrying out the interviews in different environments (see de Vaus, 1996: 110).

10

Reporting Findings

In this chapter:

- Audiences and the ways research is reported
- Disseminating research
- Styles of presentation
- What can and cannot be claimed
- The visual presentation of data
- Writing a research report

To be a good researcher you must present your findings clearly and rigorously – to help others make sense of *your* social research. Like so much else in social research, the more often you do it the better you get. This chapter, as was the case in the previous ones, is not about giving you the perfect recipe or algorithm, but about where to start from and what kind of things to consider. It is intended to be practical rather than discursive, though this does not imply that there is no debate about the best way of doing this.

I begin the chapter with a brief description of the various methods used to report and present research. I then look at strategies researchers use to persuade their audiences of the validity and reliability of their results. This demonstrates the very different styles of quantitative and qualitative research, but also shows that they can be combined in the same document. Finally, I briefly describe the layout of a typical research report.[1]

Audiences and the ways research is reported

In previous chapters (1 and 8) I have spoken of social research embodying both elements of science and commitment. The balance between these comes to the fore in presenting the research. So often here the researcher takes the role of the intermediary between the (hopefully) rigorous objectivity of the investigation and the political or social commitment of the audience (who may well be the sponsors of the research in the first place). In policy research or market research this will usually be the case. The researcher must do two things: first, convince a (politically or socially) committed audience that the findings are reliable and valid and, second, show what the limits are of those findings.

A different kind of convincing may be the case when one's audience are fellow researchers or social scientists. Here the necessary emphasis may well be on method, the novelty of the findings and how they relate to past research. Within these two broad camps of non-social science and social science audiences there are many variations and hybrids. This particularly becomes the case as more professionals in the public and voluntary sector have research training.

The audiences for research are varied, but so also are the media in which one reports findings. Box 10.1 shows the principal ways in which research is reported and the sectors most likely to use them.

Box 10.1 Methods of reporting research

Research reports

Most research, apart from small *ad hoc* projects, will be presented in a research report. Market research and in-house public sector research may be confined to this, along with oral presentations, but in the academic sector especially, a report of research is a necessary but not a sufficient condition of dissemination.

Technical report

Because reports are often aimed at those who wish to learn about the findings and conclusions, rather than the methods or technical issues, technical reports are often produced for larger research projects. The main report may only briefly describe methods, but a technical report, which is not always called this, will contain a detailed description of the methodological issues, methods used and sometimes cross-tabulations and frequencies, etc. not presented in the main report. See for example Lynn (1992).

Working papers

Research projects may go on for months or even years and researchers will want to present preliminary findings for their contemporaries in a discipline, for their organization or for the funders. Working papers are provisional and are rarely cited as authoritative because the findings are usually provisional and a number of caveats are entered. Nevertheless they can provide useful feedback in

---

	an ongoing project and are an opportunity for the researcher to take stock.
Briefings	These can range from the formal and set piece occasions where research is launched to the world, to more interactive and informal meetings of researchers and their audience. Formal briefings, to which the press may be invited, take place at the end of the research and are usually fairly non-technical and aimed at a wider audience. In local authority research these may be briefings to elected representatives as well as policy officers. Interim briefings, on the other hand, may be at a more 'grass roots' level and a little more technical.
Seminar papers	Strictly speaking, these should be short presentations with plenty of opportunity for discussion, but they take a number of different forms. They may be work in progress, or they may be a way in which findings can be directly used to inform policy and practice. A seminar of senior police officers, for example, may be presented with some findings from a local crime survey and the officers may then discuss how this impacts on local policing policy and what might be done as a result of the research.
Conference papers	Quite often conference papers are work in progress or deliberately presented to stimulate discussion. In this sense conference sessions can be a little like seminars. The conference is a good place to 'network' and get to know people, but also, if you are a new researcher, a place to try out your (often preliminary) research.
Books	Books reporting research (sometimes rather pompously known as monographs) are mainly the province of academics. Very often they report on a whole research programme (or programmes) (see Wilson, 1997, for example), or may be a series of books reporting on large-scale research such as the British Social Change and Economic Life Initiative (SCELI).[2] Single research projects (sometimes originating in PhD research) become books and books often summarize and bring together findings reported in other forms such as reports and journal articles.

Journal articles	As with all academic disciplines, a great deal of social science research is reported in refereed journals. Indeed, papers in such journals have increasingly become a measure of researchers' productivity and success. Certainly, publishing them is necessary for academic advancement. The skills in writing journal articles are somewhat different to writing reports and books. Often they are fairly short and require the writer to be succinct, but rigorous. Journal articles are usually anonymously reviewed by researchers with knowledge of the area in question.
On-line journals	On-line journals (such as Sociological Research Online http://www.socresonline.org.uk/) are increasingly used. The rules and procedures are similar to other journals, but often papers can appear much more quickly, in, say, four months as opposed to up to three years for paper journals.
Newspapers/popular journals	Particularly if your research is in a currently 'sexy' area, your research may be reported in the popular press. How well it is reported will vary. Writing for popular journals or magazines is often the best way to get research findings over to a wider public.

The choice of the means of dissemination of results will depend on who it is you wish to communicate with and why. This may be dictated by who the research is being done for, for example government department-sponsored research will be subject to reporting restrictions (see Chapter 8). Some research, say, by a transport operator on who uses their buses/trains, when and why, may be of little interest to anyone outside the company. Some academic research may be very subject specific, or technically quite difficult and therefore only suitable for a very specific audience. A great deal of research has many audiences and findings will be reported in different ways and at different levels of technical accessibility. Some examples of how research findings have been disseminated are presented in Box 10.2.

Box 10.2   Research dissemination

Example one

The European Union funded a project aimed at assessing the secondary learning effects of three non-conventional youth training programmes. This involved an international collaboration and evaluation of two theatre projects and a circus school in Liverpool, Lisbon, Portugal and Mannheim, Germany. The research deployed a variety of qualitative methods as a means of addressing what skills young people gained from these training programmes that they might not from more traditional courses. After conducting extended one-to-one interviews with key personnel, a researcher from each country interviewed groups of young trainees and also conducted one-to-one interviews with past and present trainees. The researchers then filmed and evaluated the training benefits of performances by each of the three projects, and used this material as a basis for further discussion with the key personnel who were identified earlier in the research. The course materials were also analysed. The findings served to highlight the potential benefits of 'youth-centred' training programmes concerned with broad skills to do with self-confidence and self-belief. They were disseminated, in the first instance, through a research report submitted to the European Union. The project constituted one project among many funded by the European Union's 'Youth for Europe' initiative. Results were also disseminated at various international conferences bringing together various youth researchers undertaking a variety of similar projects. The dissemination of the results presented an interesting cross-cultural dilemma, insofar as research cultures in different countries have contrasting ideas about what represents a prestigious outlet for research findings (e.g. the relative merits of producing books or refereed journal articles can vary from one country to another). Having completed the research, this represented a key focus for discussion for partners from each of the three countries. The main intention was that this research should have far more than an academic audience and that the findings could have a real impact on youth policy which it was believed, has in the past, been economically driven, rather than driven by the needs of young people themselves (see Banha et al., 1999).

Example two

Shelter UK, Plymouth City Council and South and the West Devon Health Authority funded a project aimed at showing the size and characteristics of the homeless population in Plymouth. The research was multi-method using multiple enumerations, a sample survey and focus groups. There were three main audiences: (a) local policy-makers and politicians with an interest in housing and health issues; (b) national and European homelessness campaigners and policy-makers; (c) methodologists and statisticians. The first audience were targeted through the publication of a report (Williams et al., 1995), a press launch and a one- day conference; the second through a European Union initiative on homelessness, refereed and popular journal articles and the third audience of methodologists through a chapter in an edited book and a journal article (Williams, 1999a; Williams and Cheal, 2001).

Styles of presentation

In an entertaining little book written many years ago Darrell Huff showed us how people can lie with statistics, or indeed *how to* lie with statistics! (Huff, [1954] 1973). The book was originally published at a time when people still had enormous faith in statistics and in science (and social science) to tell the whole truth and nothing but the truth. Since then the public mood has changed to a distrust of statistics and often a fear and loathing of science (Tallis, 1995). How this came to happen is a long story (Williams, 2000a: Chapter 4), but one thing most social scientists agree on is that there is no one version of the whole truth and nothing but the truth. That doesn't mean we cannot or should not pursue truth (see Chapter 1), but that our data can often be interpreted or presented in different ways.

Inevitably, then, reported research must end up being what Alan Bryman has called a *rhetoric of persuasion* (Bryman, 1998: 142).[3] We aim to persuade our audience that our findings are the most authentic possible story we could tell. Note here I use the term 'story', this is not to suggest that our reported research is fiction, but that it must be plausible, coherent and logically consistent. Thus structured much as a story would be. Indeed, I always feel that the very best reported research draws the reader in just like good fiction. The rhetorical devices will differ and depend on who the audience are, or the kind of research undertaken. There are marked differences, for example, between how qualitative and quantitative research are presented.

Here is an example of each:

1   The next two columns of Table 1.7 show how the two migration streams contributed to these aggregate changes. The net changes experienced by those moving from metropolitan to LDNM (low density non metropolitan counties) were broadly similar in pattern to the aggregate of the two, apart from the lack of overall growth in the labour force as a result of exits and entries (Champion and Atkins, 2000: 12)

2   Additionally, it became apparent that source areas become more distant as time passed, old ties were broken and new social networks developed. And

certain respondents expressed the desire to remain in Newquay because social conditions in source areas had worsened.

Jim: *Home* (Doncaster) *used to be on par with here to me – just as fast, but then it's got to be ... when I was home after the miners' strike and all that when everything was getting closed down and all that, Newquay seemed busier still than back home – (even) in winter.* (Elzey, 1998: 137)

Both reports of research describe migration from metropolitan to non-metropolitan areas, but they are very different in style and in what is being claimed. The first is a secondary analysis of large numeric data set of longitudinally linked Census data (see Chapter 9) and the second is micro-level study of young migrants to a seaside town. The first depends on fairly broad aggregate concepts such as 'labour force' , 'migrant streams' and 'metropolitan and non metropolitan low density areas.' The description is of very large numbers of people moving over ten-year periods.

The second report is of a depth interview between the researcher and respondent. It describes a personal experience of comparing Doncaster with Newquay and thus explaining why this individual (Jim) chose to remain in Newquay.

The first research shows who and how many people moved from metropolitan areas to LDNM areas, the second shows why a particular individual did so. The style of language is also very different with the first using the impersonal third person of science and the second quoting verbatim the respondent's words.

Both are different, but both are rhetorics of persuasion. The first persuades through an implicit reliance on dependability of a scientific analysis of trustworthy data. The second uses the recorded words of a respondent (an eyewitness account) to convince the audience of the truth of the matter. Bryman sees these styles of writing as imbued with realism and writers presenting their results as 'a definitive picture of an objective, external reality' (1998: 154). This may be an unexamined realism and a weaker version than that which I discussed in Chapter 1, but nevertheless through such rhetoric researchers wish to persuade their audience that they have uncovered something interesting and important about social reality.

It should not be assumed that these styles are contradictory or mutually exclusive. As I noted in the previous chapter, many designs will use qualitative and quantitative methods and it is not unusual to find reports or articles which blend the two styles. For example:

The overwhelming conclusion to be drawn from Table 7.33 is that the majority of respondents in all areas (the least was Warwickshire 67.1%) did not feel rural areas could manage with fewer health services than urban areas. When qualified, the reasons were often those of equity with other areas and of the impositions of providing health care over a large area with a low population density.

I think per head of the population you need slightly more [health services] to account for the distances as services are spread thinner over a wider area. The number of miles a doctor has to travel to a patient. And older people have more difficulty in getting to any of the services. To travel via public transport if they have none of their own costs a lot of money and time. [2243 Northumberland] (Cloke et al., 1994: 142)

In this example large-scale data from 12 counties are compared, but these data are rendered more plausible and given more 'depth' with the above quote from a depth interview with a GP in Northumberland.

The examples from Champion and Atkins and from Elzey were from publications mainly aimed at an academic or at least social science-trained audience. The style of the Champion and Atkins extract, though very clear to someone with a training in quantitative research, would appear 'difficult' or 'obscure' to the lay person. Actually the style is elegant and compact and allows a lot to be said in a few words. The Cloke et al. extract is from a report on lifestyles in rural England. It was published by the Rural Development Commission (an independent government funded body) and written (mostly) by academics. Yet the intended audience was much wider and would have included national and regional politicians and policy-makers and those providing services in rural areas. The style is consequently more accessible to the lay person.

What can and cannot be claimed?

Style is not everything. Unscrupulous researchers (both quantitative and qualitative) can use stylistic devices to persuade audiences of findings that are not valid or reliable. I once listened to a presentation to local councillors of findings from a project on attitudes to housing development. Survey findings had not been conducive to the policy the council had adopted, but a few individuals in subsequent focus groups had made comments that were. The researchers played down the survey findings and emphasized those of the focus groups. Neither the survey or focus group data were 'wrong', but the presentation was dishonest because it did not contextualize the findings to a lay audience perhaps unable to assess validity.

However, all of us face the dilemma at some time of what to present, what to emphasize. Clear hypotheses and their operationalization (see Chapter 2) will help, because the test is, what do the findings do for the hypothesis? Unfortunately findings rarely confirm or refute hypotheses conclusively and quite often even our research hypothesis is 'two tailed' (see Chapter 7). Under these circumstances it might be necessary to offer two or more scenarios to the audience.

For example:

- Contradictory findings may emerge from a set of depth interviews, in which case it may be the contradictions themselves which are interesting. Howard Becker maintained (cited in Seale, 1999: 74) that negative instances should give us greater methodological confidence in a qualitative study. That they have been found suggests a rigour in method and a need that they be explained.

- Column and row percentages in cross-tabulations may show quite a different story, often when no dependent variable can be named. This may require us to present both row and column percentages, though it might suggest that dependent variables should be selected, at least experimentally, and more analyses conducted.

Which data to present, or how strong the claim is to be made are genuine dilemmas, but there are some methodological pitfalls we can avoid. Here are a few of the commoner ones.

Quantitative research

ASSOCIATION AND CAUSATION.   In bivariate analysis we speak of variables being associated or correlated, even though we might suspect A 'caused' B (see Chapters 2 and 7 for discussion of this). Even in multivariate analysis, to speak of A causing B is a very strong claim. Instead, it is safer to use the language of 'best fitting model' and 'odds ratios' (see Tacq, 1997; Dale et al., 2000: Chapter 7).

THE ECOLOGICAL FALLACY.   This is an error whereby claims are made about individuals, or smaller groups, on the basis of data about larger groups. Higher levels of data can tell us nothing about lower ones. To claim, for example, that a cross-tabulation of metropolitan–non-metropolitan migration can tell us anything about specific migration into Newquay, would be to commit an ecological fallacy (for a detailed account of this and possible solutions see King, 1997).

STATISTICAL SIGNIFICANCE.   Not all associations are significant ones. In academic writing one would normally report the statistical significance of a table, but this will not always be appropriate in reports of research aimed at lay audiences (though such statistics may appear in appendices or technical reports). Nevertheless one should not normally present non-significant findings, especially as a key finding. Under some circumstances they may be reported as 'illustrative'. Quite often a table will contain one or two cells which are not significant. In this case the table can be retained, but the insignificance should be noted.

Qualitative research

Knowing how much to generalize from those studied to wider groups is by far the biggest problem in qualitative research. For example:

> Finally, we have demonstrated how ideas about childhood inform our understanding of particular spaces, showing for example how the idea that children's place is in the home and that they are either at risk, or need to be considered

risky, within public space is dependent on ideas of children as angels (innocence and lacking competence) or, less often, as devils (unsocialised beings whose activities need to be controlled). (Holloway and Valentine, 2000: 779)

This is a quotation from the conclusion of a paper reporting an observational case study of three schools with the additional citation of data from other qualitative sources.[4] The research itself was perhaps rigorous, but more is being claimed in the above quote about wider social phenomena than would be claimed from a large-scale sample survey. The claims made rely on a great deal of implicit assumptions of the correctness of prior theory about the character of the children and that the data from the schools can be widely generalized.

USING NUMBERS. Numbers are not necessarily absent from qualitative research and as I suggested in the last chapter, 'bridges' from quality to quantity can be made. One might even say that all qualitative research uses the simplest and most important property of number, presence or absence, 1 or 0. Yet every qualitative researcher will have been faced at some point with describing the sample in terms of more or less. If 17 out of 20 interview respondents broadly agreed on the way they described an event, or shared an opinion, not to talk in terms of 'more' seems churlish. As I have argued earlier, in Chapter 3, *moderatum* generalizations about qualitative findings are not just permissible, they are unavoidable. However, while one can speak in terms of the proportions internally of the characteristics or opinions of a group of respondents (more, most, a few, about half, etc.), this is quite a different matter from more generalized external claims, which need much more thought and qualification.

Conclusions and recommendations

The reporting of research usually takes the form of a classic logical syllogism (Weston, 1992), where the sections or chapters of the evidence become premises and the conclusion follows from this. Conclusions can take a strong and weak form. The strong form is simply the completion of the syllogism, the inescapable findings of the research lead us to conclude X. Now apart from some very safe conclusions to be drawn from statistics, this rarely happens. In reality, the writer will usually look for congruencies between the current data and past research and draw weaker conclusions hedged with caveats. For example:

Even if that is not the case, these distributions may show only the general level and we should expect a rise of intolerance toward strangers with increasing intercultural contacts between these countries. Moreover, almost all Western and Eastern countries show strong links between the dimension 'strangers' and 'social deviants'. This means, in conclusion, that the intolerance may be easily transferred from one object to another and might become politicised, thereby creating a highly dangerous climate. (Westle, 1998: 59)

This is the final paragraph of a paper in which Bettina Westle presents a great deal of cross-national statistical data. If one reads the sentences carefully it can be seen that she conjectures from her findings and on the basis of other findings (discussed earlier in the paper) speculates on future states.

I think this is reasonable if social research is to be relevant and certainly does not reduce our objectivity. In this particular specialist area Westle is probably in as strong, or stronger position than anyone to make such speculations. However, this does not give us licence for wild speculation that goes well beyond what our data would support. We will leave that for writers in popular physics and evolutionary psychology!

In reports for public or campaigning bodies, charities or the private sector (in market research), researchers are often expected to go beyond speculation and to make recommendations for action. I personally prefer not to do this; competence in research does not necessarily equate with competence in strategic or tactical policy, though I accept that often one is forced to make suggestions. Sometimes this is fairly easy. In my own homelessness research I often found that local authorities and other organizations do not standardize their monitoring of clients who are homeless. Standardization is a fairly modest and safe recommendation that permits a fairly accurate continuing estimate of numbers homeless and consequently permits better resource allocation (Williams et al., 1995: 48-9). In other cases research will suggest the existence of a problem or problems to which there may be several solutions. These solutions may in fact be known to researchers from their previous work. Under these circumstances it is perhaps one's substantive disciplinary knowledge that is as useful, or more useful, than research skills.

The visual presentation of data

The rhetoric of persuasion is quite often best served by presenting data in a visual form through using a histogram, a bar chart, a line graph or a pie chart. These can be very effective in showing the size of particular phenomena in relation to others.

When data are to be reported to an academic audience who have skills in reading tables, then these are to be preferred because they can summarize a great deal of sometimes quite complex data in very little space. However, the reader, or the seminar participant, needs to know what to look for, or at least needs to be told what to look for. For lay audiences charts get the point over quickly and simply. SPSS and Microsoft Excel offer a range of graphics for various kinds of charts, allowing quite complex data to be shown visually. It is fairly easy to experiment to find the most visually apt display.

PIE CHARTS   See Figure 10.1. When there are just a few categories to display a pie chart clearly shows relative size, but pie charts lose their visual impact with more than 6 or 7 categories, especially if some of these are very small. More categories can be displayed if contrasting colours can be used.

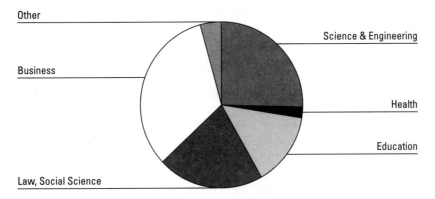

Figure 10.1   *Subject area of university degree*

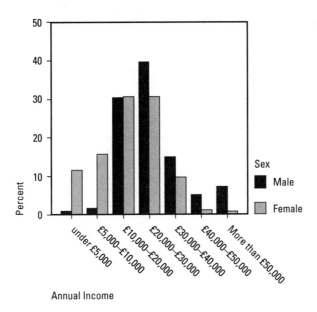

Figure 10.2   *Income by Sex*

BAR CHARTS   See Figure 10.2. Bar charts can be used instead of pie charts when more categories need to be displayed. Both these and pie charts can be used for nominal variables. The principal difference between pie and bar charts is that the former emphasizes the relative contribution of the categories to the total and the latter emphasizes the frequency of cases, in each category, relative to each other. The most useful aspect, however, is that more than one variable can be displayed fairly easily. In the example here the earnings of males and females can be compared. More complex displays, with more categories can be achieved through making the bars thinner or using '3 D' displays.

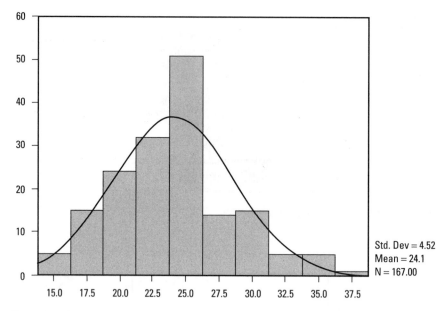

Figure 10.3   *Age at birth of first child (histogram)*

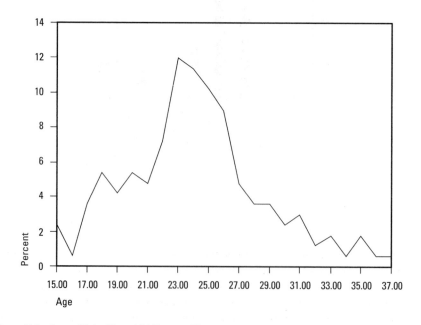

Figure 10.4   *Age at birth of first child (line graph)*

HISTOGRAMS   See Figure 10.3. Histograms are used to display single continuous variables such as age etc. They are a good visual way of showing information about the distribution of scores (in SPSS you can produce additional 'box plots' which show any values that lie some way from a normal distribution). In the example here the data are fairly normally distributed, though most data in social science are not. Note how a normal curve has been fitted to show how the distribution varies from it.

LINE GRAPHS.   See Figure 10.4. Line graphs are related to histograms and use the same levels of data. The example here uses the same data as in Figure 10.3 and shows an alternative way of presenting it. Line graphs are better than histograms at showing trends over time, such as unemployment, mortality rates, numbers of live births, student results etc. For this reason they are popular with economists. As with bar charts a great deal of comparative data can be summarised in line graphs.

Writing a research report

Box 10.1 listed several different ways in which research can be reported and ideally this chapter would describe the format of each in some detail. Unfortunately that would be a book in itself, so for two reasons I have decided to concentrate on describing only one – the research report. First, most research findings will be disseminated via a report, whatever other additional means are used. Second, research reports are the most likely means by which first-time researchers will report their findings.

The kind of research report written will depend on the nature of the research, methods used, the audience and purpose of the research. Here are some examples of the kind of research report written.

'GOVERNMENT' RESEARCH REPORT.   These might be the result of research undertaken by a government department, or by universities or independent research centres for government. Projects are usually large scale and the report may have several authors. The writing style is sparse and usually in the third person. If quantitative, tables will be described in some detail and if qualitative data may be presented in the form of case studies.

UNIVERSITY RESEARCH REPORTS.   These are similar, but usually not reporting such large-scale research. In this and the previous example the intended audience may include practitioners, policy-makers, charities, academics and local campaigning groups. Even though much academic social research gets reported in journals, a funding requirement is often an end of project report (see for example the British Economic and Social Research Council at http:www.esrc.ac.uk). Often reports have only a local circulation, but with the advent of the World Wide Web researchers can achieve wider dissemination by posting research reports on web sites. A visit to university web sites will usually list key reports, especially those produced in research centres.

THE VOLUNTARY SECTOR REPORT. The voluntary sector commission carry out research, partly to assess the extent of the issue or problem they are concerned with, but also to use results for campaigning purposes. Reports by, or for, charities or campaigning groups, aimed at demonstrating the extent or nature of an issue will often be very visual, with photographs and graphical representation of data. They will usually contain only a minimum of technical detail (though there may be an accompanying, less lavish, technical report) and will summarize key data in an eye-catching way.

COMMUNITY RESEARCH REPORTS. More than any other kind of report this focuses on simplicity and direct communication to the lay person. Technical jargon is avoided and numeric data simplified and usually visually represented. Methodological description is minimal or absent.

PHD AND MPHIL THESES. Though strictly not a research report (they are usually much longer, PhD theses are around 80,000 words), this may be the first report researchers write. There is much in common with a research book ('monographs'). Though obfuscation should be avoided, PhD theses are nevertheless written with an audience of specialists (the examiners) in mind and must deal in great depth with previous literature, methodology/methods and findings. There will usually be a quite long discussion of findings and appendices containing materials relevant but not directly referred to. Writing style is not journalistic and the style of visual presentation is clear, but sober (see Rudestam and Newton, 2000).

STUDENT DISSERTATIONS. These are really miniature versions of PhD or MPhil theses, in which researchers learn the tricks of the trade: the reporting conventions, the style of academic writing and how to discuss previous and past findings.

What goes into a report?

Every report is slightly different and in this as in presentation generally there is no single recipe. What follows are some brief notes on what a typical report might contain.

SUMMARY OF KEY FINDINGS, OR ABSTRACT. Usually reports will list up to a dozen key findings, perhaps as bullet points; in more 'academic' reports there may be an abstract summarizing the research and its findings. Summaries of key findings will often form the basis of press releases or research presentations.

ACKNOWLEDGEMENTS. Not essential but the right thing to do! Acknowledgements list all of the people and organizations that helped.

CONTENTS. A list of what will be found in the report (see Box 10.4). Reports will often employ a hierarchical numbering system:

1.

1.1

1.1.1

1.1.2

2

2.1

Box 10.4 is the contents page of an actual report and might be compared with the indicative one. The example is of a report of secondary analysis of Census and other data relating to local socio-economic conditions. The audience were policy makers in health and local authorities, regional representatives of central government, the voluntary sector and academics, pretty much in that order. In an important section in this report was a discussion of the issues surrounding deprivation and how it had been operationalized in the current research. The next section is a justification for the re-analysis of the data, that current use of the index of local conditions was not sensitive to the settlement patterns or the nature of deprivation in Devon and Cornwall. Around one third of the report is detail contained in annexes. Annex 3 described in more detail government policy on resource allocation and their response to poverty. This section was written by someone outside of the research team who had been 'bought in' for his particular expertise.

Box 10.4   The contents page of a research report

Interpreting the Index of Local Conditions: Relative Deprivation in Devon and Cornwall by Judy Payne

List of Tables and Figures

Preface

Executive Summary

1. Introduction
2. Defining and Measuring Deprivation
3. Central Government Resource Allocation
4. Main Features of the Index of Local Conditions
5. District Comparisons at the National, Regional and County Levels
6. Distribution at the Sub-District Level
7. Other Issues
8. Conclusions and Recommendations

Bibliography

Annex 1 – The Identification of Deprivation

Annex 2 – Sub-Indices

Annex 3 – Central Government Policy Responses (Eric Harrison)

Annex 4 – Most Deprived Enumeration Districts

INTRODUCTION OR BACKGROUND TO THE RESEARCH.   This moves from the general to the specific. In the first paragraph it is a good idea to say what the current research is and what the research question is. There will usually follow a discussion of previous research and the research problem itself (why is non-participation in local government elections such a problem? Why is the government so keen on lifelong learning?)

   Academic studies may contain a separate and more detailed discussion of literature in the area, indeed the literature review is a set piece section or chapter in PhD/MPhil theses and student dissertations.

METHODS AND METHODOLOGICAL DISCUSSION.   The length of this will really depend on the type of report and one's audience. The description of methods may occupy only one paragraph, or they may run to several thousand words (or they may be in a separate technical report or appendix).

FINDINGS.   In a fairly small report this may comprise one section, but in most larger research reports it will be broken down into sections or 'chapters' corresponding to particular topic areas. If one section/chapter is used for findings it should be broken down into numbered sections.

CONCLUSIONS/RECOMMENDATIONS.   Conclusions summarize findings and return to the research question or questions and show how (and how well) these have been answered by the research. In academic research the discussion will usually show how the research has contributed to theoretical understanding. It may confirm or cast doubt upon a body of theory and may add to it as a result of either of these outcomes.

Conclusion

Good research reporting is an exercise in communication. There are no strict rules about how we should report research to particular audiences, though there will be an optimum way of communicating to those audiences. In this short chapter I have tried to give a feel for typical strategies of reporting research and how these are at least partly determined by the nature of the research (broadly quantitative or qualitative) and the audience itself. Finally, the reporting of research, often referred to as dissemination, is not something just to think about when the data are all analysed. Indeed, many funders insist that a programme of dissemination is set out in the initial funding bid. The detail of presentation is embedded in data analysis. For example, in the creation of clear and appropriate table titles and value labels in survey analysis, or a consideration of which particular respondent quotes might be used as illustrative when analysing qualitative data.

Try this

Obtain a report of research in one of the formats described above, read it and try to answer the following questions:

1 Was the research question clear?
2 To what extent did the research answer the question(s)?
3 Was the methodological discussion clear and appropriate?
4 Were all the findings presented? If not, why were particular findings chosen?
5 Does the evidence (quantitative or qualitative) support the claims made?
6 Is the reporting set out clearly and Is it visually appropriate to the type of audience aimed at?
7 Could other means of reporting be used? Were they?
8 Who sponsored the research?
9 Were recommendations made and if so were they appropriate?

Suggested further reading

There are a number of good practical books on doing social research projects, as a student or in the community. Two that have good writing up sections are Judith Bell's *Doing Your Research Project* (1999) and David and Irene Hall's *Practical Social Research* (1996). Social research, like any other scientific activity, has styles of writing peculiar and special to it. These styles require practice, but a good starting point for doing this is Lee Cuba and John Cocking's *How to Write about the Social Sciences* (1997).

Notes

1 Note that in this chapter I use the term 'reports of research' to indicate all or any of the means we use to report research, and 'research, reports' as a particular form of reporting.

2 See for example, Anderson et al. (1994); Gallie et al. (1993); MacEwan Scott (1994). The SCELI initiative was a programme of research aimed at studying 'the nature and determinants of employer labour force policies, worker experiences of employment and the labour market, the changing dynamics of household relations and the impact of changes in the employment structure on social integration and social stratification in the community (Gallie et al., 1993: v).

3 Bryman uses this term to indicate quantitative and qualitative methods as 'contrasting ways of persuading audiences of the cogency of their truth claims' (1998: 142). While my use of the term is somewhat different, I do not think the two usages need be mutually exclusive.

4 A sample survey of ICT in schools was used but this did not seem to inform the generalizing claims as cited.

References

Adorno, T. (with Aron, B.; Hertz, M. and Levinson Morrow, W.) (1982) *The Authoritarian Personality*. New York: Norton.

Agar, M. (1980) *The Professional Stranger*. London: Academic Press.

Ahmad, W. (1999) 'Ethnic statistics: better than nothing or worse than nothing?', in D. Dorling, and S. Simpson, (eds), *Statistics in Society: The Arithmetic of Politics*. London: Arnold.

Albrow, M. (1990) *Max Weber's Construction of Social Theory*. London: Macmillan.

Aldous, P. (2001) 'Young people and migration choices in Cornwall', unpublished PhD thesis. Plymouth: University of Plymouth.

Aldridge, A. and Levine, K. (2001) *Surveying the Social World: Principles and Practice in Survey Research*. Buckingham: Open University Press.

Anderson, M., Beckhoffer, F. and Gershuny, J. (eds) (1994) *The Social and Political Economy of the Household*. Oxford: Oxford University Press.

Archer, M. (1995) *Realist Social Theory: The Morphogenetic Approach*. Cambridge: Cambridge University Press.

Argyrous, G. (2000) *Statistics for Social and Health Research*. London: Sage.

Arnott, J. (1999) *The Long Firm*. New York: Soho Press.

Babbie, E. (1995) *The Practice of Social Research* (7th edition). Belmont, CA: Wadsworth.

Banha, A., Gaspar, A., Gomes, M., Miles, S. and Pohl, A. (1999) 'Catching the trapeze in a life-long learning society: a comparative discussion of unconventional strategies for disadvantaged young people', in A. Walther and B. Stauber (eds), *Lifelong Learning in Europe: Differences and Divisions*, vol. II, *Strategies of Social Integration and Individual Learning Biographies*. Tübingen: Neuling Verlag. pp. 223–35.

Barbour, S. and Kitzinger, J. (eds) (1999) *Developing Focus Group Research: Politics, Theory and Practice*. London: Sage.

Barker, E. (ed.) (1982) *New Religious Movements: A Perspective for Understanding Society*. New York: Edwin Mellen Press.

Barnes, J. (1979) *Who Should Know What? Social Science, Privacy and Ethics*. Harmondsworth: Penguin.

Barton, J. (1958) 'Asking the embarrassing question', *Public Opinion Quarterly*. 22: 67–8.

Bell, J. (1999) *Doing Your Research Project: A Guide for First Time Researchers in Education and the Social Sciences*. 3rd edn. Buckingham: Open University Press.

Bennett, T. (1988) 'An assessment of the design, implementation and effectiveness of Neighbourhood Watch in London', *Howard Journal of Criminal Justice*, 27 (4): 241–55.

Berger, P. and Luckmann, T. (1961) *The Social Construction of Reality*. London: Allen Lane.

Berry, B.J.L. (1976) 'The counterurbanisation process: urban America since 1970', in B. Berry (ed.), *Urbanisation and Counterurbanisation*. New York: Arnold.

Bhaskar, R. (1978) *A Realist Theory of Science*. (2nd edition). Hemel Hempstead: Harvester.

Bhaskar, R. (1986) *Scientific Realism and Human Emancipation*. London: Verso.

Bhaskar, R. (1998) *The Possibility of Naturalism* (3rd edition). London: Routledge.

Bittner, E. (1967) 'The police on Skid Row: a study in peace keeping', *American Sociological Review* (32) 5: 699–714.

Blalock, H. and Blalock, A. (1971) *Methodology in Social Research*. New York: McGraw-Hill.

Bloor, M. (1978) 'On the analysis of observational data: a discussion of the worth and uses of inductive techniques and respondent validation', *Sociology*, (12) 3: 3–10.

Bolton, A., Pole, C. and Mizen, P. (2001) 'Picture this: researching child workers', *Sociology*, 35, 2: 501–18.

Bourdieu, P. and Wacquant, L.J. (1992) *An Invitation to Reflexive Sociology.* Cambridge: Polity Press.

Brewer, J. and Hunter, A. (1989) *Multi-method Research: A Synthesis of Styles.* London: Sage.

Bruce, S. (1994) *The Edge of the Union.* Oxford: Oxford University Press.

Bryant, L., Chandler, J. and Bunyard, T. (1995) *The Integration of Sea Service: A Report to the Royal Navy on the Integration of the WRNS into the Royal Navy.* Plymouth: Faculty of Human Sciences, University of Plymouth.

Bryman, A. (1988) *Quantity and Quality in Social Research.* London: Routledge.

Bryman, A. (1998) 'Quantitative and qualitative research strategies in knowing the social world', in T. May, and M. Williams, (eds), *Knowing the Social World.* Buckingham: Open University Press.

Bryman, A. (2001) *Social Research Methods.* Oxford: Oxford University Press.

Bryman, A. and Burgess, R. (1994) (eds) *Analysing Qualitative Data.* London: Routledge.

Bryman, A. and Cramer, D. (2001) *Quantitative Data Analysis with SPSS Release 10 for Windows: A Guide for Social Scientists.* London: Routledge.

Buck, M., Williams, M. and Bryant, L. (1993) 'Housing the Cornish, containing the crisis', *Cornish Studies,* 2nd series (1): 97–108.

Bulmer, M. (1979) 'Concepts in the analysis of qualitative data', *Sociological Review,* 27 (4): 651–79.

Bulmer, M. (ed.) (1982) *Social Research Ethics.* London: Macmillan.

Bulmer, M. (1984) *The Chicago School of Sociology.* Chicago: Chicago University Press.

Burgess, R. (1984) *In the Field: An Introduction to Field Research.* London: Routledge.

Burns, D. and Williams, M. (1989) *Neighbourhood Working: A New Approach to Housing Provision.* Bristol: SAUS.

Bunting, C. (2002) 'I spy with my science eye', *Times Higher Education Supplement,* 12 April: 17.

Butcher, H. (1990) *Local Government and Thatcherism.* London: Routledge.

Byrne, D. (1998) *Complexity Theory and the Social Sciences:* An Introduction. London: Routledge.

Byrne, D. (2002) *Interpreting Quantitative Data.* London: Sage.

Campbell, D. and Stanley, J. (1966) *Experimental and Quasi Experimental Designs for Research.* Boston: Houghton Mifflin.

Canclini, N.G. (1992) 'Culture and power: the state of research', in P. Scannell, P. Schlesinger, and C. Sparks (eds), *Culture and Power.* London: Sage.

Carter, B. (2000) *Realism and Racism.* London: Routledge.

Casti, J. (1991) *Searching for Certainty.* London: Abacus.

Chalmers, A. (1990) *Science and its Fabrication.* Buckingham: Open University Press.

Chalmers, A. (1999) *What is This Thing Called Science?* (3rd edition). Buckingham: Open University Press.

Champion, T. and Atkins, D. (2000) 'Migration between metropolitan and non metropolitan areas in England and Wales', in R. Creeser and S. Gleave, (eds), *Migration within England and Wales using the ONS Longitudinal Study.* London: The Stationery Office.

Cilliers, P. (1998) Complexity and Postmodernism: Understanding Complex Systems. London: Routledge.

Clarke, A. (1999) *Evaluation Research.* London: Sage.

Clegg, F. (1982) *Simple Statistics.* Cambridge: Cambridge University Press.

Clifford, J. and Marcus, G. (eds) (1986) *Writing Culture: The Poetics and Politics of Ethnography.* Berkele, CA: University of California Press.

Cloke, P. (1985) 'Counterurbanisation: a rural perspective', *Geography,* 70, 13–23.

Cloke, P., Milbourne, P. and Thomas, C. (1994) *Lifestyles in Rural England.* Salisbury: Rural Development Commission.

Cockburn, C. (1977) *The Local State.* London: Pluto.

Coghlan, D. and Brannick, T. (2001) *Doing Action Research in Your Own Organization.* London: Sage.

Coleman, A. (1990) *Utopia on Trial: Vision and Reality in Planning Housing.* London: Hilary Shipman.

Collett, T. (1998) *Best Value: Customer Satisfaction with Housing Services*. Truro/Plymouth: Carrick District Council/University of Plymouth, Department of Sociology.

Comley, T. (2001) 'Getting it right on-line', *Research Guide to Internet Technology*. London: Market Research Society.

Converse, J. and Presser, S. (1986) *Survey Questions: Handcrafting the Standardized Questionnaire*. Thousand Oaks, CA: Sage.

Cook, T. and Campbell, D. (1979) *Quasi Experimentation: Design and Analysis Issues for Field Settings*. Chicago: Rand McNally.

Cressey, D. (1950) 'Criminal violation of financial trust', *American Sociological Review*, 15: 738–43.

Cuba, L. and Cocking, J. (1997) *How to Write about the Social Sciences*. Harlow: Longman.

Cunningham, L., Young, C. and Lee, M. (2000) 'Methodological triangulation in measuring public transportaion service quality', *Transportation Journal*, 40 (1): 35–47.

Dale, A., Arber, S. and Proctor, M. (1988) *Doing Secondary Analysis*. London: Unwin Hyman.

Dale, A., Fieldhouse, E. and Holdsworth, C. (2000) *Analyzing Census Microdata*. London: Arnold.

Dale, A. and Marsh, C. (1993) *The 1991 Census User's Guide*. London: HMSO.

Dandeker, C. and Mason, D. (1999) 'Diversity in the UK armed forces: the debate about the representation of women and minority ethnic groups', in J. Soeters and J. van der Meulen (eds), *Managing Diversity in the Armed Forces: Experiences from Nine Countries*. Tilburg: Tilburg University Press and Purdue University Press.

Darga, K. (1999) *Sampling and the Census*. Washington, DC: AEI Press.

David, M. (2002) 'Problems of participation: the limits of action research', *International Journal of Social Research Methodology*, 5 (1): 11–19.

Denzin, N. (1970) *The Research Act in Sociology*. Chicago: Aldine.

Denzin, N. (1978) 'The logic of naturalistic inquiry', in N. Denzin (ed.), *Sociological Methods: A Source book*. New York: McGraw-Hill.

Denzin, N. (1983) 'Interpretive interactionism', in G. Morgan (ed.), *Beyond Method: Strategies for Social Research*. Beverley Hills, CA: Sage.

Denzin, N. (1989) *Interpretive Interactionism*. London: Sage.

Denzin, N. and Lincoln, Y. (eds) (1994) *Handbook of Qualitative Research*. Thousand Oaks, CA: Sage.

Denzin, N. and Lincoln, Y. (eds) (1998a) *The Landscape of Qualitative Research*. Thousand Oaks, CA: Sage.

Denzin, N. and Lincoln, Y. (eds) (1998b) 'Introduction' in N. Denzin, and Y. Lincoln, (eds), *The Landscape of Qualitative Research*. Thousand Oaks, CA: Sage.

de Vaus, D. (1996) *Surveys in Social Research* (2nd edition). London: Routledge.

Devine, F. and Heath, S. (1999) *Sociological Research Methods in Context*. London: Macmillan.

Dey, I. (1993) *Qualitative Data Analysis: A User Friendly Guide for Social Scientists*. London: Routledge.

Diamond, I. (1999) 'The census', in D. Dorling and S. Simpson (eds), *Statistics in Society: The Arithmetic of Politics*. London: Arnold.

Dines, A. (1997) 'A case study of the ethical issues in health promotion – mammography screening: the nurse's position', in M. Sidell et al. (eds), *Debates and Dilemmas in Promoting Health: A Reader*. Buckingham: Open University Press.

Dorling, D. and Simpson, S. (eds) (1999) *Statistics in Society: The Arithmetic of Politics*. London: Arnold.

Douglas, J. (1967) *The Social Meanings of Suicide*. Princeton, NJ: Princeton University Press.

Downie, R. (1971) *Roles and Values: An Introduction to Social Ethics*. London: Methuen.

Durkheim, E. ([1896] 1952) *Suicide*. London: Routledge and Kegan Paul.

Elzey, R. (1998) 'In-migration to Newquay: migrants' lifestyles and perspectives on environments', *Cornish Studies*, 2nd series, 6: 127–42.

Evans, J. (1995) *Feminist Theory Today: An Introduction to Second Wave Feminism*. London: Sage.

Evans, J. St B.T. and Over, D.E. (1996) *Rationality and Reasoning*. Hove: Psychology Press.

Eve, R., Horsfall, S. and Lee, M. (eds) (1997) *Chaos, Complexity and Sociology*. Thousand Oaks, CA: Sage.

Fay, B. (1996) *Contemporary Philosophy of Social Science*. Oxford: Blackwell.

Fielding, J. and Gilbert, N. (2000) *Understanding Social Statistics*. London: Sage.

Fielding, N. (1981) *The National Front*. London: Routledge and Kegan Paul.

Fielding, N. (1982) 'Observational research on the National Front', in M. Bulmer (ed.) *Social Research Ethics*. London: Macmillan.

Fielding, N. (1993) 'Ethnography', in N. Gilbert (ed.), *Researching Social Life*. London: Sage.

Fink, A. (1995a) *How to Sample in Surveys*. Thousand Oaks, CA: Sage.

Fink, A. (1995b) *The Survey Handbook*. Thousand Oaks, CA: Sage.

Fink, A. (1998) *Conducting Research Literature Reviews: From Paper to the Internet*. London: Sage.

Fisher, S. (1993) 'The pull of the fruit machine: a sociological typology of young players', *Sociological Review*, 3: 41.

Frankenburg, R. (1957) *Village on the Border*. London: Cohen and West.

Fraser, N. (1989) *Unruly Practices: Power, Discourse and Gender in Contemporary Social Theory*. Cambridge: Polity Press.

Frey, J. and Oishi, S. (1995) *How to Conduct Interviews by Telephone and in Person*. Thousand Oaks, CA: Sage.

Fromm, E. (1977) *The Anatomy of Human Destructiveness*. Harmondsworth: Penguin.

Fuller, S. (2000) *The Governance of Science*. Buckingham: Open University Press.

Furnham, A. (1996) 'Attributions for the increase in urban homelessness', *Journal of Social Behavior and Personality*, 11 (1): 189–200.

Gallie, D., Marsh, C. and Vogler, C. (eds) (1993) *Social Change and the Experience of Unemployment*. Oxford: Oxford University Press.

Galliher, A. (1964) 'Plainville: the twice studied town', in A. Vidich, J. Bensman and M. Stein (eds), *Reflections on Community Studies*. New York: Harper and Row.

Geertz, C. (1979) 'Deep play: notes on the Balinese cockfight', in P. Rabinow and M. Sullivan (eds), *Interpretive Social Science: A Reader*. Berkeley, CA: University of California Press.

Geertz, C. (1994) 'Thick description: toward an interpretive theory of culture', in M. Martin and C. McIntyre (eds), *Readings in the Philosophy of Social Science*. Cambridge, MA: MIT Press.

Giddens, A. (1984) *The Constitution of Society*. Cambridge: Polity Press.

Gilbert, N. (1993) *Analyzing Tabular Data: Loglinear and Logistic Models for Social Researchers*. London: UCL Press.

Glaser, B. and Strauss, A. (1967) *The Discovery of Grounded Theory*. Chicago: Aldine.

Glass, G. (1984) *Statistical Methods in Education and Psychology*. London: Prentice-Hall.

Goffman, E. (1959) *The Presentation of Self in Everyday Life*. Garden City, NY: Doubleday.

Goffman, E. (1961) *Asylums*. New York: Anchor.

Goldthorpe, J. (2000) *On Sociology: Numbers, Narratives and the Integration of Research and Theory*. Oxford: Oxford University Press.

Goldthorpe, J., Lockwood, D., Bechhofer, F. and Platt, J. (1969) *The Affluent Worker in the Class Structure*. Cambridge: Cambridge University Press.

Gomez, S., Cheal, B., Bunyard, T. and Williams, M. (1999) *Young People in Torbay with Severe Housing Need*. Plymouth: University of Plymouth, Department of Sociology.

Goode, L. and Bartunek, J. (1990) 'Action research in an unbounded setting', *Consultation*, 9 (3) 209–28.

Griffin, J. (1977) *Black Like Me*, 2nd edn. Boston: Houghton Mifflin.

Guba, E. and Lincoln, Y. (1982) 'Epistemological and methodological bases of naturalistic inquiry', *Education Communication and Technology Journal*, 30: 233–52.

Hacking, I. (1983) *Representing and Intervening: Introductory Topics in the Philosophy of Natural Science*. Cambridge: Cambridge University Press.

Hakim, C. (1982) *Secondary Analysis in Social Research*. London: Allen and Unwin.

Hakim, C. (2000) *Research Design: Successful Designs for Social and Economics Research*. London: Routledge.

Halberg, M. (1989) 'Feminist epistemology: an impossible project', *Radical Philosophy*, 53: 3–7.

Halfpenny, P. (1982) *Positivism and Sociology: Explaining Social Life*. London: Allen and Unwin.

Hall, D. and Hall, I. (1996) *Practical Social Research: Project Work in the Community*. London: Macmillan.

Hammersley, M. (1989) *The Dilemma of Qualitative Method: Herbert Blumer and the Chicago School*. London: Routledge.

Hammersley, M. (1995) *The Politics of Social Research*. London: Sage.

Hammersley, M. (1996) 'The relationship between qualitative and quantitative research: paradigm loyalty versus methodological eclecticism', in J. Richardson (ed.), *Handbook of Research Methods for Psychology and the Social Sciences*. Leicester: BPS Books.

Hammersley, M. (1998) *Reading Ethnographic Research*. 2nd edn. Harlow: Longman.

Hammersley, M. (2000) *Taking Sides in Social Research: Essays in Partisanship and Bias*. London: Routledge.

Hammersley, M. and Atkinson, P. (1995) *Ethnography: Principles in Practice*. 2nd edn. London: Routledge.

Hammersley, M. and Gomm. R. (2000) 'Bias in social research', in M. Hammersley, *Taking Sides in Social Research*. London: Routledge.

Harding, S. (1986) *The Science Question in Feminism*. Milton Keynes: Open University Press.

Harding, S. (1996) 'Rethinking standpoint epistemology: what is "strong objectivity"?', in E. Fox Keller and H. Longino (eds), *Feminism and Science*. Oxford: Oxford University Press.

Hari, J. (2001) 'How to divide "us" from "them"', *New Statesman*, 19th November: 14.

Hartsock, N. (1987) 'The feminist standpoint: developing the ground for a specifically feminist historical materialism', in S. Harding (ed.), *Feminism and Methodology*. Milton Keynes: Open University Press.

Hattersley, L. and Creeser, R. (1995) *Longitudinal Study 1971–1991: History, Organisation and Quality of Data*. OPCS Series LS no. 7. London: HMSO.

Hays, W. (1993) *Statistics*. 4th edn. New York: Holt, Rinehart and Wilson.

Herrnstein, R. and Murray, C. (1994) *The Bell Curve: Intelligence and Class Structure in American Life*. New York: The Free Press.

Herskovits, M. (1953) *Franz Boas*. New York: Scribner.

Hobbs, D. (1988) *Doing the Business: Entrepreneurship, Detectives and the Working Class in the East End of London*. Oxford: Clarendon.

Hobbs, D. (1995) *Bad Business*. Oxford: Oxford University Press.

Hobbs, D. and May, T. (eds) (1993) *Interpreting the Field: Accounts of Ethnography*. Oxford: Oxford University Press.

Holdaway, S. (1982) 'An inside job: a case study of covert research on the police', in M. Bulmer (ed.), *Social Research Ethics*. London: Macmillan.

Holloway, S. and Valentine, G. (2000) 'Spatiality and the new social studies of childhood', *Sociology*, 34 (4): 763–84.

Holton, G. (1993) *Science and Anti-Science*. Cambridge, MA: Harvard University Press.

Homan, R. (1991) *The Ethics of Social Research*. Harlow: Longman.

Horrowitz, I. (1983) *C. Wright Mills: An American Utopian*. New York: Free Press.

Howell, K. (2000) *Discovering the Limits of European Integration: Applying Grounded Theory*. Huntington, NY: Nova Science Publishers.

Howitt, D. and Cramer, D. (2001) *A Guide to Computing Statistics with SPSS for Windows*. London: Prentice-Hall.

Hoyle, R. (1999) *Statistical Strategies for Small Sample Research*. Thousand Oaks, CA: Sage.

Huff, D. ([1954] 1973) *How to Lie with Statistics*. Harmondsworth: Penguin.

Humphreys, L. (1970) *The Tea Room Trade*. London: Duckworth.

Jackson, J. (1986) *Migration*. London: Longman.

Jephcott, P. with Robinson, H. (1971) *Homes in High Flats*. Edinburgh: Oliver and Boyd.

Jones, T. (1998) 'Interpretive social science and the "native's" point of view', *Philosophy of the Social Sciences*, 28 (1): 32–68.

Kimmel, A. (1996) *Ethical Issues in Behavioral Research*. Cambridge, MA: Blackwell.

Kincaid, H. (1996) *Philosophical Foundations of the Social Sciences: Analyzing Controversies in Social Research*. Cambridge: Cambridge University Press.

King, G. (1997) *A Solution to the Ecological Inference Problem: Reconstructing Individual Behavior from Aggregate Data*. Princeton, NJ: Princeton University Press.

Kinnear, T. and Taylor, J. (1996) *Marketing Research: An Applied Approach*. New York: McGraw-Hill.

Kirby, M. (1999) *Stratification and Differentiation*. London: Macmillan.

Körner, S. (1955) *Kant*. Harmondsworth: Penguin

Korsgaard, C. (1996) *Creating the Kingdom of Ends*. Cambridge: Cambridge University Press.

Kuhn, T. (1970) *The Structure of Scientific Revolutions* (2nd edition). Chicago: Chicago University Press.

Lakatos, I. (1978) *The Methodology of Scientific Research Programmes. Philosophical Papers*. Vol. 1 Eds J. Worrall and G. Curry. Cambridge: Cambridge University Press.

Lakatos, I. and Musgrave, A. (eds) (1970) *Criticism and the Growth of Knowledge*. Cambridge: Cambridge University Press.

Lamb, S. (1997) 'Gender differences in mathematics participation: an Australian perspective', *Educational Studies*, 23 (1): 105–25.

Lassell, M. (1962) *Wellington Road*. London: Routledge and Kegan Paul.

Layder, D. (1990) *The Realist Image in Social Science*. London: Macmillan.

Layder, D. (1993) *New Strategies in Social Research: An Introduction and Guide*. Cambridge: Polity Press.

LGA (1999) *Whose Zone is it Anyway? The Guide to Area Based Initiatives*. London: Local Government Association.

Lindesmith, A. ([1947] 1968) *Addiction and Opiates*. Chicago: Aldine.

Lindner, R. (1996) *The Reportage of Urban Culture: Robert Park and the Chicago School*. Cambridge: Cambridge University Press.

Lipton, P. (1991) *Inference to the Best Explanation*. London: Routledge.

Little, D. (1991) *Varieties of Social Explanation*. Boulder, CO: Westview Press.

Litwin, M. (1995) *How to Measure Survey Reliability and Validity*. Thousand Oaks, CA: Sage.

Locke, K. (2001) *Grounded Theory in Management Research*. London: Sage.

Longino, H. (1990) *Science as Social Knowledge: Values and Objectivity in Scientific Enquiry*. Princeton, NJ: Princeton University Press.

Lundberg, G. (1939) *Foundations of Sociology*. New York: Macmillan.

Lundberg, G. (1947) *Can Science Save Us?*, New York: Longmans Green.

Lurie, A. (1967) *Imaginary Friends*. London: Heinemann.

Lynd, R. and Lynd, H. (1929) *Middletown: A Case Study in American Culture*. New York: Harcourt Brace.

Lynn, P. (1992) *Survey of Single Homeless People*. London: Social and Community Planning Research.

Lyon, S. and Busfield, J. (eds) (1996) *Methodological Imaginations*. Basingstoke: Macmillan.

Lukes, S. (1973) *Emile Durkheim: His Life and Work: A Historical and Critical Study*. Harmondsworth: Penguin.

MacEwan Scott, A. (ed.) (1994) *Gender Segregation and Social Change*. Oxford: Oxford University Press.

Madge, J. (1963) *The Origins of Scientific Sociology*. London: Tavistock.

Malinowski, B. (1937) *Sex and Repression in Savage Society*. London: Routledge and Kegan Paul.

Manicas, P. (1987) *A History and Philosophy of the Social Sciences*. Oxford: Blackwell.

Marsh, C. (1988) *Exploring Data: An Introduction to Data Analysis for Social Scientists*. Cambridge: Polity Press.

Martin, M. and McIntyre, L.C. (eds) (1994) *Readings in the Philosophy of Social Science*. Cambridge, MA: MIT Press.

Martin, S. (2001) 'Re-evaluating public service improvement: the early impacts of the Best Value regime', *Policy and Politics*, 29 (4): 447–50.

Mason, J. (1996) *Qualitative Researching*. Thousand Oaks, CA: Sage.

Mauthner, M. (1998) 'Bringing silent voices into a public discourse: researching accounts of sister relationships', in J. Ribbens and R. Edwards (eds), *Feminist Dilemmas in Qualitative Research: Public Knowledge and Private Lives*. London: Sage.

May, T. (ed.) (2002) *Qualitative Research in Action*. London: Sage.

May, T. (1998a) 'Reflexivity in the age of reconstructive social science', *International Journal of Social Research Methodology*, 1 (1): 7–24.

May, T. (1998b) 'Reflections and reflexivity', in T. May and M. Williams (eds), *Knowing the Social World*. Buckingham: Open University Press.

May, T. (2000) 'A future for critique? Positioning, belonging and reflexivity', *European Journal of Social Theory*, 3(2): 157–73.

May, T. (2001) *Social Research* (3rd edition). Buckingham: Open University Press.

May, T. and Williams, M. (eds) (1998) *Knowing the Social World*. Buckingham: Open University Press.

McCluskey, J. (1993) *Reassessing Priorities: The Children Act 1989 – A New Agenda for Homeless Young People?*, London: CHAR.

McKinney, J. (1966) *Constructive Typology and Social Theory*. New York: Appleton-Century-Crofts.

Merton, R. (1968) *Social Theory and Social Structure*. New York: Free Press.

Miles, S., Pohl, A., Stauber, B. and Walther, A. (2002) *Communities of 'Youth': Cultural Practice and Informal Learning*. Aldershot: Ashgate.

Mill, J. (1987) *On the Logic of the Moral Sciences*. London: Duckworth.

Mills, I. and Teague, A. (1991) 'Editing and imputing data in the 1991 Census', *Population Trends*, 64: 30–7.

Mitchell, L. (1999) 'Combining focus groups and interviews: telling how it is; telling how it feels', in S. Barbour and J. Kitzinger (eds), *Developing Focus Group Research: Politics, Theory and Practice*. London: Sage.

Morley, D. (ed.) (1978) *The Sensitive Scientist*. London: SCM.

Moser, C. and Kalton, G. (1971) *Survey Methods in Social Investigation*. (2nd edition). London: Heinemann Educational.

Mouzelis, N. (1995) *Sociological Theory: What Went Wrong? Diagnoses and Remedies*. London: Routledge.

Murie, A. (1983) *Housing Inequality and Deprivation*. London: Heinemann.

Nelkin (2000) 'Less selfish than sacred? Genes and the religious impulse in evolutionary psychology', in Rose, H. and Rose, S. *Alas Poor Darwin: Arguments Against Evolutionary Psychology*. London: Janathan Cape.

Newport, F., Saad, L. and Moore, D. (1997) *Where America Stands*. New York: John Wiley and Sons.

Newton, R. and Rudestam, K. (1999) *Your Statistical Consultant: Answers to your Data Analysis Questions*. Thousand Oaks, CA: Sage.

Newton-Smith, W. (1981) *The Rationality of Science*. London: Routledge and Kegan Paul.

Oakley, A. (1981) 'Interviewing women: a contradiction in terms?, in H. Roberts (ed.), *Doing Feminist Research*. London: Routledge.

Oakley, A. (2000) *Experiments in Knowing: Gender and Method in the Social Sciences*: Cambridge: Polity Press.

Ò Dochartaigh, N. (2001) *The Internet Research Handbook*. London: Sage.

O'Hear, A. (1997) *Beyond Evolution*. Oxford: Oxford University Press.

Okely, J. (1994) 'Thinking through fieldwork', in A. Bryman and R. Burgess (eds), *Analysing Qualitative Data*. London: Routledge.

O'Neill, J. (1993) 'Ethics', in W. Outhwaite, and T. Bottomore (eds), *Blackwell Dictionary of 20th Century Social Thought*. Oxford: Blackwell.

Oppenheim, A. (1992) *Questionnaire Design, Interviewing and Attitude Measurement*. London: Pinter.

Papineau, D. (1978) *For Science in the Social Sciences*. London: Macmillan.

Parsons, T. (1968) *The Structure of Social Action*. 3rd edn. New York: Free Press.

Parsons, T. and Shils, E.A. (eds) (1951) *Toward a General Theory of Action*. New York: Harper & Row.

Pawson, R. (1989) *A Measure for Measures: A Manifesto for Empirical Sociology*. London: Routledge.

Pawson, R. (2000) 'Middle range realism', *Journal of European Sociology*, XLI (2): 283–325.

Pawson, R. and Tilley, N. (1997) *Realistic Evaluation*. London: Sage.

Payne, G. (1996) 'Imagining the community: some reflections on the community study as a method', in S. Lyon and J. Busfield (eds), *Methodological Imaginations*. Basingstoke: Macmillan.

Payne, J. (1995) *Interpreting the Index of Local Conditions: Relative Deprivation in Devon and Cornwall*. Plymouth: Plymouth Business School.

Perry, R., Dean, K. and Brown, B. (1986) *Counterurbanisation: Case Studies in Urban to Rural Movement*. Norwich: Geo Books.

Philips, D. (1987) *Philosophy, Science and Social Inquiry: Contemporary Methodological Controversies in Social Science and Related Applied Fields of Research*. Oxford: Pergamon.

Phillips, J. (1999) *How To Think About Statistics*. 6th edn. New York: Freeman.

Platt, J. (1996) *A History of Sociological Research Methods in America 1920–1960*. Cambridge: Cambridge University Press.

Polsky, N. (1969) *Hustlers, Beats and Others*. New York: Anchor Books.

Popper, K. (1959) *The Logic of Scientific Discovery*. London: Routledge.

Popper, K. (1989) *Conjectures and Refutations: The Growth of Scientific Knowledge*. 5th edn. London: Routledge.

Pratt, A. (1994) *Uneven Development: Industry, Space and Society*. London: Pergamon.

Rallings, C. and Thrasher, M. (1994) *Explaining Election Turnout: A Secondary Analysis of Local Election Statistics*. London: HMSO.

Rallings, C., Thrasher, M. and Downe, J. (1996) *Enhancing Local Electoral Turnout: A Guide to Current Practice and Future Reform*. York: Joseph Rowntree Foundation.

Rapoport, R. and Rapoport, R. (1971) *Dual Career Families*. Harmondsworth: Penguin.

Ribbens, J. and Edwards, R (1998) *Feminist Dilemmas in Qualitative Research: Public Knowledge and Private Lives*. London: Sage.

Richards, L. and Richards, T. (1994) 'From filing cabinet to computer', in A. Bryman and R. Burgess (eds), *Analyzing Qualitative Data*. London: Routledge.

Riley, G. (ed.) (1974) *Values, Objectivity and the Social Sciences*. Reading, MA: Addison-Wesley.

Ritzer, G. (2000) *Classical Sociological Theory*. Boston: McGraw-Hill.

Roberts, H (ed.) (1981) *Doing Feminist Research*. London: Routledge.

Robson, C. (2002) *Real World Research* (2nd edition). Oxford: Blackwell.

Rock, P. (1979) *The Making of Symbolic Interactionism*. London: Macmillan.

Rose, D. and O'Reilly, K. (eds) (1997) *Constructing Classes: Towards a New Social Classification for the UK*. Swindon: ESRC/ONS.

Rose, D. and Sullivan, O. (1996) *Introducing Data Analysis for Social Scientists*. Milton Keynes: Open University Press.

Rose, H. (1983) 'Hand brain and heart: a feminist epistemology for the natural sciences', *Signs*, 9: 73–90.

Rosenau, P. (1991) *Post-Modernism and the Social Sciences: Insights, Inroads and Intrusions*. Princeton, NJ: Princeton University Press.

Roszak, T. [1968] (1995) *The Making of a Counter Culture: Reflections on the Technocratic Society and Its Youthful Opposition*. Berkeley, CA: University of California Press.

Rudestam, K. and Newton, R. (2000) *Surviving Your Dissertation: A Comprehensive Guide to Content and Process* (2nd edition). London: Sage.

Ruspini, E. (2000) 'Longitudinal research in the social sciences', *Social Research Update* 28: http://www.surrey.ac.uk/sru/SRU28.html.

Sagan, C. (1996) *The Demon Haunted World: Science as a Candle in the Dark*. London: Headline.

Sarantakos, S. (1998) *Social Research* (2nd edition). Basingstoke: Macmillan.

Savage, M. (2000) 'Mind the credibility gap'. *Research*, 415, December: 17.

Scriven, M. (1980) *The Logic of Evaluation*. Inverness, CA: Edgepress.

Seale, C. (1999) *The Quality of Qualitative Research*. London: Sage.

Shapin, S. (1979) 'The politics of observation: cerebral anatomy and social interests in the Edinburgh phrenology disputes', in R. Wallis (ed.), *On the Margins of Science: The Social Construction of Rejected knowledge*. Sociological Review Monograph 27. Keele: University of Keele.

Shipman, M. (1988) *The Limitations of Social Research*. Harlow: Longman.

Sidell, M., Jones, L., Katz, J. and Peberdy, A. (1997a) (eds), *Debates and Dilemmas in Promoting Health: A Reader*. Buckingham: Open University Press.

Sidell, M., Jones, L., Katz, J. and Peberdy, A. (1997b) 'Introduction', in M. Sidell et al. (eds), *Debates and Dilemmas in Promoting Health: A Reader*. Buckingham: Open University Press.

Silverman, D. (1985) *Qualitative Methodology and Sociology*. Aldershot: Gower.

Singleton, R., Straits, B. and Straits, M. (1988) *Approaches to Social Research*. New York: Oxford University Press.

Siu, P. (1987) *The Chinese Laundryman: A Study of Isolation*. New York: New York University Press.

Skinner, Q. (ed.) (1985) *The Return of Grand Theory in the Human Sciences*. Cambridge: Canto.

Skvoretz, J. (1998) 'Theoretical models: sociology's missing links', in A. Sica, *What is Social Theory: The Philosophical Debates*. Malden, MA: Blackwell.

Smithson, J. (2000) 'Using and analysing focus groups: limitations and possibilities', *International Journal of Social Research Methodology*, 3 (2): 103–21.

Spradley, J. (1970) *You Owe Yourself a Drunk: An Ethnography of Urban Nomads*. Boston: Little Brown.

Stevens, A. (ed.) (2000) *The Advanced Handbook of Methods in Evidence Based Healthcare*. London: Sage.

Stinchcombe, A. (1968) *Constructing Social Theories*. New York: Harcourt, Brace and World.

Strauss, A. and Corbin, J. (eds) (1997) *Grounded Theory in Practice*. Thousand Oaks, CA: Sage.

Suttles, G. (1968) *The Social Order of the Slum*. Chicago: University of Chicago Press.

Sutton, P. (2000) *Explaining Environmentalism: In Search of a New Social Movement*. Aldershot: Ashgate.

Tacq, J. (1997) *Multivariate Analysis Techniques in Social Science Research: From Problems to Analysis*. London: Sage.

Tallis, R. (1995) *Newton's Sleep: Two Cultures and Two Kingdoms*. London: Macmillan.

Tashakkori, A. and Teddie, C. (1998) *Mixed Methodology: Combining Qualitative and Quantitative Approaches*. Thousand Oaks, CA: Sage.

Tauber, A. (ed.) (1997a) *Science and the Quest for Reality*. London: Macmillan.

Tauber, A. (1997b) 'Introduction', in A. Tauber (ed.), *Science and the Quest for Reality*. London: Macmillan.

Taylor, C. (1994) 'Interpretation and the sciences of man', in M. Martin and L.C. McIntyre (eds), *Readings in the Philosophy of Social Science*. Cambridge, MA: MIT Press.

Tyler, S. (1984) 'The poetic turn in postmodern anthropology – the poetry of Paul Frederich', *American Anthropologist*, 86: 328–36.

Thomas, R. and Purdon, S. (1994) 'Telephone methods for social surveys', *Social Research Update* 8: http://www.soc.surrey.ac.uk/sru/SRU8.html.

Thomas, S. (1999) *Designing Surveys that Work*. Thousand Oaks, CA: Corwen Press.

Thompson, S. (1996) 'Paying respondents and informants', *Social Research Update* 14: http://www.soc.surrey.ac.uk/sru/SRU14.html.

Tonkiss, F. and Passey, A. (1999) 'Trust, confidence and voluntary organisations: between values and institutions', *Sociology*, 33 (2): 257–74.

Tyler, S. (1986) 'Post-modern ethnography: from document of the occult to occult document', in J. Clifford and G. Marcus (eds), *Writing Culture: The Poetics and Politics of Ethnography: A School of American Research Advanced Seminar*. Berkeley, CA: University of California Press.

van Frassen, B. (1980) *The Scientific Image*. Oxford: Oxford University Press.

van Zijl, V. (1993) *A Guide to Local Housing Needs Assessment*. Coventry: Institute of Housing.

Vertovek, S. (1994) 'Multi-cultural, multi-Asian, multi-Muslim Leicester: dimensions of social complexity, ethnic organisation and local government interface', *Innovation*, 7 (3): 259–76.

Vidich, A. and Bensman, J. (1960) *Small Town in Mass Society: Class, Power and Religion in a Small Community*. New York: Anchor Books.

Vogt, W. (1998) *Dictionary of Statistics and Methodology: A Nontechnical Guide For the Social Sciences* (2nd edition). London: Sage.

Wallis, R. (1976) *The Road to Total Freedom: A Sociological Analysis of Scientology*. London: Heinemann.

Warwick, D. (1982) 'Tearoom trade: means and ends in social research', in M. Bulmer (ed.), *Social Research Ethics*. London: Macmillan.

Webb, E., Campbell, D., Schwartz, R., Sechrest, L. and Grove, J. ([1966] 1981) *Non Reactive Measures in the Social Sciences*. Boston: Houghton Mifflin.

Weber, M. (1974) '"Objectivity" in social science and social policy' in G. Riley (ed.), *Values, Objectivity and the Social Sciences*. Reading, MA: Addison-Wesley.

Weber, M. ([1906] 1975) *Roscher and Knies: The Logical Problems of Historical Economics*. New York: Free Press.

Weber, M. ([1925] 1978) *Economy and Society: An Outline of Interpretive Sociology*. New York: Bedminster.

Westergaard, J. and Resler, H. (1975) *Class in a Capitalist Society*. London: Heinemann.

Westle, B. (1998) 'Tolerance', in J. van Deth (ed.), *Comparative Politics: The Problem of Equivalence*. London: Routledge.

Weston, A. (1992) *A Rulebook for Arguments*. London: Hackett.

Whyte, W.F. ([1943] 1955) *Street Corner Society*. 2nd edn, Chicago: University of Chicago Press.

Williams, A. and Williams, M. (2002) *Learning in Guernsey: Findings of the Learning Trends Survey in Guernsey 2001*. St. Peter Port: States of Guernsey Education Council.

Williams, M. (1998) 'The social world as knowable', in T. May and M. Williams (eds), *Knowing the Social World*. Buckingham: Open University Press.

Williams, M. (1999a) 'Using capture-recapture to estimate the size of the homeless population', in D. Aramov (ed.), *Coping with Homelessness: Issues to be Tackled and Best Practices in Europe*. Aldershot: Ashgate.

Williams, M. (1999b) 'Single case probabilities and the social world: the application of Popper's propensity interpretation', *Journal for the Theory of Social Behaviour*, 29 (2): 187–201.

Williams, M. (2000a) *Science and Social Science: An Introduction*. London: Routledge.

Williams, M. (2000b) 'Interpretivism and generalisation', *Sociology*, 34 (2): 209–24.

Williams, M. (2000c) 'The value of objectivity and objectivity as a value', *Proceedings of the IEEE International Symposium on Technology and Society*. Rome: IEEE/La Sapienza.

Williams, M. (2000d) 'Social research: the emergence of a discipline?', *International Journal of Social Research Methodology*, 3 (2): 157–66.

Williams, M. (2002) 'Generalizations in interpretive research', in T. May (ed.), *Qualitative Research in Action*. London: Sage.

Williams, M. and Champion, T. (1998) 'Cornwall, poverty and in migration', *Cornish Studies*, 2nd series, 6: 118–26.

Williams, M. and Cheal, B. (2001) 'Is there any such thing as homelessness? Measurement, explanation and process in "homelessness" research', *Innovation*, 14 (3): 239–53.

Williams, M. Cheal, B. and Gomez, S. (1995) *Homelessness in Plymouth: Report of Research – Stage 2*. Plymouth, University of Plymouth.

Williams, M. and Cox, S. (1994) *Homelessness in Plymouth: Report of Research–Stage 1*. Plymouth: University of Plymouth, Department of Sociology.

Williams, M. and Harrison, E. (1995) 'Movers and stayers: a comparison of migratory and non-migratory groups in cornwall'. *Cornish Studies*, Exeter: University of Exeter Press.

Williams, M. and May, T. (1996) *Introduction to Philosophy of Social Research*. London: Routledge.

Willis, P. (1977) *Learning to Labour*. Farnborough: Saxon House.

Wilson, W. (1997) *When Work Disappears: The World of the New Urban Poor*. New York: Vintage.

Winch, P. ([1958] 1990) *The Idea of a Social Science and its Relation to Philosophy*. London: Routledge.

Wright, E.O. (1997) *Class Counts: Comparative Studies in Class*. Cambridge: Cambridge University Press.

Znaniecki, F. (1934) *The Method of Sociology*. New York: Farrar and Rinehart.

Index